Scottish Woodland History

Other books of interest from Scottish Cultural Press

The History of Soils and Field Systems
S Foster and T C Smout (eds.)
1 898218 13 7

Scotland since Prehistory: Natural Change and Human Impact
T C Smout (ed.)
1 898218 03 X

Fragile Environments:
The use and management of Tentsmuir National Nature Reserve, Fife
Graeme Whittington (ed.)
1 898218 77 3

Scotland's Rural Land-use Agencies: The history and effectiveness
in Scotland of the Forestry Commission, Nature Conservancy Council
and Countryside Commission
Donald G Mackay
1 898218 31 5

Robert Burns – A Man for All Seasons:
The natural world of Robert Burns
John Young
1 898218 60 9

Scottish Woodland History

Edited by T C Smout

SCOTTISH CULTURAL PRESS
EDINBURGH

First published 1997
Scottish Cultural Press
Unit 14, Leith Walk Business Centre,
130 Leith Walk
Edinburgh EH6 5DT
Tel: 0131 555 5950 • Fax: 0131 555 5018
e-mail: scp@sol.co.uk
http://www.taynet.co.uk/users/scp

British Library Cataloguing in Publication Data
A catalogue record for this book is available from the British Library

ISBN: 1 898218 53 6

This book is published with the aid of a grant from Historic Scotland

Printed and bound by
BPC-AUP Aberdeen Ltd

Contents

List of illustrations   vi
List of tables   vii
Introduction   1

Part I

1   Highland Land-use before 1800: Misconceptions, Evidence and Realities   5
    Chris Smout

2   Ancient Trees in Scotland   24
    Peter R Quelch

3   Plant Indicators of Long-established Woodland: 40
    A Preliminary Test in North-east Scotland
    John Miles and Alan Miles

4   The Great Myth of Caledon   47
    David J Breeze

5   Medieval Woodland History from the Scottish Southern Uplands: 52
    Fine Spatial-scale Pollen Data from a Small Woodland Hollow
    Richard Tipping

6   Old Managed Oaks in the Glasgow Area   76
    Martin Dougall and Jim Dickson

Part 2

7   Exploiting Semi-natural Woods, 1600–1800   86
    Chris Smout and Fiona Watson

8   Rights and Responsibilities: Wood-management as seen through   101
    Baron Court Records
    Fiona Watson

9   Cutting into the Pine: Loch Arkaig and Rothiemurchus   115
    in the Eighteenth Century
    Chris Smout

10   Changes in Native Woodland in Assynt, Sutherland, since 1774   126
    Robin Noble

11   Birchwoods in a Deeside Parish   135
    Neil A MacKenzie and Robin F Callander

12   A History of two Border Woodlands   147
    A H H Smith

13   Coppice Management in Highland Perthshire   162
    Christopher Dingwall

14   The Woods of Strathspey in the Nineteenth and Twentieth Centuries   176
    B M S Dunlop

15   Beinn Eighe National Nature Reserve: Woodland Management   190
    Policy and Practice 1944–1994
    Tim Clifford and Andrew Forster

Index   207

List of Illustrations

Chapter 1

Fig. 1	Strathnavar and Loch Loyal according to Pont.	8
Fig. 2	Strathnavar and Loch Loyal according to Blaeu's Atlas.	9
Fig. 3	Loch Carron and Strathcarron according to Pont.	13
Fig. 4	Part of Strathspey according to Pont.	14
Fig. 5	Loch Tay according to Pont.	15

Chapter 2

Fig. 1	Fused oak coppice (part felled). Dalkeith Park.	35
Fig. 2	Overgrown pollard oaks. Dalkeith Park.	35
Fig. 3	Ancient hollow oak with pronounced basal swelling. Dalkeith Park.	36
Fig. 4	Massive ancient oak. Dalkeith Park.	36
Fig. 5	Burry oak pollard with basal swelling. Inverbeg, Loch Lomond.	37
Fig. 6	Typical roadside overgrown ex-pollard sycamore, South Loch Tayside road.	38
Fig. 7	Typical roadside overgrown ex-pollard oak, South Loch Tayside road.	39

Chapter 5

Fig. 1	(a) location of the Southern Uplands, of (b) Upper Eskdale in southern Scotland, and of (c) the site of Over Rig within the upper catchment of the River White Esk, with localities in upper Eskdale.	54
Fig. 2 (a–e)	Complete pollen stratigraphy for the post-late Iron Age ditch fill OR-85 3/B at Over Rig.	56–60
Fig. 3	Plot of the ^{14}C dates obtained on the ditch fill sediments against depth.	62

Chapter 6

Fig. 1	General view of the Cadzow Oaks.	77
Fig. 2	Stagheaded oak with massive epicormic outgrowth and some lower bough dieback.	79
Fig. 3	One of the most severe cases of dieback, revealing the hollow centre to the trunk.	80
Fig. 4	View across part of the ancient inner core of Garscadden Wood with Drumchapel behind.	82
Fig. 5	Away from the houses but still within the ancient inner core of Garscadden Wood.	83
Fig. 6	Garscadden Wood.	83

Chapter 8

Fig. 1	Incidence of wood-cutting in the Appin of Dull, expressed as a percentage of tenants summoned to court, 1650–1738.	105
Fig. 2	Incidence of wood-cutting in Rannoch, expressed as a percentage of tenants summoned to court, 1701–1736.	105

Chapter 10

Fig. 1	Changes in native woodland in Assynt.	128

Chapter 11

Fig. 1   Location map of Highland Deeside and the Parish of Finzean.   137
Fig. 2   The Parish of Finzean.   138
Fig. 3   Birch woodland in Finzean parish, 1947–1985.   142

Chapter 12

Fig. 1   The location of Tinnis Stiel and Black Andrew Woods.   151

Chapter 13

Fig. 1   Detail from James Stobie's map of Dunkeld, 1780.   165
Fig. 2   Detail from Charles Steuart's painting of Dunkeld from the east, 1765.   166
Fig. 3   Detail from Charles Steuart's painting of the Black Lynn Falls on the   169
          River Braan, 1765.
Fig. 4   Detail from plan of the Atholl plantations by T Steuart, 1820.   173

Chapter 15

Fig. 1   The age distribution of sample trees *(Pinus sylvestris)* from Beinn Eighe   193
          pinewood in 1953 (after McVean 1953).
Fig. 2   The size distribution of sample trees *(Pinus sylvestris)* from Beinn Eighe   201
          native woodland in 1990 (Clifford 1991).

List of Tables

Chapter 2

Table 1   Fallen deadwood in Lady Park Wood compared with natural temperate   26
           broadleaved woodland and managed and overstood coppices.
Table 2   Variation in Tree Form.   33

Chapter 3

Table 1   Species thought to indicate old woodland around Banchory.   43

Chapter 5

Table 1   Simplified sediment or litho-stratigraphy of the sediments infilling OR-   55
           85 3/B at Over Rig.
Table 2   Details of the ^{14}C dates obtained on the ditch fill sediments.   61
Table 3   Details of the pollen morphology of certain taxa recorded and the taxa   64
           employed in the construction of the cumulative curves for pastoral and
           arable indicators.

Introduction

Chris Smout

This book was conceived at a one-day conference on Scottish woodland history held in April 1995 by the Institute for Environmental History, University of St Andrews, at the Scottish Natural Heritage Countryside Centre, Battleby, Perthshire, attended by 150 people. Six of the present chapters were developed from papers delivered that day. Another seven came about from an invitation to the audience to add further new work. Two are reprints of articles published elsewhere.

The result shows the extraordinary variety and vibrancy of research into woodland history carried on in Scotland today by all manner of people, ranging from practising ecologists, foresters and conservationists to academic archaeologists, palynologists and historians. The first group is driven by the professional need to know how semi-natural woodland systems have worked in historical time, in order to identify what is left and perpetuate what is valuable. The second group is inspired partly by the wish to help the first, and partly by the need to understand the past environment as the context for human settlement and behaviour.

The book reflects all of these concerns, but is unified by all the contributors' love for the ancient woods. The opening chapter reflects on land-use history, the importance of getting it right and the materials that are at hand for its study, not least the enigmatic cartographic sketches of Timothy Pont (c. 1590). The next five chapters are remarkable, among other things, for the span of methodologies brought to bear. Peter Quelch opens our eyes to the archaeology of living trees, showing us how to identify an outgrown pollarded or coppice stool, and what the significance of such discoveries on the ground are to documentary studies. John and Alan Miles tackle the critical question of how, in their part of Scotland (Deeside), ground flora might act as indicator species for ancient woods, effectively applying north of the border the methodology adumbrated by George Peterken in England. David Breeze returns to the original sources of Roman antiquity to consider the historical foundations for belief in a Great Wood of Caledon, and finds them shaky. Richard Tipping brings to bear the formidable science of a palynologist to investigate the past history of ground-cover in the south-west, with conclusions for medieval farming history as well as for woodland history. Martin Dougall and Jim Dickson look at the medieval oaks of Cadzow near Hamilton and the remnant ancient wood at Garscadden amid the Drumchapel housing estates of Glasgow, using the approach associated in England with Oliver Rackham: a close survey of the trees themselves and an appreciation of the archaeology of the site where they are found.

All the chapters in the second part of the book deal with semi-natural woodland in the last 400 years, most of them as case studies in specific localities. The first, however, discusses more generally the problem of how far management in the past has been sustainable, and concludes that whatever formal or informal systems may have operated originally, rising populations of Highlanders and their animals were putting the woods at risk by the late eighteenth century: conversely, ironmasters and other direct commercial exploiters of timber were (in the medium term) generally more likely to improve practice than to extirpate the resource upon which they depended. Fiona Watson, in Chapter 8, conducts a pioneering exploration of baron court records on the Breadalbane and Menzies estates and shows how differing lords had differing management philosophies, and how danger to the woods lay ultimately in depriving the ordinary tenant of any interest in their preservation. Chapter 9 investigates the exploitation of Caledonian pine woods on two other Highland estates, both of which attracted and disappointed external speculators yet proved of high value to local people, although the latter were not always scrupulous in their exploitation. These three chapters are limbs of a larger project on sustainable woodland management history in Scotland, funded by the Global Environmental Change Initiative of the Economic and Social Research Council.

In Chapter 10, Robin Noble takes us to Assynt and questions the usual attribution of decay of the woods in the far north-west to sheep and deer: most of the woods present in 1774 are present still. Neil MacKenzie and Robin Callandar next show how in Deeside birch and pine have alternated on the same lands over the past three centuries, the broadleaf invading as the conifer was cut, and retreating as it was replanted, often without significant alteration in the overall acreages of either. Alexander Smith deals with the very different valley of the Yarrow Water in the south-eastern Borders, showing how the Buccleuch estate gradually extended management control and modern forestry practices over what had been ancient and decaying wood, probably used mainly for pasture. Christopher Dingwall's examination of coppice management around Dunkeld shows the oak-bark industry in full swing, and uses art history to illustrate its early development on the Atholl estate.

In the penultimate chapter, Basil Dunlop surveys the treatment of native woodlands in Speyside over the last 200 years, too often a sorrowful tale of neglect and insensitivity at the very core of the Caledonian pine resource. Finally, Timothy Clifford and Andrew Forster explore the problems and uncertainties faced by the Nature Conservancy and its successors in managing the pine woods of Beinn Eighe since its acquisition in 1951 as the first Scottish

National Nature Reserve. Anyone who thinks that it is going to be easy to decide on woodland policy in the next fifty years should read this chapter and reflect: fashions in management plans clearly have a much shorter life than trees.

Three broad impressions linger in the mind after completing the editorial task. First, how many ways there are of investigating woodland history: indeed, if it is not interdisciplinary it will often be inadequate. Secondly, how rewarding good local studies can be: given the exceptional geographical diversity of Scotland, close examination of particular localities is where woodland history has to start. Thirdly, how necessary it nevertheless is to be able to draw back from the local and attempt some synthesis. This final task is less attempted here: it is premature to expect it.

Nevertheless, there will be a lot more research directed to all these ends. The other main outcome of our Battleby conference was the formation of a Scottish Woodland History Discussion Group, which now has 90 members and an ongoing programme of meetings.* Enthusiasm for the woodland heritage has come a long way since 1935 when R Angus Galloway, of the Royal Scottish Forestry Society, wrote to the newly formed National Trust for Scotland in an attempt to persuade them to purchase a remnant of old Caledonian pine forest with a view to its preservation for posterity; he reported back in 1936 that the Forestry Commission had agreed to set aside 42 acres of Glen Loy as the first of a series of projected Caledonian pine woodland remnants to be 'retained in their original state' (Lambert, in prep.). It received an immense fillip from the publication of Steven and Carlisle's brilliant and scholarly monograph on the native pinewoods (1959) and M L Anderson's posthumous two-volume history of forestry (1967). It gained scientific depth from the labour of McVean and Ratcliffe (1962), impetus from papers in two symposia (Jenkins [ed.] 1986; Aldhous [ed.] 1995), stimulus from James Lindsay's remarkable thesis of 1974, and breadth from the recent inventory surveys of Scottish native woodlands. It assumed new institutional forms with the creation of Reforesting Scotland and other native woodland groups in the 1980s and 1990s, and focused on the recreation of native woodland in the Millennium Forest project that achieved official backing in 1995. The volume presented here is born in this ferment of interest and activity. It offers the scholarship of its contributors to the under-standing and management of Scottish native woodlands as they exist today, and as they may become in the future.

* *Anyone wishing to join the discussion group should write to the Secretary, Institute for Environmental History, University of St Andrews, St Andrews, Fife KY16 9QW.*

References

Aldhous, J R (ed.), *Our Pinewood Heritage* (Forestry Commission, RSPB, SNH, 1995)
Anderson, M L, *A History of Scottish Forestry* (2 vols., London, 1967)

Jenkins, D (ed.), *Trees and Wildlife in the Scottish Uplands* (NERC Institute of Terrestrial Ecology, Banchory, 1985)

Lambert, R A 'A History of Nature Conservation and Recreation in the Cairngorms *c.* 1880–1975' (Ph.D. thesis, in preparation, University of St Andrews)

Lindsay, J, 'The Use of Woodland in Argyllshire and Perthshire between 1650 and 1850' (unpublished Ph.D. thesis, University of Edinburgh, 1974)

McVean, D N and Ratcliffe, D A, *Plant Communities of the Scottish Highlands* (Nature Conservancy Monograph 1, HMSO, London, 1962)

Steven, H M and Carlisle, A, *The Native Pinewoods of Scotland* (Edinburgh, 1959)

1. Highland Land-use before 1800:

Misconceptions, Evidence and Realities

Chris Smout

There is no full-length modern ecological history of the Highlands or even a sketch of it, but many people have a set of ideas which guide their overall view of how the landscape has changed over the last two millennia. It was neatly summarised in 1990 by the following digest of the Green Party Manifesto for the Highlands, as described in *Scotland on Sunday*.

> The Great Wood of Caledon existed between the last Great Ice Age and about 1,000 years ago, extending across the Highlands to the outer isles. Neolithic settlements began the destruction of the forest, and the Vikings made a second major impact, burning large areas in warfare. Then in the 17th and 18th centuries the Great Wood was cleared for iron smelting in the west and, more recently, for timber, cattle, deer and sheep.
>
> This long and complex history of ecological devastation has left the Highlands almost totally deforested and in the final phase of vegetation and soil degeneration.

The origin of this historical theory, with its overtones of a lost Eden destroyed by man's greed, particularly his recent greed, is not hard to discern. It owes almost everything to that masterpiece of popular ecology, Frank Fraser Darling's *Natural History in the Highlands and Islands* (1947), which in turn drew heavily on James Ritchie's pioneering *Influence of Man on Animal Life in Scotland* (1920). Ritchie himself had drawn material from certain Victorian writers, especially Nairne (1892), though his own book was a highly original and important synthesis. Nevertheless, it is high time we reconsidered this sketch in the critical light of modern archaeological and historical scholarship, and discussed some of the sources that can throw light on the problem.

First of all, how real was the Great Wood of Caledon? Tipping (1994) has well summarised the position as understood today. In the aftermath of the last Ice Age some type of forest cover indeed covered the Highlands from edge to edge, apart from the high tops, though pine and oak did not grow on the islands and the Flow country of the north, where such cover as there was consisted largely of birch and hazel. There is, however, no evidence that even in Roman times, 2000 years ago, the forest was still anything like this extent. Modification of the environment was begun by man in the Mesolithic period, and became significant in the Neolithic. In the Bronze Age and the Iron Age, metal tools were added to fire and the tooth of domestic animals as a means of human impact on the natural world. Climatic change and human activity in the millennia between the Mesolithic and the Roman period encouraged the formation of blanket peat: it is striking that carbon dating of Scots pine from bogs and loch sides has shown few to be younger than 4000 years old. Just how much of the original forest cover of Scotland had vanished by the time of the birth of Christ is hard to say, but very possibly considerably more than half of it. We suspect that islands like Lewis and Lowland counties like Fife were disafforested by the end of the Iron Age, and it is sobering that beneath the ancient pine woods of Loch Garten on Speyside lie the traces of Neolithic cultivation and that the shores of Loch Pityoulish were first cleared about 1000 BC. One of the most striking discoveries of archaeology in the last generation has been the realisation that at about the time of the Roman arrival in Scotland the population of Britain may have been about five million, or probably as large as it was at any time during the Middle Ages (Cunliffe 1985), and the abundance of such traces of human occupation as crannogs in the Highlands suggests that the region was as developed (in relative terms) as any other. O'Sullivan (1977) considers that in north-west Scotland the pine forests were largely replaced by blanket-bog (except on steep slopes and other unfavourable areas) before any large scale impact by man, but that in the Eastern Highlands, human activity was the main destructive agent, stretching over a period from about 1700 BC to about 1000 AD. Forest destruction cannot in Scotland be blamed on the Romans in the same way as it might, for example, be attributed to them in the vicinity of their iron and glass works in the south of England, as they were here only briefly, pursued no industrial activities, and in any case failed to occupy the Highlands. The forest clearers were obviously native farmers.

Popular understanding of the forestry history of the medieval period has also been bedevilled by some very peculiar stories. The Vikings are said to have set fire to wide areas of natural forest as part of their campaigns of ravage and rapine: the Wolf of Badenoch is reported to have done much the same (Darling 1947). Even if firing woodland was part of their strategy, it is very doubtful if medieval man had the ability to inflict permanent damage on the environment by a casual military campaign: a fire in a pine wood (such as would happen anyway from time to time naturally as a result of lightning strike) would be followed by general regeneration unless there was already either a dense population of grazing animals to devour the seedlings, or climatic conditions were such that wet and peat-covered ground would inhibit successful seeding. In either case the underlying cause of disafforestation would be farming or climatic change, not the rabid warfare of military hooligans. It is likely enough, however, that woodland cover continued to decline through the Middle Ages, though the balance of probability strongly suggests that much of the cover had gone before 1000 AD and the culprit, as before, would be the fire, the cattle, the sheep and the goats of the Highland peasant, aided by periods of climatic deterioration such as the so-called 'Little Ice Age' commencing in the later fourteenth century and not really over before the late seventeenth century. A very rough estimate by Walker and Kirby (1989) is that by the end of the Middle Ages only about four percent of the Scottish land-surface was still covered by wood; since the estimate for the Mesolithic period is 50 to 60 percent, we may conclude (if they are correct) that nine-tenths of the wood had gone before there was any question of the intrusion of outsiders, or external market forces.

From this it naturally follows that there might not be much substance in the allegation that 'in the seventeenth and eighteenth centuries the Great Wood was cleared for iron smelting in the west, and more, recently, for timber, cattle, deer and sheep'. Such a summary is a travesty of seventeenth and eighteenth century land management practices. We should be equally cautious in accepting without exploration and qualification the notion that the Highlands, as a result of 'a long and complex history of ecological devastation' are now in 'the final phase of vegetation and soil degeneration'. Fraser Darling was wont to describe the Highlands as having become a 'wet desert' as a result in particular, of sheep grazing, since the eighteenth century. Today we quite like certain wet deserts, having spent a great deal of effort and money in saving the greatest of them all, the Flow country of Caithness and Sutherland, for its intrinsic wildlife and wilderness interest. We can also quite like sheep farming: the Scottish Wildlife Trust has become a sheep farmer in order to maintain the characteristic flora of the serpentine Grey Hills in Ayrshire, one of its largest reserves.

We should remember that Fraser Darling approached ecology initially from a farming rather than a scientific perspective, and that this led him to approve of agricultural and forestry reclamation policies about which we have considerable reservations today. He even went so far as to write privately, in a letter that was then cited as part of an apologia for Scottish forestry policy, that 'the Sitka spruce has been a godsend in reafforestation of Scottish hill ground of peaty character... to recreate a forest biome after a long period of soil degradation is inevitably a slow process (I think myself in terms of one or two centuries)' (Maxwell 1973). But in 1968 he was devastatingly critical of the attitudes that led the Scottish Department of Agriculture to award 50 percent grants to 'the ardent reclaimer' to cut down a birch wood to create indifferent pasture and soak up fertilisers. On his own admission he had come late to see that it was not the agricultural quality of the land that mattered: 'to put it quite baldly, scenery is money, and the Highlands are throwing away their capital' (Darling 1968). That is an observation which should be written in gold over the entrance to Highland Planning Department.

Before the end of the sixteenth century almost our only evidence for the ecological history of the Highlands has to be based upon archaeology and pollen analysis. Only thereafter do we begin to get cartographical and extensive

Figure 1: Strathnavar and Loch Loyal according to Pont.

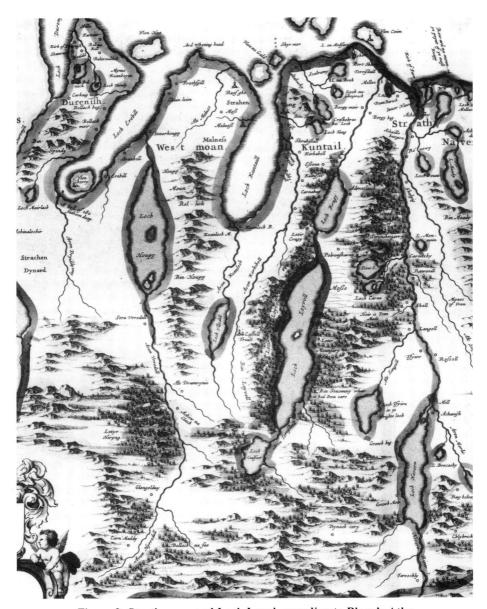

Figure 2: Strathnavar and Loch Loyal according to Blaeu's Atlas.

documentary evidence. Of the maps, the best known are Roy's military survey of 1747–55, which has been much used in, for example, the identification of surviving semi-natural woodland. It is wisest, however, to consider it in the light of Whittington and Gibson's helpful critique and explanation of how it was compiled, in a rough version (or 'protracted copy') and in a fair copy with substantial differences between them (Whittington 1986; Whittington and Gibson 1986). The authors also emphasise the usefulness of checking Roy against the numerous estate maps which exist for many parts of Highland and Lowland Scotland from the period of the first phase of improvement in the eighteenth century (see Adams 1970). These often show details even of extensive features that escaped Roy, and are in any case likely to be more accurate. It is worth emphasising that Roy's depiction of woodland and field areas was often symbolic rather than the result of detailed survey, and one should therefore view with scepticism the conclusion that his maps can tell us that, for example, seven percent of the Highlands were then covered with wood (O'Dell 1953). Certainly it may provide a rough estimate, but it is very far from an exact figure.

Much less well known than Roy, and hitherto entirely unused by scientists or ecological historians, are the sketch maps made by Timothy Pont in the very first attempt to make a cartographical survey of Scotland in the period between about 1585 and 1596. Pont did not map everything, but he travelled over a surprisingly large amount of some of the wildest and least accessible parts of the Highlands, including much of the north-west: the original sketches were published for the first time, in a very scholarly and useful edition by Jeffrey Stone in 1989. They had, however, been used by the great Dutch cartographer John Blaeu as part of his atlas of the known world, published at Amsterdam in 1654. Blaeu or his collaborators, however, simplified, altered and prettified Timothy Pont's original maps as they reduced their scale and prepared them for publication: it has, unfortunately, hitherto been only these abridged and sometimes falsified versions that have been inspected to assess Scottish woodland history.

The difference between Pont and Blaeu can be considerable, as Figures 1 and 2, depicting North-west Sutherland, demonstrate. At present modern maps indicate only traces of natural woodland around Loch Loyal (mainly a patch about 1 km long at Letterbeg on the east side at the northern end) with rather more in central Strathnavar (mainly along the river, for about 7 km between Carnachy and Syre). Blaeu, however, gives an impression of a very generously wooded area, with Loch Loyal clothed with trees on both shores from the loch to the tops of the adjacent ridges, and a further large wooded area to the south and round Loch Coulside: in Strathnavar there are again extensive wooded slopes from the stream to the tops, on the west virtually merging with those of Loch Loyal. A historian comparing Blaeu with the modern map might well conclude that disafforestation since the middle of the seventeenth century had been very extensive in the area. An examination of Pont's original survey, the only authority that Blaeu acknowledges, gives a very different impression, however. The forest around Loch Loyal appears here as a quite limited area of trees clothing both banks: of the wood round Loch Coulside and the headwaters to the south there is no trace whatever: in Strathnavar there are two quite restricted woods, which far from stretching to the tops, appear circumscribed, perhaps enclosed. This obviously amounts to substantially more wood than exists today, but by no means suggests the kind of dramatic ecological change that comes from comparing Blaeu with the modern situation. The explanation is likely to be that someone else, perhaps Gordon of Straloch who inherited Pont's material, altered and exaggerated it in order to make a more emphatic and beautiful map, secure in the knowledge that few of Blaeu's readers would travel to Sutherland to check on its accuracy. It is also interesting to compare Pont's sketch with Roy's survey a century and a half later (not illustrated here). Roy showed no wood around Loch Loyal except, roughly, where it is today, and wood in Strathnavar again much where it is today, though it is now on a reduced scale. It is interesting that Roy shows wood on Loch Loyal to the north of where Pont appears to indicate it, and along Strathnavar partly to the south of Pont's limit: but this could indicate a shift in the wood as much as an inaccuracy in Pont. A manuscript believed to be an abridgement of a lost Pont description of Strathnavar (Mitchell 1907) speaks of a trade in wood products for grain between there and Caithness, and calls the strath 'weal stored with wood'. That phrase is capable of several interpretations.

One of the features of Pont's sketch maps are the numerous comments written on them, often of significant ecological interest. 'Heir yrons made' is written both in the Pont original and the Blaeu version on the Strathnavar map on the Wood of Skail, which remains to this day full of birch, a little aspen, and much juniper, some of the latter twenty feet high. This wood is of great interest as the first in Scotland known to be associated with iron smelting. 'Brik and holyn wood' (birch and holly wood) is written on the now vanished wood to the north of Skail, the Wood of Stronchergary, in Pont but not in Blaeu. Such remarks were usually edited out in Blaeu and occur only in the Pont originals. 'Heir is much blak moss', 'heir is a green slett with fowles', 'heir perle', 'fair lynks and bent', 'heir build wyld geese', 'many wolfs in this cuntry', are typical entries for Sutherland. There are several references to studs of horses evidently running wild. 'Heir ar black flies in this wood... soucking mens blood' is the most heartfelt comment, from Loch Stack. North of Loch Sealge, in Wester Ross, is the remark 'excell: Hunting place wher are deir to be found all the year long, as in a mechtie Parck of nature'. The woods that Blaeu shows on the fringes of this area have all now vanished.

The notes transcribed in the seventeenth century, thought to be from a lost Pont manuscript, (Mitchell 1907) also contain a lot of extremely valuable ecological information along similar lines, including the observation that Strathnavar 'never lacks wolves, more than ar expedient', and several references to woodland – for example to a 'fair hollyn wood' in Glensheil, and Kintail 'watered with divers rivers covered with strait glenish woods' – that is, with many narrow woods along the watercourses. The number of references to holly is striking: it is a tree that is now seldom dominant in a wood even in the west, and is among the first to be grazed out as a sapling by sheep, deer or cattle.

Most arresting of all is the description of Loch Maree:

> Upon this Lochew, do grow plentie of very fair firr, hollyn, oak, elme, ashe, birk and quaking asp, most high, even, thicke and great, all-longst this loch... Loch Mulruy... is compasd about with many fair and tall woods as any in all the west of Scotland, in sum parts with hollyne, in sum parts with fair and beautiful fyrrs of 60, 70, 80 foot of good and serviceable timmer... in other places ar great plentie of excellent great oakes, whait may be sawin out planks of 4 sumtyms 5 foot broad.

It is unfortunate that Pont never left a finished map of this area, but the very superlatives of his description indicate that he thinks it was exceptional. This great wood has changed and largely gone on Loch Maree, but surely it was an unusual survivor of natural woodland even in 1600.

Figures 3–5 illustrate some of the other Pont maps for different parts of the Highlands. Figure 3, Loch Carron with Strathcarron, and Figure 5, Loch Tay, are interesting for their portrayal of natural woodland, more or less where it still survives today (unless cut out and replaced by conifers), and not of appreciably greater extent. The comments on the latter, 'fair salmond, trouts, eeles, pearle', include the non-ecological information, 'a king drowned in Loch Tay'. Figure 4, part of Speyside, is particularly difficult to grasp – not as full of woods as might be expected, though Abernethy and its forest is clear enough: of interest here is the plenitude of placenames, indicating a well-populated valley around 1600, certainly not some kind of wild Caledonian forest awaiting discovery by outsiders. Blaeu omitted almost all the woodland in Speyside and Perthshire, as his maps of this area were on a small scale and he wished to give priority to places. In this case his maps give the impression of less forest than Pont. It is therefore essential to examine the original sketches to get the full richness of detail for the landscape at the turn of the sixteenth and seventeenth centuries. Another extremely interesting map (known as Pont 13, not illustrated) was his highly finished sketch, never utilised by Blaeu, of Loch Eil and Loch Leven, showing 'many Firr Woods heir along' between the head of Glencoe and Kinlochleven, where there is now little of any age. Of course the Pont maps must always be regarded as sketches and not as surrogates for modern measured surveys.

Early maps are rare, and though they are invaluable for the glimpses they give us of the appearance of the land, we have to look elsewhere for day-to-day details about how the land was used. For this we must turn to collections of estate papers. Some are still *in situ* in the muniment rooms of the great houses: like Inveraray for the Dukes of Argyll, Dunvegan for Macleod of Macleod, Blair Atholl for the Dukes of Atholl. The National Register of Archives (care of

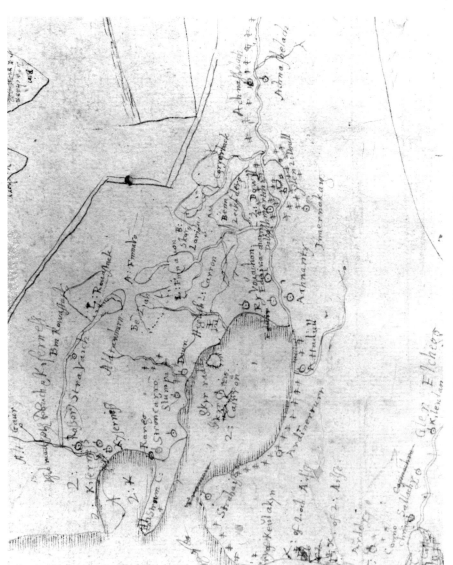

Figure 3: Loch Carron and Strathcarron according to Pont.

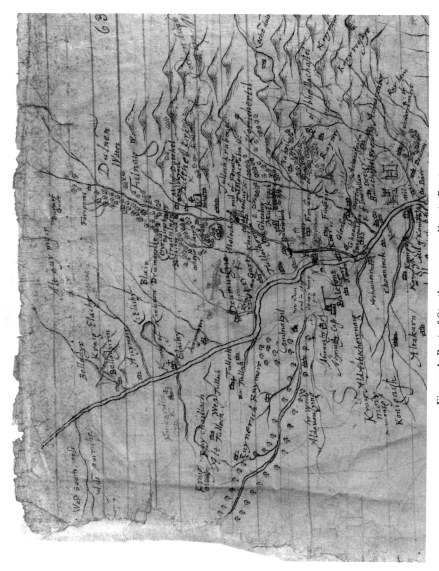

Figure 4: Part of Strathspey according to Pont
(north is at foot of page, Abernethy on the left).

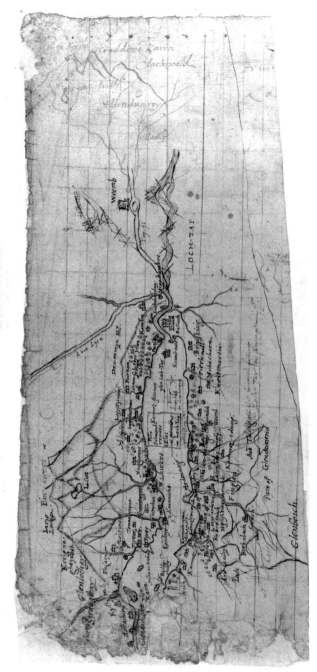

Figure 5: Loch Tay according to Pont.

the Scottish Record Office) has listed most of them. Others are among the 'Gifts and Deposits' section in the Scottish Record Office in Edinburgh: like Grant of Grant, Breadalbane and Montrose (the latter an important source for the history of Loch Lomondside woodland). A few have been, at least in part, published by the Scottish History Society, and other historical publishing societies. The problems for the interested amateur trying to extract information from them can nevertheless be formidable. For one thing, unpublished records before about 1700 can be very difficult to read. For another, unless the reader is a trained historian, the meaning and arrangement of estate papers can be most obscure. They tend to have been examined from the points of view that have traditionally interested historians – to trace the rise and fall in the fortunes of a family, for example, or to elucidate movements in rent and changes in tenure. Some types of detail that could very much interest an ecologist have hardly been searched for at all: sheep to cattle ratios, identified long ago by Fraser Darling as a crucial variable, are a good example. What might be discovered is illustrated by the published survey of farms in Assynt in 1799, where ten farms had a ratio of sheep to cattle varying from 4:5 to 1:5, with a mean of 1:3 (Adam 1960). In this case there were vastly more cattle than sheep, but to get a modern equivalent one would also need to know about animal sizes (Gibson 1988). A research project to comb Highland estate papers systematically to reveal such infor-mation could be very rewarding.

One thing that estate papers can easily yield is information on forestry practices, and the work that has already been done on this in the last 20 years completely overturns the traditional view of seventeenth and eighteenth-century despoilation of the forests. It is indeed possible that exploitation of the area round Loch Maree and Loch Ewe in the seventeenth and earlier eighteenth century for iron smelting and other purposes was of an irresponsible cut-and-run character. The woods may have been so exceptionally rich and so undervalued by the local lairds that this could happen, as it did in seventeenth-century Ireland. Even here, though, the islands on Loch Maree, accessible to the iron masters but not to grazing animals, are covered with Caledonian pine, so one must have doubts about who or what was the true agent of disafforestation. The iron masters who moved into the Western Highlands in search of charcoal reserves in the later eighteenth century using imported English ore, however, usually had no interest whatever in exhausting the woods. Their preferred path to maximise the yield of oak was to coppice, so one impact of the iron masters would be to encourage and preserve oak at the expense of other trees, such as the holly, birch, pine and aspen referred to by Pont. Large and ancient oaks, no doubt, would be felled for timber, and the stools managed to harvest a succession of young growth suitable for charcoal production. This would alter the nature of the woods, but certainly not extirpate them. They were carefully fenced and cut in rotation: as long as the fence was maintained, nothing else was needed to ensure long-term sustainable resources (Lindsay 1974; 1975a; 1975b; 1977). Another use of oak-woods, very common in the West Highlands and in areas like Loch Lomondside and the Trossachs, was for tan bark. The woods on the Montrose estates in this area were coppiced in exactly the same way (Lindsay 1974; 1975b; Tittensor 1970).

In each case the intrusion of outside commercial interests gave a new value to woodland that before had been used mainly as wood pasture. What was valued was generally preserved, and properly documented examples of broadleaf woods actually destroyed by this kind of activity are hard to come by. What undoubtedly occurred in some places was the decay of coppiced oak woodland in the nineteenth century, when the Highland iron furnaces went out of operation as coal-fired plants replaced the charcoal-fired ones, and as chemical substitutes were found for the natural tannin in oak bark. Then the fences were neglected again, sheep were allowed in and regeneration ceased. It is easy to see how a neglected coppice could die out when it lost value, and even how the story of its exploitation by the iron masters could be blamed, albeit wrongly, for its end. But the eighteenth and early nineteenth centuries were a good time for the oak woods, or at least for the remnants that had survived until 1700.

The situation in the Caledonian pine woods was somewhat different, and it is helpful to distinguish between the western woods, where heavy rainfall and blanket peat made regeneration difficult, and the eastern woods, where the seed took root much more easily. It is in the west that most damage was probably done by casual felling of ancient pines, on estates such as those at the head of Loch Leven where Pont had noted much pine not subsequently to be found. In the east, notably on Speyside, Deeside and to a lesser extent Rannoch, professional foresters were employed by the estates to supervise the exploitation and maintenance of the woods, because in this area there was in fact a fair climatic environment for regeneration, if minimal care was taken to fence and to restrict animal browsing. Even here of course, there were neglectful owners and good ones. The Jacobite Robertsons of Struan let the Black Wood of Rannoch go to ruin, but their successors, the Commissioners for Annexed Estates, spent time and money refencing it and protecting it from fire (Lindsay 1975c). Much is often made of the 60,000 trees contracted to be felled by English outsiders, the York Buildings Company, when they purchased an interest in the Grant estates at Abernethy in 1728, but one cannot help but notice that the Abernethy Forest is still there. On balance, however, it seems likely that there was a good deal less left of the old pine woods by 1800 than there had been in 1600.

The real enemies of the eastern pines in the eighteenth century, in fact, are not those who wished to conduct lumbering operations, for they gave the woods value, and therefore a purpose for their preservation and renewal. Decline rather took place when the wood could not be sold because of the extremely successful competition from Norwegian, Swedish and Baltic suppliers of pine and spruce timber, whose product was delivered so cheaply within Scotland that it was scarcely worth the effort to cut Scots pine in the Highlands for the market. Only where there was some interruption of foreign supplies due to warfare, such as during the hostilities against the French between 1793 and 1815, did it pay to ship even Speyside timber south: otherwise it had to depend on very local users for low quality wood. In Aberdeenshire itself, the builders of country houses found that it paid to buy from abroad rather than from Deeside (Thomson 1991). Consequently, some owners in the Cairngorm area began to regard their forests as game preserves for sport rather than as economically important sustainable resources, even evicting the tenants within their bounds. As soon as they underwent this change of use, natural regeneration within them was prevented by browsing deer (Watson 1983). This protection appears, however, to have come too late for the capercaillie, which had been exterminated by about 1770, perhaps by a combination of thinning habitat and heavy pressure from an increasing human population (Harvie-Brown 1897).

If the surviving woods were not preserved for commercial forestry or hunting, they would have been used for wood pasture. In England the import-ance of this land use in broad-leafed woodlands has long been recognised, but in Scotland only quite recently. Old upland woods often occupied a fluctuating area, perhaps with a core of ancient trees and an area round about that was sometimes a wood and sometimes not, depending on grazing and cutting pressures. A remarkable example of very ancient, spreading oaks can be found just west of Firbush Point on Loch Tay, where oaks with a crown diameter of up to 90 feet can be found growing in the remains of an ancient tumbled dyke, but with more recent deciduous trees, birch, cherry, and alder, growing around them. The famous ash-wood at Rassell in Wester Ross, with its spreading crowns, did not, notes Peterken (1985), 'regenerate in an older, closed woodland'. The same open structure of spreading branches can be seen in many of the 'granny pines' of, for example, the Black Wood of Rannoch or Glen Affric, which again seems to indicate trees growing wide apart. These oldest Scots pines are in this respect quite unlike their Scandinavian equivalents, where a forest appears to have been clear felled and then allowed to regenerate as a stand of even age.

In such woods, the main enemy of natural regeneration in the seventeenth and eighteenth century would hardly have been the Lowlander's Blackface and Cheviot sheep, which so often bear the brunt of the blame, as these only became an important element in Highland land use after about 1760, and then only spread gradually before the nineteenth century. It would have been the Highlanders own grazing and browsing animals – cattle, small horses, small sheep akin to the St Kilda and Shetland breeds, and perhaps especially goats: 100,000 goat and kid skins were exported from Scotland to London in 1698, which gives a vivid impression of how common the goat must have been in the traditional Highland economic system (Smout 1963). It is true that all the grazing animals would have been tended by children, but the effectiveness of this control would depend firstly on the value that the peasants put on having a wood resource at all, and secondly on the strength of regulation in the common interest.

We need not doubt that where trees had survived until the seventeenth and eighteenth centuries the local population had a use for them – as timber for building purposes, for tool making and fencing, as bark for tanning leather and preserving ropes and nets, and even as resources for making 'fir candles' from resinous cores of pines and ropes from their roots (Grant 1961). Trees and grazing could be maintained together in a way akin to the *dehesa* of Spain, and the maintenance of the habitat might not have to depend entirely on natural regeneration: saplings could be raised in nursery grounds on the tenants' own kailyards and crofts, and planted out – protected from grazing animals – when they were a little older, as described in the regulations of Glenorchy Baron court in the early seventeenth century.

There are, however, indications that traditional ways of controlling wood pastures through such baron court regulations, perhaps seldom truly effective for long under Highland conditions, were starting to collapse in the eighteenth century, partly under pressure from increasing numbers of animals and people, partly because wood pasture and commercial forestry were incompatible uses for natural woodlands. Individualistic ways of thought were increasingly replacing communal ones. In Sutherland, the notorious factor and clearer Patrick Sellar made a most interesting survey of the natural woods on the estate in 1816 (Adam 1972). The Wood of Skail, extant in Pont's day when it was a site for local iron smelting, recorded by Roy, and existing still, was described as 'pretty free from damage' but consisting 'in a great measure of stunted Birch trees, which, being, every Winter, cropped by tenants horses and cattle make no progress'. His management plan consisted of felling the crooked timber for boat building, selling the bark to fishermen to cure their lines, nets and sails, while giving room for 'Young vigorous plants to come forward'. At Letterbeg on Loch Loyal he found the wood consisting 'Entirely of Birch of pretty good size', but beyond hope because of tenant damage. Elsewhere in Strathnavar he reported 'woods... which have already begun to shoot out since the removal of the tenantry. That part thinned last Year, by the [incoming] tenant, shews a new appearance of health'. Where he found woods damaged by unauthorised bark peeling, he searched out the local tenants who had been responsible and evicted them. On the existing old Sutherland birches, frequently with two or more stems from the same bole, the trunks are often extremely calloused: this could well indicate damage from such peeling. It is clear that he expected the new sheep farmers to protect regeneration, and reported that they had done so. Afterwards, of course, in the later nineteenth and twentieth centuries, the woods were neglected again and reduced to their present parlous state when the sheep got in. But it is interesting to find so infamous a historical villain as Patrick Sellar momentarily (if ruthlessly) on the side of helping natural woods to recover from earlier misuse.

Despite the notoriety of the clearances, it is worth reminding ourselves that steadily increasing peasant population was the most critical feature of the ecological history of the seventeenth and eighteenth centuries throughout the Highlands (Dodgshon 1981), and that it reached a maximum at the census of

1841 (Flinn 1977). So many people must have meant very few roe and red deer compared to present levels. Before the coming of the potato in the second half of the eighteenth century, rising population was fed partly by subsistence husbandry (growing oats and bere, raising sheep and goats) and partly by an exchange of Highland black cattle and wood products for Lowland oatmeal (Gibson and Smout 1989). A commercial economy, in this sense, was in place long before 1745, and (contrary to popular belief) the failure of the Jacobite risings probably made very little difference to the economic history of the Highlands.

In these circumstances in the seventeenth century one major predator – the wolf – was lost: unsurprisingly, considering its propensity to prey on sheep and cattle, particularly if deer numbers fell. But other interesting mammals, the beaver, the bear and the auroch, had been lost some time in the long period between pre-history and 1600 when there had been only a very little external trade (Ritchie 1920; Nairne 1892). In the case of Highland history, the notion that the intervention of the external trader leads to disaster, while a primitive people untouched by commerce stay in balance with the environment (Darling 1947) is hard to sustain. A more useful lesson from the Highlands is that man preserved what he valued, for whatever reason, and wasted or destroyed what he did not.

The least known factor of all about the environment in the seventeenth and eighteenth centuries is the state of the herbage. Fraser Darling and others have been very insistent that the arrival of commercial modern sheep farming on a large scale (from about 1790 onwards) had a very deleterious effect on the land they grazed: 'two centuries of extractive sheep farming in the Highland hills have reduced a rich natural resource to a state of desolation'. If this is true, we can now form only a very imperfect view of eighteenth century heathland and pasture flora, even woodland flora, from what survives today: but equally everything we know about Highland pastoral farming before 1790 suggests real grazing pressures, though with different animals. At least we would expect moors with more *erica* heathland, less *nardus* and other coarse grasses, because it does appear to be the case that a long-term consequence of heavy sheep grazing and associated muirburn has been the replacement of heather by such grasses. It was the opinion of a very good Victorian observer (Nairne 1892) that sheep rearing on a large scale had had 'a distinct effect' upon the Highland forests, as the area under wood ceased its natural expansion, 'the young seedlings being all eaten up, while the herbage got so rough that there was not a suitable bed for the seed to fall in'. Cattle had kept coarse herbs down and trampled the seed into the ground, so that, given fencing, 'wherever they fed in the proximity of a wood, a luxuriant crop of trees invariably made its appearance'. With sheep this effect simply ceased. 'Then came another enemy of the woods – deer – within the last half century. Natural reproduction can never go on in or about the forest where deer are present...' This summary has some force, but it should not allow us to ignore evidence for overgrazing and neglect in the earlier period. The truth seems to be that, because wood was often undervalued, fencing was very generally ignored, and the benevolent effects of cattle grazing usually did not follow as far as trees were concerned. The very heavy game bags reported by early sportsmen like Colonel Thornton in the 1780s, as well as the appalling raptor slaughter of the Victorian period (Thornton 1804; Ritchie 1920), nevertheless suggest that the eighteenth-century ecosystem may have been able to support a much larger volume of prey species than the modern Highland environment. But at the present state of knowledge this is hard to prove.

Finally, a plea must be made for conservationists to give history a foremost place in all their work. It is notoriously difficult to speak in a country like Scotland of a 'natural landscape', a 'natural wood' or a 'natural environment' of any kind, if by that we mean a feature unmodified by people. Some beaches, some small islands, some mountain tops fall into this category, but not much else. It has become customary to speak of 'semi-natural' features, especially for woodland, but in a way this begs the question: almost everything is semi-natural, in that it has features of nature about it, even a lawn with its rich flora of daisies and dandelions. There is much to be said for talking about 'historic landscapes' or 'cultural landscapes' (Birks 1988), because that term concentrates the attention on how a landscape existed and persisted at a particular period in the past, and on what we need to know in terms of economic and cultural history in order to preserve or recreate such a landscape. To recreate the environment of the Mesolithic, as it was when yet relatively untainted by man, might indeed be possible, given the will, the money and the imagination. It would be a different thing, however, from recreating the landscape indicated by Timothy Pont in his maps, and that again different from recreating the coppiced oak woodlands of the eighteenth-century iron industry at Loch Etive or Loch Fyne, or the farms heavily grazed by cattle but scarcely at all by sheep at Assynt in 1799, or the Wood of Skail when it was grazed by horses and cattle in 1816. As we move to a more informed understanding of Scotland's natural heritage, we need to realise the extent to which it is Scotland's historic heritage as well. The ecologist and the historian could fruitfully plan a partnership of research and interpretation.

References

Adam, R J (ed.), *Home's Survey of Assynt* (Scottish History Society, 1960)

Adam, R J (ed.), *Papers on Sutherland Estate Management* (Scottish History Society, 1972)

Adams, I, *A Descriptive List of Plans in the Scottish Record Office* (2 vols., Edinburgh, 1970)

Birks, H H *et al., The Cultural Landscape – Past, Present and Future* (Cambridge, 1988)

Cunliffe, B W, 'Man and landscape in Britain, 6000 BC–400 AD', *The English Landscape, Past, Present and Future*, ed. Woodell, S R J (Oxford, 1985)

Darling, F F, *Natural History in the Highlands and Islands* (London, 1947)

Darling, F F, 'Ecology of land use in the Highlands and Islands', *The Future of the Highlands*, eds. Thomson, D S and Grimble, I (Edinburgh, 1968)

Dodgshon, R, *Land and Society in Early Scotland* (Oxford, 1981)

Flinn, M W (ed.), *Scottish Population History from the Seventeenth Century to the 1930s* (Cambridge, 1977)

Gibson, A J S, 'The size and weight of cattle and sheep in early modern Scotland', *Agricultural History Review*, 36 (1988), 162–71

Gibson, A J S and Smout, T C, 'Scottish food and Scottish history', *Scottish Society 1500– 1800*, eds. Houston, R A and Whyte, I D (Cambridge, 1989), pp. 59–84

Grant, I F, *Highland Folk Ways* (London, 1961)

Harvie-Brown, J A, *The Capercaillie in Scotland* (Edinburgh, 1897)

Lindsay, J M, 'The use of woodland in Argyllshire and Perthshire between 1650 and 1850', (unpublished Ph.D. thesis, University of Edinburgh, 1974)

Lindsay, J M, 'Charcoal iron smelting and its fuel supply: the example of Lorn furnace, Argyllshire, 1753–1876', *Journal of Historical Geography*, 1 (1975a), 283–98

Lindsay, J M, 'The history of oak coppice in Scotland', *Scottish Forestry*, 29 (1975b), 87–95

Lindsay, J M, 'Some aspects of timber supply in the Highlands, 1700–1850', *Scottish Studies*, 19 (1975c), 39–53

Lindsay, J M, 'Forestry and agriculture in the Scottish Highlands, 1700–1850', *Agricultural History Review*, 25 (1977), 23–36

Maxwell, H A, 'Coniferous plantations', *The Organic Resources of Scotland: Their Nature and Evaluation,* ed. Tivy, J (1973)

Mitchell, A (ed.), *Geographical Collections relating to Scotland* (3 vols., Scottish History Society, 1907)

Nairne, D, 'Notes on Highland woods, ancient and modern', *Trans. Gaelic Society of Inverness*, 17 (1892), 170–221

O'Dell, A C, 'A view of Scotland in the middle of the eighteenth century', *Scottish Geographical Magazine*, 69 (1953), 58–63

O'Sullivan, P E, 'Vegetation history and the native pine woods', *Native Pinewoods of Scotland,* eds. Bunce, R G H and Jeffers, J N R (Institute of Terrestrial Ecology, 1977)

Peterken, G F, 'The status of native woods in the Scottish uplands', *Trees and Wildlife in the Scottish Uplands*, ed. Jenkins, D (Institute of Terrestrial Ecology, 1985)

Ritchie, J, *The Influence of Man on Animal Life in Scotland* (Cambridge, 1920)

Smout, T C, *Scottish Trade on the Eve of Union 1660–1707* (Edinburgh, 1963)

Stone, J C, *The Pont Manuscript Maps of Scotland: Sixteenth-century Origins of a Blaeu Atlas* (Tring, 1989)

Thomson, A, 'The Scottish timber trade, 1680–1800' (unpublished Ph.D. thesis, University of St Andrews, 1990)

Thornton, T, *A Sporting Tour through the Northern Parts of England, and a Great Part of the Highlands of Scotland* (1804)

Tipping, R, 'The form and fate of Scotland's woodlands', *Proceedings of the Society of Antiquaries of Scotland*, 124 (1994), 1–54

Tittensor, R M, 'History of Loch Lomond oak woods', *Scottish Forestry*, 24 (1970), 100–118

Walker, G J and Kirby, K J, *Inventories of Ancient, Long-established and Semi-natural Woodland for Scotland* (Research and Survey in Nature conservation, NCC, Peterborough, 1989)

Watson, A, 'Eighteenth-century deer numbers and pine regeneration near Braemar, Scotland', *Biological Conservation*, 25 (1983), 289–305

Whittington, G, 'The Roy Map: the protracted and fair copies', *Scottish Geographical Magazine*, 102 (1986), 18–28

Whittington, G and Gibson, A J S, *The Military Survey of Scotland, a Critique* (Aberdeen, 1986)

Acknowledgements

Thanks are due to Scottish Natural Heritage for permission to reproduce this material from A Bachell, ed., *Highland Land Use: Four Historical and Conservation Perspectives* (NCCS, Inverness, 1991). Small amendments have been made to that version. The plates are reproduced by kind permission of the National Library of Scotland.

2. Ancient Trees in Scotland

Peter R Quelch

> That many semi-natural woodlands have survived over the last century and
> half is due not so much to enlightened management, as to the ability of trees
> as organisms to endure for very long periods, providing they are not
> physically removed from the landscape. (Smout and Watson, this volume.)

Semi-natural woodland condition

Many semi-natural broadleaved woodlands in Scotland, and also parkland,
hedgerow and roadside trees, have been allowed to grow relatively undisturbed
since their last period of economic management well over 100 years ago.

The negative aspect of this neglect has been a lack of regeneration, mainly
due to widespread grazing of semi-natural woodlands this century. However,
since many of the stands were last coppiced during the late nineteenth century
before going into neglect, in fact semi-natural broadleaved woodlands today are
characterised by predominantly middle aged stems (100–150 years). Because of
the longevity of oak, these stands are perhaps only a third of their potential age,
and there is scope to develop a cohort of much older stems for the future.

It is fortuitous that oak dominated the abandoned nineteenth-century
coppices, as it is a long-lived and hardy species, allowing large areas of ancient
woodland to survive grazing and neglect. If the woods had been predominantly
birch, hazel or ash when abandoned to grazing, many more ancient woodland
sites would now be treeless pastures. Indeed there are many areas shown on the
1750s Roy maps as semi-natural woodland, which are currently bare save for a
few scattered trees surviving. A remnant flora of bluebells or even dogs mercury
may persist under the bracken, making these areas prime targets for restoration
to native woodland. Future surveys might record these sites to assist in planning
the creation of new native woodlands, under a category such as 'Currently
Unwooded Roy Sites' (CURS).

A further consideration is that many currently open and decrepit stands of
birch, which perhaps used to contain pine, oak and ash before exploitation for

timber, are also priority sites for regeneration with a wider range of native species to match local soil and site, before they too are lost.

Some observers feel that the semi-natural oakwoods have artificially high levels of oak compared to other species and that this detracts from their naturalness. This may be so when compared to an ideal model of post-glacial wildwood, but that is not what we have in Scotland today. The oaks have been through at least 200 years of commercial exploitation for coppice, tanbark, and charcoal, and despite that (or sometimes perhaps because of that), they have survived. Carried through with them are the ground flora, the fungi and epiphytes, the insects, and the whole biodiversity of ancient semi-natural woodland habitats, to the present day. The ideal species composition in the future is a matter for debate, and is inextricably linked to the future utilisation, management and silviculture of native woods.

Old growth and deadwood

There is widespread agreement that enhanced quantities of old stems and deadwood will strongly benefit the nature conservation value of all types of semi-natural woodlands through the creation of nesting holes, rotting wood habitat for saproxylic insects and fungi, and niches for lichens, bryophyte and fern epiphytes. Indeed ecologists are now questioning the pursuit of regeneration and recoppicing on a large scale (Hambler and Speight 1995). Although coppicing is often carried out for conservation benefits, there is sometimes greater biodiversity in the old growth neglected coppice, and in managers allowing a transition towards high forest.

The same authors argue however that a 'diversity of conservationists' may also benefit biodiversity, and that there is merit in a variety of management systems in semi-natural woodlands, reflecting the varying objectives of owners and managers. There is of course scope for restoring small areas of coppice in Scotland to traditional management for historic and conservation reasons (Quelch 1994). Nevertheless, the majority of semi-natural stands in Scotland will be managed in high forest silvicultural systems, especially in the Highlands where interactions with deer, and a desire to minimise fencing would make restoration of extensive oak coppice regimes particularly difficult and of questionable ecological value.

The most natural woodlands in Europe, of which Bialowieza National Park in Poland is one of the best examples, have impressive old oak, ash, pine, lime and other trees up to 600 years old, as well as enormous volumes of standing and fallen deadwood. Some nature reserves in Britain are attempting to build up deadwood levels (see Table 1 from Peterken 1995).

There is however much scope in Scottish woodlands to maintain and increase the dead and dying wood habitat which ancient trees afford *par excellence*.

Table 1: Fallen deadwood in Lady Park Wood compared with natural temperate broadleaved woodland and managed and overstood coppices

Woodland Type	Volume of fallen deadwood (m³ per ha)
Mixed coppices in rotation, 0–20 years growth	1–12
Mixed coppices overstood, 30–60 years growth	4–31
Lady Park Wood, young-growth stands	36
Lady Park Wood, old-growth stands	46
Natural temperate forest, Bialowieza National Park, Poland	52–94

(Quoted in Peterken 1995, using data from Kirby 1992.)

It will be useful now to review the range of types of ancient trees in Scotland, to help towards ensuring that more foresters, conservationists, planners and others recognise ancient trees for what they are, and afford them a higher value. They deserve a little more care, both in woodland and in the wider countryside.

Ancient tree species

An ancient tree is an individual tree of any species, of any stem form or shape, older than about half of its natural life span. The 'Veteran Tree Group' has now changed its name to 'Ancient Tree Forum' (K Alexander, pers. comm.) so there is widespread agreement on the use of the description 'Ancient Tree' (although the above generalised definition is my own). Rackham (1994) points out that what constitutes antiquity depends on the species, and he wisely declines to give a simple definition of an ancient tree.

In the Scottish context, a birch, rowan, aspen, alder or gean over 100 years might be considered ancient in the same way as elm, ash, beech or sycamore over 150, oak over 200 (see Figures 1–5) or yew over 300 years.

Non-native trees frequently become ancient trees, particularly sycamore, common lime, sweet chestnut, European larch and European silver fir, and those planted in the parks and avenues of country houses are themselves now ancient trees (Rackham 1994). This applies equally to Scotland where many of the biggest and oldest trees survive in the eighteenth-century designed landscapes, including the neglected pollards discussed below.

The presence of any species of ancient tree in park and hedgerow is usually a scenic asset as well as a wildlife habitat. Individual non-native ancient trees in semi-natural woodlands can also be an ecological and historical asset, especially in the absence of native ancient trees. They should not be removed without consideration of the balance of benefits. My own observations show for example that massive old beech within semi-natural ex-coppiced oakwoods can provide woodpecker nesting holes and deadwood for bracket fungi to exploit (and no doubt saproxylic insects), during a period when the oak is still too small to provide these niches. Old sycamore and beech, especially if remnants from previous long periods of wood pasture, can act as temporary repositories of ancient woodland species, particularly lichens, and can transfer species to restored adjacent native woodlands in due course (e.g. Achnatra Wood, Inveraray). One of the main management problems with ancient trees in wood pasture is that there are often no intermediate age classes of future host trees coming on (e.g. Cadzow oaks, Hamilton).

If non-native trees (usually beech and sycamore) are contributing nuisance levels of seedlings particularly in regeneration enclosures, then killing the trees by ringbarking (rather than felling) will at least preserve the deadwood habitat for many years, while removing the seed source. Regular pollarding may preserve the ancient tree habitat and suppress seed production without actually killing the tree. Binggeli (1994) maintains that a proportion of sycamores do not set viable seeds and it would be worth checking significant ancient trees for empty nutlets, as these individuals pose no invasive threat to the woodland.

Other non-native species of ancient trees which are not actively regenerating such as common lime can be left intact, partly for their habitat value, but also as historical markers. They demonstrate that this woodland went through a plantation phase or, for example, that a previous laird liked occasional European larch on the boundaries of his oak coppices. Further documentary research might discover the significance of such unexpected trees.

Ancient tree stem form

Not only do some species, notably oak and yew, naturally have greater longevity than birch and rowan, but how long a tree lives is also strongly influenced by the way it has been managed or treated in the past. There are three main types of stem form, with variants, which give direct evidence of the past history of the tree and the woodland:

a. *Maiden* – individual stem grown from seedling or transplant.
b. *Coppice* – a tree cut at ground level which sprouts again.
c. *Pollard* – a tree cut above ground level, typically at 2–3 m, and which shoots from the top of the cut stump (bolling).

These main types, and important variants, are described below.

Maiden

These are the typical trees of plantations and forest but also of parks, gardens and open heath colonised by trees. Their shape is mainly influenced by physical factors such as exposure to wind and the proximity of other trees. When close-grown on good soils they become tall and slender, but when open-grown develop a short tapered stem with wide branching crown. Pruning of side branches does not materially affect their basic shape.

Coppice

Coppicing effectively rejuvenates the tree every time it is cut and in theory a coppice tree, ungrazed, could survive indefinitely. Westonbirt Arboretum has a small-leaved lime ring of approximately 18m diameter which has been DNA tested to show that it is all one genetic individual, and estimated to be 2000 years old (J White, pers. comm.). It is being conserved through recutting the coppice stems, which were last cut in 1939. This illustrates an important principle of coppicing, that the tree stems and roots begin to age from the last time they were cut, and without periodic coppicing at intervals of less than 50 years, the stem will grow old and decline in vigour. Because their root system is inherently poor, it is common for large overgrown coppice stems to break apart at ground level and collapse. They can regrow from new shoots provided grazing is at low levels, and species like wych elm, hazel and small-leaved lime frequently do this and rejuvenate themselves naturally. However oak and ash tend to die if old coppice breaks apart; very good examples may be seen in oak at Dalkeith Old Oaks, where an enormous overgrown medieval oak coppice is in various stages of decline (see Figure 1).

Good examples of old oak coppice stools are seen in Methven Wood, Perth, and in Bailefuil Wood, Strathyre, where oak stools, including one of 8.1 m circumference, and with stems of about 140 years, are being recoppiced in a plan to ensure longevity of unusually fine stools and to secure regeneration in open areas from standard trees.

Coppice with standards

A variation of coppicing, this system is halfway between coppice and high forest, where a matrix of coppice is interspersed with widely spaced maiden trees. This was a common practice in the oakwoods of central Scotland and is particularly obvious on east Loch Lomondside (e.g. Inchcailloch or Ross Wood). Even when the oak coppice was singled by estate foresters, following abandonment of the system, the two age-classes of ex-coppice and the standards are usually apparent. In fact the standards will not all usually be the same age in any one stand as a few new ones were recruited at each coppice rotation, and a few mature ones cut.

Singled coppice

Many oakwoods may appear to be of maiden trees perhaps planted in the nineteenth century, until closer inspection shows that they are singled stems from old coppice stools. Partly decayed stumps at the base of the oak are often visible as they can take a long time to rot away. Even the heartwood of suppressed stems may still be standing, growing out of the old stump adjacent to the living tree. Foresters tended to single coppice on good soils lower down the slope to encourage the best stems to grow on to sawlog size. However they often did not treat the poorly grown stools higher up the slope, and these can still be recognised as unsingled stools. Good examples can be found at Plora Wood, Innerleithen, and in Ledmore Oakwood, Spinningdale.

If the singling work was done perhaps 80 years ago, it can be difficult to recognise remains of the previous coppice stool, particularly in lowland woods where no stools were left untreated. However, an ex-coppice stem always tends to remain somewhat one-sided, or with a swept base, and are disliked by timber merchants as their timber does not compare with that of well grown maidens. Indeed foresters in Normandy would rather cut old oak coppice and replant or regenerate, than single and retain (store) the ex-coppice stems until maturity.

Swept or J-shaped trees can also arise on steep ground, caused by minor landslips or from heavy snow damage. Horizontal trees with curved upgrowing crowns or new stems arising from branches can of course arise from windthrown trees. This can give rise to unusual tree shapes, particularly when whole coppice stools blow over and resume vertical growth gradually!

Fused coppice

Long abandoned coppice stems, especially if stools are widely spaced with plenty of light, can occasionally grow together or fuse (see Figure 1). This occurs in oak and birch, but also in elm, gean, sycamore and others. Stems often fuse for only one or two metres, but sometimes much higher. In time, open-grown fused stems can appear similar to an old neglected pollard. Proof of their origin lies in the cut stump which clearly shows several stems fused into one. Fused coppice is found mainly in hedgerows and roadsides, but also on woodland boundaries and within open grazed woods.

Natural coppice

It would be wrong to assume that all multi-stemmed trees today arose from deliberately managed coppice, since episodes of grazing and fire can give rise to stands of multi-stemmed natural coppice in birch and even hazel. Indeed of all British trees, hazel seems to grow as if it preferred coppicing, and if this does not happen through man's efforts, it will throw up new coppice-like shoots all around the older main stem whenever a break in grazing pressure allows. As with small-leaved lime, wych elm and some willows, it can also perpetuate itself vegetatively by layering when old stools break up and touch the ground. Heavy and persistent grazing can upset this apparent resilience however and hazel stools will readily die if new shoots are persistently browsed and not allowed to get away.

Bundle planting

A spectacular form of tree can be produced from a bundle of trees planted in the same hole together. As they grow they blend together and look like fused coppice except that there is no central space between them. True coppice tends to grow outward after each cutting, leaving an increasing gap in the centre of the stool. Bundle planting, usually with beech, was deliberately done for landscape effect, to gain impressive wide crowned trees quickly (Green 1995). They are therefore usually visible from a large country house, and good examples are surprisingly numerous in Scotland (e.g. Carstramon Wood, Gatehouse of Fleet).

Hedges

Occasionally hedges, again typically beech, are simply left to grow on, and many prominent lines of trees in rural and suburban situations can be seen to be overgrown hedges, with multiple fusing and branching up to 2–3 metres, and normal stems above that level. Very occasionally hedges are actually maintained as such even when very tall, and the Meikleour beech hedge in Perthshire is an outstanding example.

Pollards

Although it is very unusual in Scotland to find a classic rural pollard of the type still to be seen in parts of France and England, there are many examples of overgrown pollards (see Figure 2). Typically they have a pronounced candelabra shape, and are not uncommon throughout lowland Scotland in parks, hedgerows and roadsides, and are particularly associated with eighteenth century designed landscapes.

The main reason for pollarding in other countries was to provide a supply of fuel and domestic wood, while allowing regrowth above the height that grazing livestock and deer could reach. Another important reason, with a long tradition, was to use the cut shoots to feed livestock as dried leaf fodder, as bark to nibble in the winter, and as whole leafy shoots cut in late summer.

Pollarding and shredding (pruning branches for fodder high into the tree) was common practice in Scandinavia until recently (Austad 1989), and also in the Lake District due to the Norse influence. Here the traditional pollarding practice known as 'cropping' is being revived for historical, landscape and conservation reasons by the National Trust (J Derbyshire, pers. comm.). Guidelines for tenant farmers on how to do the work have been drawn up based on some years of trial and experience (Mercer 1994).

There is apparently only fragmentary evidence of this sort of tree cropping in Scotland but an important example in the Ochils has been studied recently (Wallis 1994). Pollards are essentially a feature of wood pasture and the ash and elm in this example show the pronounced buttress swelling in some burry trees promoted by decades of trampling and the nibbling of shoots at the base of the tree. Identical types of hollow, overgrown ash tree pollards can be seen in the cropped wood pasture of upper Borrodale. The trees in the Ochils may have undergone only a limited phase of pollarding however. The study showed that there were extensive timber sales on this site in 1844, and there is no evidence of the woodland having been replanted. It is likely that some poor trees were not felled and the remaining woodland thrown open to grazing, with casual pollarding during the nineteenth century. Pollarding is a way in which a tenant farmer could obtain wood, when the main woodlands on the estate were not available to him. It is common in the Lake District and many parts of Scotland to see old overgrown ash, sycamore or elm pollards in or close to farmyards for this very reason.

Research into this forgotten aspect of rural life could be revealing. Dendrochronological studies looking for evidence of a repeated pollard sequence in the tree rings tend not to find that. However, a clear sequence is only likely in managed pollards cut on a regular cycle as in willow on riverbanks, whereas the cropping of trees for fodder by farmers was done on a much more casual basis. It is unlikely that all the branches were cut on a tree at once, forcing the tree into a period of slow growth which would show up on the ring sequence. Traditional practice (i.e. not the product of a revival) has been observed in the Lake District where branches were cut and thrown to sheep almost in the passing, with a few cut here and a few there (C Brown, pers. comm.). After stripping by sheep the branch wood dried quickly and was very useful as fuel.

An approach to research into this topic was shown by Haeggstrom (1994) who studied old landscape paintings throughout Europe to find contemporaneous evidence of pollarding.

Pollard restoration

Restoring pollards by pruning often massive limbs which have not been cut for a century or more is being undertaken in England partly for historical reasons, but also to help prolong the lives of very old trees in the landscape, and as wildlife habitats (Read 1991). Experience is growing on how best to do the work without causing such a shock to the tree that it dies. It is however expensive and somewhat dangerous work needing skilled contractors.

There is scope to carry out similar work in Scotland, particularly in those medieval deerparks where pollarding was traditionally carried out (e.g. Lochwood, Beattock). Individual trees in parks and designed landscapes could be preserved by repollarding, and a proportion of the best trees could be treated in the ash/elm wood pastures. It seems an eminently practical way for tree surgeons to lighten the crown of some dangerous trees without removing the ancient tree itself. Overgrown roadside ex-pollards, which have been topped at 2–3 m, and pruned to that height for a period at least, can be seen on many roads in Scotland. Good examples are on the south Loch Tayside road (see Figures 6 and 7), while the massive sycamores on the roadside at Comrie Golf Course are most impressive.

Stub trees

Rackham (1990) describes these low boundary pollards, which are usually on a woodbank and cut periodically at 1 or 2 m height for fuelwood and to maintain boundaries. These are not common in Scotland although the occasional low pollard is sometimes found on old boundary dykes (e.g. Woodhall Dean, Dunbar).

A form of ancient tree that is relatively common in central and west Scotland however is an 'alder stub' which is neither coppice nor pollard. They perhaps started life as coppice stools at ground level but were cut successively higher until a massive fused stub is formed. Examples of over 2 m diameter can be found and they are a most impressive sight. Since they are now usually situated in wood pastures, if re-cut the new shoots would be above grazing level, and would ensure the perpetuation of these unique trees.

Ageing of ancient trees

It is a simple matter to count the rings of felled coppice stems to estimate when the stools were last cut. However it is very difficult to age the actual stool. The rate of stool diameter growth for any species depends on many factors such as soil nutrient and moisture, elevation, exposure, condition of roots, stool spacing, competition from other trees and coppice rotation period. It is not therefore possible to accurately assess the total age of a coppice stool, but estimation techniques are given in Rackham (1990) and White (1994).

Similarly, the date of last pollarding can be estimated by increment borers or by counting rings on cut limbs, though frequently old pollards will be hollow in the main stem making accurate age estimation impossible. For trees in designed landscapes however there may be documentary records of dates of planting.

Hollow yew trees, often though not always found in churchyards, are notoriously difficult to age. Britain's oldest tree may be the Fortingall Yew in Perthshire, now only represented by fragments on the circumference of what was once a great hollow tree (Dixon 1994), and estimated to be 5000 years old.

Discussion

Scotland does have excellent examples of all the types of tree outlined above and summarised in Table 2. Many exhibit growth of epiphytic lichens, mosses, liverworts and ferns unequalled in Britain and perhaps Europe. There are also magnificent ancient trees in the native pinewoods which I have not attempted to describe.

This chapter will have succeeded in its aims if it encourages people to

Table 2: Variation in Tree Form

	Maiden	Coppice	Pollard
Brief Definition	Single stem, from seedling (self seeded or planted).	Cut at ground level, multi-stemmed	Cut at 2–3m, shooting above

Main Examples	*Plantation* trees
	Open grown trees
	Park trees
	Standards (in coppice)
		In Rotation: 0–30 years
		Young: 30–80 (stem age not stool)
		Old: 80–200
		Ancient: 200+ (e.g. Dalkeith oak)
			Overgrown pollards (previously lopped at 2–3 m)
			Situated at:
			  roadside
			  hedgerow
			  park
			  woodland boundary
			  wood pasture

Variants	*Forked trees* (high or low) *Ancient oak* (stunted, tapered, hollow, in wood pasture – e.g. Cadzow) *Ancient yews* *Ancient shrubs* (e.g. hawthorn, derived during wood pasture) *Trees within trees* (e.g. rowan seeded into hollow oak) *Lime trees* (with naturally bushy outgrowths around trunk)	*Coppice with standards* *Singled coppice* (thinned to one or two stems per stool) *Fused coppice* (multiple stems fused into one) *Ancient stools* (old or young stems) *Natural coppice* (multiple stems arising following lapse in grazing) *Bundle planting* (multi-stemmed but not actually coppice; fused stems grown up together)	*Urban pollards* (street/ garden) *Restored pollards* (recent pruning of long neglected heavy limbs, typically leaving long branch stubs) *Stub trees* (low pollards (1 m) on woodland boundaries) *Alder stub* (massive fused coppice or low pollard, now 1–3 m high stub)

Common Variants (can occur in all three main form types)

Burry trees
Swollen buttress trees, (usually on current or previous wood pasture).
Swept (curved and up-growing stems from windthrown trees or landslip).
Layering (lateral spread following collapse of bush, coppice or pollard, branches touching ground and rooting).
Overgrown hedges (fused stems up to 3 m, normal growth above).

---

observe ancient trees. The best ancient trees are more likely to survive if they are better known and better appreciated, though the work of identifying them is essentially a local task. It is disappointing for example, that the very best example of medieval deer park oaks at Cadzow, Hamilton, still seemed to be under vague threat of possible development when the Native Woodland Discussion Group visited the site in 1992.

Until very recently many of the best examples of ancient trees and woodland in Scotland have been regarded as important only as wildlife habitats, and not as ancient living entities in their own right. Recent fellings of ancient trees in Windsor Park, despite protest, does little to encourage optimism for the future of ancient trees in Britain. Some of the Cadzow oaks are reputed to have been planted by King David I (died 1153) and would have already been stout trees when William Wallace was making history with Robert the Bruce!

It is hoped that the Woodland History Discussion Group will encourage further academic and practical work on the ancient trees of Scotland.

References

Austad, I, 'Tree Pollarding in Western Norway', *The Cultural Landscape, Past, Present & Future*, ed. Birks, H *et al.* (C U P, Cambridge, 1989)

Binggeli, P, 'Controlling the Invader', *Tree News* (1994)

Dickson, J H, 'The Yew Tree in Scotland', *Scottish Forestry*, 48 (1994)

Green, E, 'Advantages of Bundle Planting', *Tree News* (1995)

Haeggstrom, C A, 'Pollards in Art', *Botanical Journal of Scotland*, 46 (1994)

Hambler, C and Speight, M R, 'Biodiversity Conservation in Britain – Science Replacing Tradition', *British Wildlife*, 6 (1995)

Kirby, K J, 'Accommodation of deadwood – a missing ingredient in coppicing?', *Ecology & Management of Coppice Woodlands*, ed. Buckley, G P, (Chapman & Hall, London, 1992)

Mercer, L, 'Pollard Guidelines' (unpublished report, National Trust, Grasmere, 1994)

Peterken, G F, 'Lady Park Wood Reserve – the First Half Century', *British Wildlife*, 6 (1995)

Quelch, P R, 'Coppicing in Scotland', *Native Woodland Discussion Group, Newsletter*, 20 (1994)

Rackham, O, *Trees and Woodland in the British Landscape* (London, 1990)

Rackham, O, 'Ancient Trees', *Tree News* (1994)

Read, H J (ed.), *Pollard and Veteran Tree Management* (City of London Corporation, London, 1991)

Wallis, J, 'An investigation into the biological, cultural and conservation significance of Myreton Wood' (M.Sc. dissertation, University of Stirling, 1994)

White, J, 'Estimating the Age of Large Trees in Britain', *Research Information Note 250* (Forestry Commission, 1994)

Figure 1: Fused oak coppice (part felled). Dalkeith Park.

Figure 2: Overgrown pollard oaks. Dalkeith Park.

Figure 3: Ancient hollow oak with pronounced basal swelling. Dalkeith Park.

Figure 4: Massive ancient oak. Dalkeith Park.

Figure 5: Burry oak pollard with basal swelling. Inverbeg, Loch Lomond.

Figure 6: Typical roadside overgrown ex-pollard sycamore, South Loch Tayside road.

Figure 7: Typical roadside overgrown ex-pollard oak, South Loch Tayside road.

3. Plant Indicators of Long-established Woodland:

A Preliminary Test in North-east Scotland

John Miles and Alan Miles

Introduction

Can plants indicate ancient or long-established broadleaved woodland in Scotland? The development since at least the seventeenth century of the notion that the presence of different plant species and vegetation types could indicate characteristic aspects of and differences in their environments, especially in soil and climate, was summarised by Clements (1920), a pioneering American plant ecologist and range manager. Clements' own early studies in the mid-continental prairies of Nebraska (1916, 1920) gave a seminal addition to this concept by showing clearly and forcefully that many species also indicated the biotic history of sites, in his case past grazing use.

The fact that many plant species occur naturally only under very specific ecological conditions provided much of the basis of the system of vegetation classification, or phytosociology, pioneered in continental Europe by Braun-Blanquet (1932), and now being comprehensively applied in Britain (Rodwell, 1991–95). These classified 'communities', however, are just convenient fictions, static nomenclatural pegs for patches of vegetation on which other descriptors can be hung. Yet all vegetation is essentially dynamic, and during the same half century various people in Britain became interested in vegetation changes with time, including identifying 'original' or 'primaeval' woods by reference to various plants apparently restricted to them (Peterken 1981).

The most significant advance in this new line of thinking came with Peterken's (1974) studies of 85 woods in mid-Lincolnshire which, from documentary and archaeological evidence, he regarded as relict stands of primaeval, 'primary', or – perhaps functionally the best term – 'ancient' woodland. The yardstick was that, regardless of past management, such woods should have existed continuously, or effectively so, on the same ground since trees recolonised Britain after the last glaciation. In addition, he studied over

150 'secondary' or 'recent' woods where it was known there had been long periods without woodland cover, as well as hundreds of other kinds of vegetation. The result was a list of 30-odd species showing a 'strong affinity' with ancient woods, and a further 20-odd species with a 'mild affinity'. This indicator value was attributed to these species being very slow to colonise newly-appearing 'secondary' woods. Rackham (1980) thought that the indicator value of Peterken's list broadly held across a large area of eastern England.

In contrast, Miles (1988) noted that in eighteen years of studying vegetation succession in many parts of upland Scotland, he had recorded fifteen of Peterken's (1974) ancient-woodland indicator species as colonists after disturbance or during succession. Given that, at least in northern Scotland, native pinewoods and birchwoods tend to regenerate outside their boundaries, and thus effectively to move around over the centuries (Miles and Kinnaird 1979; Callander 1986), it should not be surprising if their ground flora is also relatively mobile. Nevertheless, Miles (1988) also noted that, in his experience, most of Peterken's indicator species and a few more northern species 'do indicate the likelihood of old or former woodland sites in the [Scottish] uplands, especially if several are present'. He also noted of the fifteen 'Peterken species' he had found as colonists, 'although they can colonise secondary woodland and quarries, I have never found most doing so further than 100–200 m from a seed source'. Such limited colonising ability is quite consistent with the notion of gradually shifting birchwoods and pinewoods, as most birch and pine seeds fall within 50–100 metres of the parent trees (Miles and Kinnaird 1979).

In 1993, a need by the junior author to do an investigation as part of a Higher Geography assessment gave the opportunity to make a preliminary test of the value of plants as indicators of old woodland around Banchory, in north-east Scotland. This project built on a Standard Grade Geography investigation done in 1991 which mapped and quantified changes in woodland cover around Banchory since the Ordnance Survey's first 1:63360 scale map of the area was published in 1867, tracking these changes through successive 1:63360 and 1:50000 or 1:25000 scale maps (with editions or revisions of 1907, 1956, 1979, 1983 and 1993, being those immediately available in the household). Because Peterken (1981) defined 'ancient' woodland for convenience as woods existing before the year 1600, while the oldest documentary source there was time to examine in both these school studies was the 1867 map, woods shown on this latter should probably be termed 'long-established' (Walker and Kirby 1989), but for simplicity are henceforward just termed 'old'.

Methods

The study area around Banchory was delimited by the northern boundary of the 1867 map (sheet 66), the western and southern boundaries of the 1956 (sheet 40) and subsequent editions, and the easting NO 790 of the National Grid to the east, giving an area of some 130 square kilometres. Five days were spent (by A M) in recording plants at twenty-seven sites (with identifications checked by J M). The sample of sites chosen was stratified as follows:

1. eight woods with apparent continuity of broadleaved woodland cover since 1867, termed 'old' woods (NB: the 1867 map separately identified broad-leaved and coniferous woods);
2. eleven woods shown as broadleaved woodland on the 1867 map, but now under conifer plantations (probably since the 1950s), termed 'coniferized' old woods;
3. three areas of rough pasture or moorland which were shown as broadleaved woodland in 1867, termed 'former' woods;
4. five broadleaved, coniferous or mixed woods, apparently established since the 1950s, which were not shown as woodland in 1867, termed 'recent' woods.

All the sites were freely drained and had brown forest soils or iron podzols (Soil Survey of Scotland, sheet 66/67). At each site, all the species of flowering plants, ferns, mosses and toadstools seen were listed within a sample plot 20 metres square, and their relative cover of the ground was assessed by eye on a five-point scale: 1 = <1%; 2 = 1–5%; 3 = 6–20%; 4 = 21–50%; 5 = 51–100%. Species growing on the trees (epiphytes) were not identified because of lack of time. Because the above-ground parts of *Anemone nemorosa* had largely disappeared at the time (September 1993), the sites were revisited during early summer 1995 to assess this species.

Results and Discussion

Because substantial tree planting was done around Banchory from the eighteenth century by the lairds of Crathes (Anderson 1967) trees were disregarded as potential indicators of woodland antiquity.

Fifteen moss species were found: *Atrichum undulatum, Dicranum majus, D. scoparium, Hylocomium splendens, Hypnum jutlandicum, Leucobryum glaucum, Mnium hornum, M. punctatum, Plagiothecium undulatum, Pleurozium schreberi, Polytrichum commune, Rhytidiadelphus squarrosus, R. triquetrus, Sphagnum compactum, Thuidium tamariscinum*. These occurred mostly quite indiscriminately across the range of sites, and none are regarded in the literature as woodland indicators (Smith 1978).

Toadstools were found at only two sites, both old woods. However, the three species seen were all mycorrhizal (cep *Boletus edulis*, chanterelle *Cantharellus edulis* and fly agaric *Amanita muscaria*), and are believed to be associated with mid- to late-successional rather than young woods (Miles 1985).

Excluding trees, only sixty species of vascular plant were found at the twenty-seven sites, a rather low total which reflects the relatively acid soils and

Site numbers	'Old woodland' (broadleaved woodland in 1987)									'Coniferized' former old broadleaved wood										Formerly old woodland, now rough pasture or moorland			New woodland (pasture or arable land in 1867)				
	1	2	3	4	5	6	7	8	9	10	11	12	13	14	15	16	17	18	19	20	21	22	23	24	25	26	27
Bugle *Ajuga reptans*	2	4	2		2		3																				
Chickwood wintergreen *Trientalis europaea*	2	2	2	1	1			1	2	1		1	1														
Common dog violet *Viola riviniana*	2					2	2																				
Common figwort *Scrophularia nodosa*		1											2														
Golden saxifrage *Chrysosplenium oppositifolium*	1																					1					
Great woodrush *Luzula sylvatica*		1				2	1		2	1																	
Ground-ivy *Glechoma hederacea*			2																								
Hedge woundwort *Stachys sylvatica*		3																									
Herb Bennet *Geum urbanum*		3																									
Marsh ragwort *Senecio aquatica*		1																									
Primrose *Primula vulgaris*					1																						
Valerian *Valeriana officinalis*	2																										
Wood anemone *Anemone nemorosa*	3		2	1	2	4	1	2	1		1										1						
Wild strawberry *Fragaria vesca*					2																						
Wood forget-me-not *Myosotis sylvatica*					1																						
Wood horsetail *Equisetum sylvaticum*																2											
Woodsage *Teucrium scorodonia*	1	3		2																							
Wood sorrel *Oxalis acetosella*	4		4		4	3	3	3	3	2	2	3	3		2	3											
Wood stichwort *Stellaria nemorum*															2	2											
Yellow pimpernel *Lysimachia nemorum*					2																	1					
Number of species per site	8	8	5	3	8	4	5	3	4	3	2	2	3	0	3	3	1	0	0	0	1	1	0	0	0	0	0

Table 1: Species thought to indicate old woodland around Banchory (see text for key to cover ratings).

soil parent materials. These sixty species fell into four groups.

Firstly, twenty species occurred only in old, 'coniferized' and deforested former woodland sites (Table 1). They showed a gradient of decreasing relative abundance and number of species per site from old broadleaved woodland, through (on former woodland sites) larch (sites 9–12) and Scots pine (sites 13–17) plantations, to rough pasture and moorland. The two former woodland sites now planted with about thirty-year-old Sitka spruce had none of these species.

Of these twenty species, twelve were listed by Peterken (1974) as ancient woodland indicators in Lincolnshire. Two species (*Trientalis europaea* and *Stellaria nemorum*) were unlikely to have been recorded by Peterken as they naturally occur further north and west, but they are thought of as characteristic woodland plants (Clapham, Tutin and Moore, 1987). The other six species (*Ajuga reptans, Geum urbanum, Glechoma hederacea, Senecio aquatica, Stachys sylvatica, Teucrium scorodonia*) are not generally thought of as especially characteristic of woodland (Clapham *et al.* 1987), but in the authors' experience are usually woodland or woodland-edge plants in Scotland.

Secondly, eleven species that are not generally thought of as characteristic of woodland also occurred only on the old or former old woodland sites, and not in the recent woods *(Blechnum spicant, Calluna vulgaris, Digitalis purpurea, Epilobium tetragonum, Erica cinerea, E. tetralix, Filipendula ulmaria, Holcus mollis, Luzula multiflora, Rosa canina agg., Vaccinium vitis-idaea)*. However, in contrast to the first group of twenty species, their relative abundance tended to increase along the gradient from old broadleaved woodland to former old woodland now under Scots pine and to moorland.

Thirdly, thirteen species generally characteristic of disturbed conditions, and mostly of soil disturbance, were found only in former ancient woodland, variously in larch and Scots pine plantations, rough pasture, and also in woods of recent origin *(Achillea millefolia, Cerastium fontanum, Cirsium palustre, Deschampsia cespitosa, Hieracium vulgatum, Juncus conglomeratus, Ranunculus bulbosus, R. repens, Rumex acetosa, R. acetosella, Senecio jacobaea, Trifolium repens, Ulex europaeus)*.

Fourthly, there were sixteen species known to have a wide ecological tolerance and to be good colonisers which were generally widespread and frequently abundant in all types of site, even occurring in Sitka spruce plantations *(Agrostis canina, Carex binervis, Deschampsia flexuosa, Dryopteris carthusiana, D. dilatata, Galium saxatile, Holcus lanatus, Juncus effusus, Potentilla erecta, Pteridium aquilinum, Rubus idaeus, Succiza pratensis, Urtica dioica, Vaccinium myrtillus, Veronica chamaedrys, V. officinalis)*.

Conclusions

The small sample size in this preliminary study precluded a convincing statistical analysis. Nevertheless, the results encourage the belief that Peterken's

(1974) list of plant species indicating ancient woodland, may, with the addition of certain northern species (as well as the obvious deletion of species not occurring so far north), be used cautiously to infer woodland antiquity. Table 1 shows that the mean number of indicator species per site in the four groups (old broadleaved woods, the 'coniferized' former old woods, the deforested former old woods, and the recent woods) was (to the nearest whole number) 6, 2, 1 and 0, respectively, and mean percentage ground cover (using the midpoints of the scale intervals) was 42, 7, <1 and 0, respectively. The mean number of species per site was significantly greater ($P<0.10$) in old than in coniferized old broadleaved woods. Using only those species in Peterken's (1974) list, with the addition of the northern species *Trientalis europaea* and *Stellaria nemorum*, gave corresponding values of 4, 2, 1, 0 and 29%, 7%, <1% and 0%, respectively.

These results are ecologically striking, and suggest that at least two or three of the 1867 woods are ancient relicts. The reduction in numbers of indicator species in the 'coniferized' old woods was expected, as was the decline in numbers along the larch/Scots pine/Sitka spruce gradient of increasing canopy density, and hence shading of the understory. These findings suggest that more extensive studies, perhaps based on the existing inventory of ancient and long-established woodland in Scotland (Walker and Kirby, 1989) would give worthwhile insights. Particularly useful would be any insights into colonisation and extinction rates of indicator species (i.e. species adapted to habitat continuity), and also of the rare species that such long-persisting habitats tend to accumulate with time.

References

Anderson, M L, *A History of Scottish Forestry* (2 vols., Nelson, London)

Braun-Blanquet, J, *Plant Sociology. The Study of Plant Communities* (McGraw Hill, New York, 1932)

Callander, R, 'The history of nature woodlands in the Scottish Highlands', *Trees and Wildlife in the Scottish Uplands,* ed. Jenkins, D, (Abbots Ripton, Institute of Terrestrial Ecology, 1986), pp. 40–5

Clapham, A R, Tutin, T G and Moor, D M, *Flora of the British Isles* (3rd edn, Cambridge University Press, Cambridge, 1987)

Clements, F E, 'Plant succession: an analysis of the development of vegetation', *Carnegie Institute of Washington Publication* (1916), No. 242

Clements, F E, 'Plant indicators: the relation of plant communities to process and practice', *Carnegie Institute of Washington Publication* (1920), No. 356

Miles, J, 'Soil in the ecosystem', *Ecological Interactions in Soil,* eds. Fitter, A H, Atkinson, D, Read, D J, Usher, M B (Blackwell Scientific Publications, Oxford, 1985), pp. 407–27

Miles, J, 'Vegetation and soil change in the uplands', *Ecological Change in the Uplands,* eds. Usher, M B, Thompson, D B A (Blackwell Scientific Publications, Oxford, 1988), pp. 57–70

Miles, J and Kinnaird, J W, 'The establishment and regeneration of birch, juniper and Scots pine in the Scottish Highlands', *Scottish Forestry,* 33 (1979), 280–89

Peterken, G F, 'A method of assessing woodland flora for conservation using indicator species', *Biological Conservation*, 6 (1974), 239–45

Peterken, G F, *Woodland Conservation and Management* (Chapman and Hall, London, 1981)

Rackham, O, *Ancient Woodland: Its History, Vegetation and Uses in England* (Edward Arnold, London, 1980)

Rodwell, J S (ed.), *British Plant Communities* (vols. 1–4, Cambridge University Press, Cambridge, 1991–95)

Smith, A J E, *The Moss Flora of Britain and Ireland* (Cambridge University Press, Cambridge, 1978)

Walker, G J and Kirby, K J, *Inventories of Ancient, Long-Established and Semi-Natural Woodland for Scotland* (Nature Conservancy Council, Peterborough, 1989)

4. The Great Myth of Caledon

David J Breeze

Introduction

In a lecture to the North West Scotland Region of the Nature Conservancy Council in 1990 Professor T C Smout reviewed the evidence for Highland land use before 1800 (Smout, this volume). His talk was subtitled 'misconceptions, evidence and realities'. One of the misconceptions he touched on was that at the time of the Romans the Highlands were completely forested. The references of Roman (and medieval) writers to the Caledonian Forest play their part in the misconception considered by Smout. These references are frequently cited today in discussions of Scotland's countryside and have even provided the title for a book. Yet few people have gone back to the original sources. Even M L Anderson (1967) in his magisterial survey of Scottish forestry quoted the secondary source of Hector Boethius' 1596 history of Scotland rather than original Roman sources. The purpose of this note is to examine the primary literary evidence relating to the Caledonian Forest.

The evidence

The first known published reference to the Caledonian Forest is nearly 2000 years ago in 77 AD by the elder Pliny who was to die two years later in an eruption of Vesuvius. He recorded in his *Natural History* that 30 years after the Roman invasion of Britain in 43 AD Roman armies had not extended knowledge of the island beyond the neighbourhood of the Caledonian Forest. Where was that forest?

The area north of the Firth of Forth was known to the Romans as Caledonia. The historian Tacitus in his account of the campaigns of his father-in-law Julius Agricola, governor of Britain from 77 AD to 83 AD, recorded that in his sixth season (82 AD) the general led his troops across the Forth into Caledonia. In the middle of the next century the Greek geographer Ptolemy listed the tribes of Britain, which included the Caledonii, whom he recorded as stretching from the

Lemannonius gulf to the Varar estuary. The Farrar river, which flows into the Beauly Firth, retains an element of the latter place name. The Lemannonian gulf lies on the west coast and Loch Long, Loch Linnhe and Loch Fyne have all been suggested. Many scholars thus place the Caledonii in the Great Glen, which lies directly between these two points, but it has also been argued that their territory stretched round the southern and eastern edge of the Highlands (Hind 1983). In part this argument is based upon the apparent paucity of Iron Age settlement in the Great Glen, in particular in comparison to the Perthshire glens and straths. Other Roman writers, such as Martianus Capella writing in the fifth century AD and Silius Italicus in the first century, confirm the general northern location of Caledonia by linking the name with the Orkney Islands or Thule which was believed to lie beyond Orkney. The final evidence for the Caledonii survives in modern place names in Perthshire – Dunkeld, Schiehallion and Rohallion – all of which retain an element of the Caledonii in their names (Jackson 1954).

Both Tacitus and Ptolemy presumably derived their information from the campaigns of Agricola, whose army reached Moray on land, but whose fleet, Tacitus stated, circumnavigated Scotland, visiting the Orkney Islands and sighting Thule, wherever that was. However, their evidence does not exactly coincide. Tacitus always writes of a geographical area known as Caledonia, Ptolemy records a tribe, the Caledonii. Scholars have tried to marry the references, but certainty is impossible, only reasonable hypothesis. It has been suggested, for example, that the Caledonii were part of a confederacy of tribes and, being the largest, gave their name to the area occupied by the whole confederacy; or that the Caledonii had formerly occupied the whole area but had been forced to cede all but the upper straths to newcomers: certainly at one time the Caledonians were important enough to give their name to the Duecaledonius Ocean, which is placed by Ptolemy to the west or north of Scotland. In summary, all that can be said is that the land north of the Forth was known to the Romans as Caledonia and that within that area lived a tribe, the Caledonii.

Ptolemy records that 'beyond' the Caledonii was the Caledonian Forest: 'beyond' here means 'west of'. Even here, however, there is a problem. Gordon Maxwell has pointed out to me that the Greek word for 'beyond' may be a copyist error for the word for 'below', which is very similar. Since the Caledonii cannot be located exactly, and some doubt surrounds the text, it is not possible to locate the Caledonian Forest exactly. It may have lain west and north of the Great Glen; alternatively it may have covered the Grampian and Monadhliath mountains.

While it would be useful to tie down the position of the Caledonian Forest, we must accept that it is possible that the Romans themselves had no clear appreciation of its location. No Roman marching camps are known in the Highlands and it is possible that the army did no more than scout up some of the glens. Ptolemy's seemingly exact position for the forest may have been based upon travellers' tales relayed to the army. Other writers seem to have used

'Caledonian this or that' vaguely to mean something a long way off. Thus Florus, writing about 120 AD, credited Julius Caesar with chasing the southern British as far as the Caledonian forests during his invasion of 54 BC. Silius Italicus, writing in the first century AD in a poem in honour of the Emperor Vespasian (reigned 69–79), offers what is clearly another gross exaggeration, namely that during the Claudian invasion of 43 AD Vespasian had conquered Thule and led an army into the Caledonian forests (*cf.* Momigliano 1950, 41–2). Thule was simply the most northerly land known to the Romans and the implication is that the Caledonian forests were also 'somewhere up there'. Indeed the use of the plural, forests, suggests that this is a general description of northern woodland and not a reference to a specific place. Statius stated that a governor of Britain in the late 60s had won glory on the Caledonian plains when, so far as we can tell, a Roman army had not penetrated within a 100 miles of Caledonia. Lucan referred to the wild seas of Caledonia as if they were the furthest point of the island. In these and other sources 'Caledonian' seems to have been nothing more than a literary allusion to a far-away land. (It would certainly have been far away for Martianus Capella who was an African!)

This use continued throughout the Roman period and is picked up by medieval writers. Thus Nennius stated that Merlin hid in the Calidon Forest, while Geoffrey of Monmouth asserted that Arthur fought one of his twelve battles in the Celidon Wood. In medieval tradition the Wood of Celidon is somewhere in the Southern Uplands, between Dumfries and Peebles, not where any reputable Roman source places it (Alcock 1971).

Roman authors refer to woodland in other contexts. Tacitus, in describing the campaigns of the governor Agricola in the 80s AD, Cassius Dio and Herodian those of the Emperor Septimius Severus in the early third century, and the anonymous *Panegyric of Constantine* that of the Emperor Constantius Chlorus in 305 AD, all state that their armies had to fight their way through forests in order to get to grips with the enemy. Yet we must consider the nature of these literary sources. Works such as the *Life of Agricola* are full of set phrases whose purpose is to indicate to the reader that the hero of the book was a good general because he did all that was required of a good general. So we must beware of reading too much into such phrases: they may be little more than literary conventions. Furthermore, the Roman writers offer mutually contradictory descriptions of the countryside. Herodian, for example, stated that most of Britain is marshland and, in his discussion of the early third century AD campaigns of the Emperor Septimius Severus, refers to marshes more frequently than woods. Tacitus also mentions marshes in describing the first century campaigns of Agricola, while the *Panegyric of Constantine* refers to the forests and swamps of the Caledonians and other Picts. Both Tacitus and Cassius Dio, however, also record that the Caledonians used chariots, a vehicle which would require hard open terrain on which to operate. Open pasture would be required for the cattle and sheep which are also mentioned, by Cassius Dio for example. It is clearly dangerous to take out of the descriptions of these authors only what we want to believe.

There is one occasion when we can be sure that a wood was encountered. After the battle of Mons Graupius in 83 AD, Tacitus stated that the Roman army experienced difficulty in pursuing the defeated enemy into a wood. On the other hand it is also clear that the battle took place in the open, while the laying out of Roman marching camps, which could extend to 165 acres in area, demonstrates that there was plenty of open ground around. So too the construction of the Antonine Wall in turf in the 140s shows that there was open grassland in Central Scotland at that time. None of this is surprising considering that Scotland had been a settled agricultural land for over 3000 years by the time the Romans arrived (for a review of the evidence of the extent of woodland in the Roman period see Hanson and Macinnes 1980).

In summary, Roman and medieval literary references to the Caledonian Forest should be treated with caution. In view of strange stories that Roman authors recounted about the peoples and the land around the fringes of the known world some doubt must surround their accounts of the Caledonian Forest. Roman descriptions do not allow the Forest to be located with any exactitude; the sceptic might even doubt whether it existed, and that all we are dealing with is a myth repeated by many writers. Certainly the Roman authors do not provide any justification for the view that Scotland was one vast forest stretching from shore to shore when the Romans arrived. One Roman account relating to the fauna of the period rather than the flora, however, it is hoped, is believable. This is the statement by the poet Martial that a Caledonian bear took part in the opening ceremonies at the Coliseum in Rome in June 80.

Postscript

This article was originally published in *Scottish Forestry* 46, 4 (October 1992). Responses were published in *Scottish Forestry* 47, 1 (January 1993) and 47, 2 (April 1993). Attention should be drawn to the letter of Mr W W Gauld (*Scottish Forestry* 47, 2 [April 1993], 6–7) discussing the medieval sources and in particular how it came to be believed that the Wood of Celidon was located in the Southern Uplands.

References

a) Ancient References to Caledonia and the Caledonian Forest

Roman

The ancient sources listed below are conveniently collected in Rivet and Smith 1979
Anonymous: *Panegyric of Constantine*, Ch. 7
Cassius Dio: *History of Rome*, Ch. 76, vs. 12 and 13
Florus: *Epitome de Tito Livio*, Ch. 1, vs. 45
Herodian: *Histories*, Ch. 3, vs. 14
Lucan: *Pharsalia*, Ch. 6, vs. 68
Martial: *De Spetaculis*, Ch. 7, vs. 3
Martianus Capella: *De nuptis philologiae et Mercurii*, Ch. 6, vs. 666

Pliny the Elder: *Natural History*, Ch. 4, vs. 102
Ptolemy: *Geography*, Ch. 2, vs. 3, paras. 1 and 8
Silius Italicus: *Punica*, Ch. 3, vs. 597–8
Statius: *Silvae*, Ch. 5, vs. 2, para. 142
Tacitus: *Life of Agricola*, Chs. 10, 11 and 25–38

Medieval
Geoffrey of Monmouth: *Historie Regum Britanniae*, ch. 7, vs. 4; Ch. 9, vs. 3
Nennius: *Historia Brittonum*, Ch. 56

b) Modern References

Alcock, L, *Arthur's Britain* (Penguin, London, 1971)
Anderson, M L, *A History of Scottish Forestry* (Edinburgh, 1967)
Clarke, B, 'Calidon and the Caledonian Forest', *Bulletin of the Board of Celtic Studies,* XXIII, Part III (1969), 191–201
Hanson, W S and Macinnes, L, 'Forests, Forts and Fields', *Scottish Archaeological Forum* 12 (1980), 98–113
Hind, J G F, 'Caledonia and its occupation under the Flavians', *Proceedings of the Society of Antiquaries of Scotland,* 113 (1983), 373–8
Jackson, K, 'Two Early Scottish Names', *Scottish Historical Review,* 33 (1954), 14–16
Momigliano, A, 'Panegyricus Messallae and "Panegyricus Vespasiani"', *J. Roman Studies,* 40 (1950), 39–42
Rivet, A L F and Smith, C, *The Place Names of Roman Britain* (Batsford, London, 1979)

Acknowledgements

I am grateful to Mr G S Maxwell and Professor T C Smout, who read this chapter in draft, for their helpful comments.

This chapter is reprinted from *Scottish Forestry,* 46 (1992), pp. 331–5, with kind permission.

5. Medieval Woodland History from the Scottish Southern Uplands:

Fine Spatial-scale Pollen Data from a Small Woodland Hollow

Richard Tipping

Introduction

Palynological enquiries into the ways in which Scottish landscapes have changed during the present interglacial have frequently neglected the important alterations within the historic period. Although there have been exhaustive syntheses of woodland history for this period compiled from documentary and place-name sources (McVean and Ratcliffe 1962; McVean 1964; Anderson 1967), these have not in the main been supported by pollen analytical studies (Walker 1984; Lowe and Tipping 1994; Tipping 1995).

There are historical reasons for this, in the initial emphasis, engendered by the prolific Cambridge school of Sir Harry Godwin (e.g. Godwin 1975), on understanding the mechanisms and rates of formation of natural woodlands following the last glaciation, *c.* 10,000 years ago, summarised by Birks (1977). Events within the historic period were noted (e.g. Birks 1972) but commonly the chronological precision was very poor, temporal resolution of analyses limited and cultural associations inferred from inadequately researched records.

Practical reasons for this seeming lack of interest include the difficulties of resolving the chronology of pollen-bearing sediments in this period. Clearly, when the chronology of historical events can be precisely defined from documentary sources it is highly desirable to be able to identify these unambiguously from peats or lake sediments. Yet 'absolute' techniques of temporal reconstruction, largely based on a variety of radiometric methods, currently fail us (Oldfield *et al.* 1994; Oldfield, Richardson and Appleby 1995; Belyea and Warner 1994). This is partly because all such methods necessarily have measurement uncertainties, and partly because in many instances different dating techniques do not provide unique solutions to age estimates. Such age estimates cannot be used to identify dates in the way documentary records can, and the temptation to do so must be avoided (Baillie 1991; Dumayne *et al.*

1994). Future developments do offer considerable hope, however, as the identification of precisely known-age distal volcanic deposits (tephras) from Iceland is becoming more assured, particularly in northern Britain (Dugmore 1989).

Some pioneering palynological studies have been undertaken, such as those of Oldfield (1963, 1969) in southern Cumbria; Roberts, Turner and Ward (1973) in the uplands of Weardale; Barber (1981) on the western Anglo-Scottish Border; B Moffat (1985) on a monastic landscape in Sussex; Bartley and Chambers (1992) in Lancashire; Dumayne (1992) at a number of sites in northernmost England and southern Scotland; and Mackay and Tallis (1994) in the Forest of Bowland. Chronological uncertainties are clear in these studies, but enough is understood to indicate the potential of such analyses. It is apparent, for example, in this period – as in prehistory – that multi-proxy approaches to environmental reconstruction are needed. Documents do not hold all the answers to questions of environmental, social and economic change in the last several centuries; important insights are gained from suitably detailed palaeoenvironmental analyses. An as yet poorly researched advantage of such analyses is the potential of such work to test the precision of palynological reconstruction against independent data-sets. Palynologists should not be too confident of the veracity of many of their interpretations, and the historic period affords the opportunity to explore how faithfully landscape changes are reflected in the pollen record.

This chapter is a small contribution to this field of enquiry. It presents palynological data from a peat deposit in the Southern Uplands of Scotland, from upper Eskdale (Figure 1). The peat formed entirely in the post-Roman periods, within a narrow ditch associated with a late Iron Age enclosure. This rather artificial setting has one major advantage in the reconstruction of woodland history, in the very small spatial extent of the site. Sites with small surface areas tend to reflect the vegetation of a correspondingly small area around the site, often only tens of metres away (Bradshaw 1981, 1988). Analyses from such sites in Scotland are few (Tipping 1995). There are chronological weaknesses in the reconstruction from this peat, as at many other sites, such that anthropogenic changes can only be tentatively associated with particular cultural groups. Nevertheless, the data presented here are sufficiently intriguing to encourage further work.

The site at Over Rig

The archaeological site at Over Rig, south of Eskdalemuir in the valley of the River White Esk [NY 246 934], lies at *c.* 168 m OD, on a glaciolacustrine terrace some 7–8 m above the river, perched on its right (west) bank (Figure 1c). Recorded in the 1920s (RCAHMS 1920), a perceived threat from fluvial erosion led to a campaign of excavation in the mid-1980s by Roger Mercer (then of the

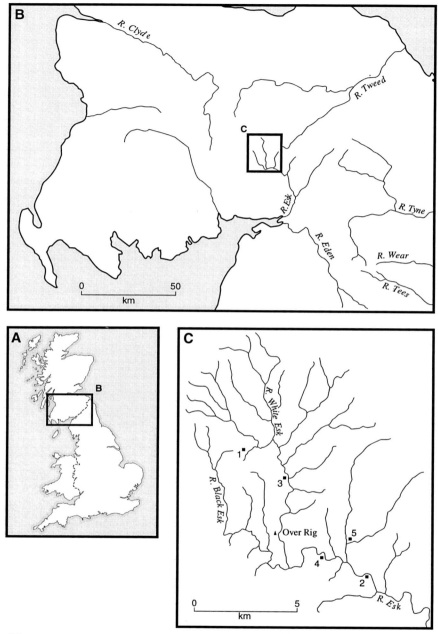

Figure 1: (a) location of the Southern Uplands, of (b) Upper Eskdale in southern Scotland, and of (c) the site of Over Rig within the upper catchment of the River White Esk, with localities in upper Eskdale referred to in the text:
1. Long Knowe; 2. Boonies; 3. Eskdalemuir; 4. Lyneholm; 5. Effgill

Dept. of Archaeology, Edinburgh University). The site lies at the base of a steep-sided (12–15°) arcuate slope, receiving drainage from Silurian mudstone and till-clad hillslopes supporting free-draining brown forest soils. The flat terrace surface at the foot of this slope is very poorly drained but in the late Iron Age supported two ring-ditch houses and other structures (Mercer, in prep.). These are isolated from the steep slopes to the west by a series of three ditches. The higher two are virtually devoid of infilling sediments, but the innermost at the junction of slope and terrace is filled with laminated silts and clays and overlying peats. This innermost ditch-fill is discussed in this chapter.

Table 1: Simplified sediment or litho-stratigraphy of the sediments infilling OR-85 3/B at Over Rig

UNIT 1 (0–9 cm)	2.5Y 5/2 greyish brown coarsely banded and finely laminated fine-coarse silts and clays; abrupt erosive boundary to
UNIT 2 (9–19 cm)	2.5Y 6/2 light brownish grey and 2.5Y 5/2 greyish brown coarsely banded and finely laminated clays and silts; abrupt conformable boundary to
UNIT 3 (19–21.5 cm)	10YR 2/2 very dark brown amorphous peat in nodules within 7.5YR 5/2 brown structureless clay; diffuse boundary to
UNIT 4 (21.5–36 cm)	7.5YR 5/2 and 7.5YR 4/2 structureless and finely laminated clays; abrupt irregular boundary to
UNIT 5 (36–124 cm)	5YR 2.5/1 black amorphous well-humified peat changing above 65 cm to 5YR 2.5/2 dark reddish brown less well-humified peat with common medium-coarse woody and fleshy plant remains, and above 80 cm to 5YR 2.5/1 black amorphous peat; sharp horizontal boundary to
UNIT 6 (124–127 cm)	5 YR 3/2 dark reddish brown organic-rich clay with rare fleshy plant remains.

The analyses to be considered come from one of the seven ditch-sections excavated, DU6 (ditch fill OR-85-3b) (in all figures representing this section the vertical (depth) axes are numbered with the lowermost ditch sediment as 0.0 cm). The lowermost sediments (0–37 cm) are laminated silts and silty clays derived during storm events from unvegetated ditch sides (Table 1). They were probably formed very rapidly, in the first few years following cessation of ditch

Figure 2: Complete pollen stratigraphy for the post-late Iron Age ditch fill OR-85 3/B at Over Rig: a) depth in cm (note that 0 cm represents the deepest sample), stratigraphy and stratigraphic units (see Table 1), sample locations within the monolith tins sampled, and tree and shrub pollen calculated as % total land pollen (t.l.p.); b) herb pollen as % t.l.p., the t.l.p. total counted which forms the base for % calculations; c) herb pollen as % t.l.p.; d) t.l.p. concentrations and grains counted per traverse, and a summary of the changes in the major life-form groups defined in Figure 2; e) aquatic pollen and spores as % t.l.p. + this group, cumulative curves for pastoral and arable indicator herb pollen (see Table 3) and miscellaneous palynomorphs recorded. (See pages 56–60.)

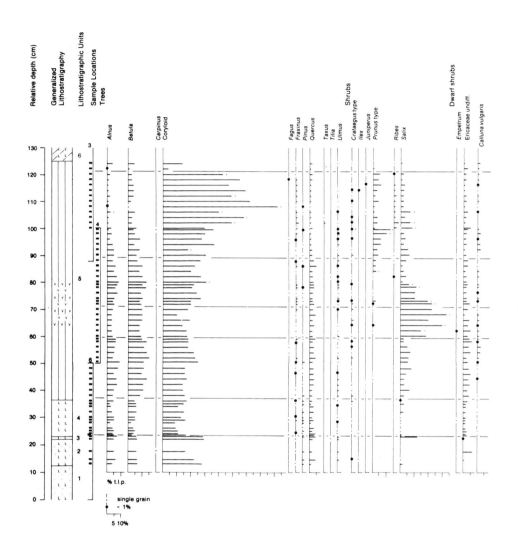

Figure 2a

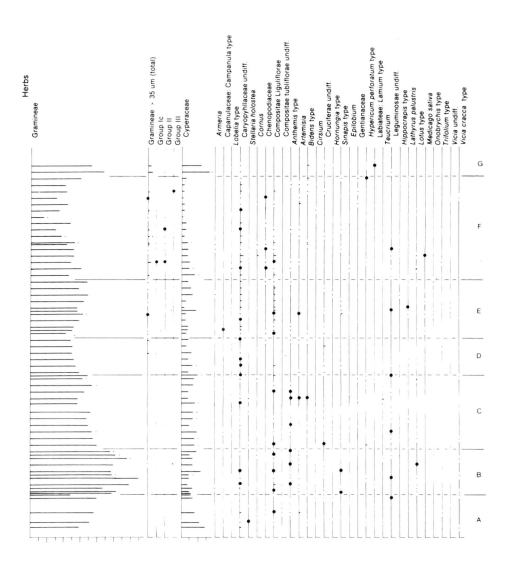

Figure 2b

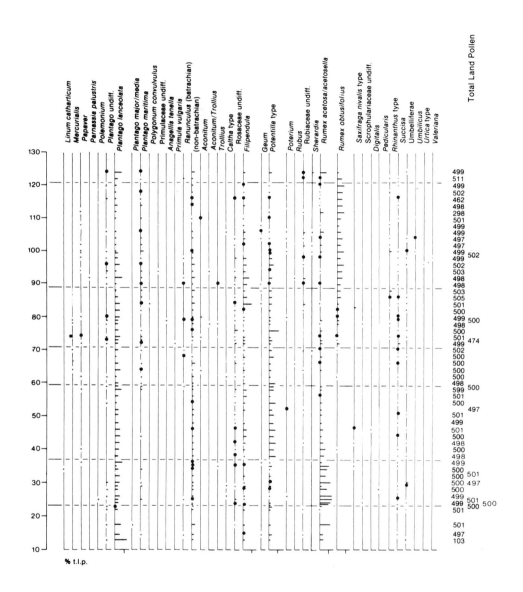

Figure 2c

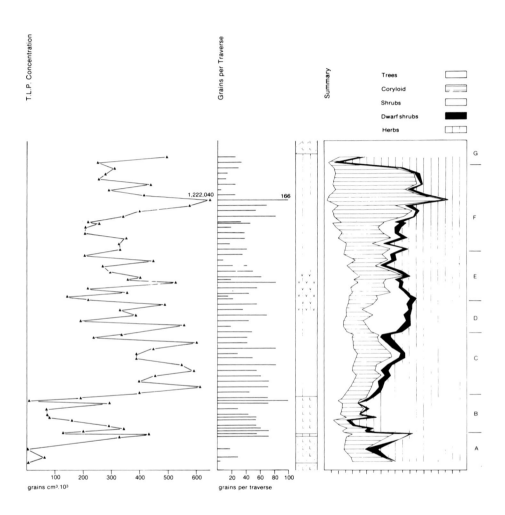

Figure 2d

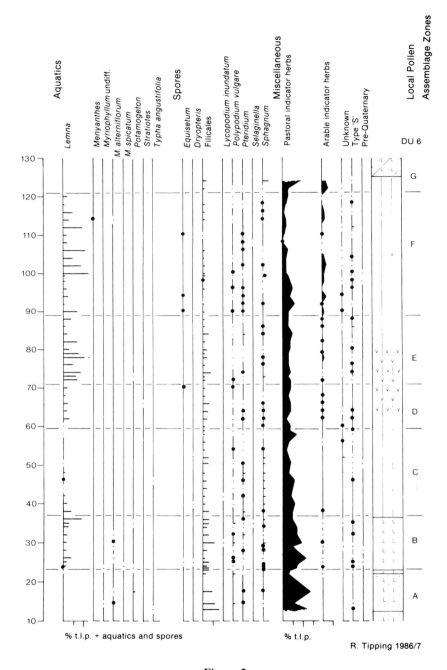

Figure 2e

digging or ditch clearance. These minerogenic sediments contain abundant pieces of wood, both worked and unworked, which have been analysed by Boyd (1988), and will be further discussed in detail elsewhere. This chapter will concentrate on the overlying organic sediments, the uppermost 90–95 cm of the fill (Table 1; Figure 2a – Generalised Lithostratigraphy/Lithostratigraphic Units).

Methods

(a) dating

Figure 3 depicts a simplified sediment stratigraphy of the fill OR-85-3b, together with the stratigraphic positions of the eleven ^{14}C dates obtained from organic deposits (see also Table 2) and the linear depth-time profile used to estimate ages. Four dates (GU-1891 to -1894) were obtained on pieces of wood from the basal laminated sediments of a number of ditch sections, and all are in good agreement in indicating an age for the initial infilling to have been very

Table 2: Details of the ^{14}C dates obtained on the ditch fill sediments

Code (GU-)	Sediment	Sample Depth	Fraction Dated	^{14}C Age $\pm 1\sigma$	δ^{13}C ‰	Cal. BC/AD $\pm 1\sigma$
1891	wood	0–30 cm	2nd humic acid	1915 ± 50	-26.5	27–130 AD
1892	wood	0–30 cm	2nd humic acid	2025 ± 145	-25.8	346 BC–127 AD
1893	wood	0–30 cm	2nd humic acid	2000 ± 75	-26.5	95 BC–68 AD
1894	wood	0–30 cm	2nd humic acid	1965 ± 50	-27.6	88 BC–72 AD
2220	amorphous peat	36–39 cm	2nd humic acid	2660 ± 70	-28.2	898–795 BC
2221	amorphous peat	60–63 cm	2nd humic acid	2620 ± 50	-28.5	825–788 BC
2222	amorphous peat	83–86 cm	2nd humic acid	2730 ± 50	-28.5	930–826 BC
2223	amorphous peat	121–124 cm	2nd humic acid	1760 ± 50	-24.8	181–340 AD
2404	wood	65–80 cm	2nd humic acid	1650 ± 80	-27.2	259–531 AD
2666	wood	65–80 cm	2nd humic acid	1860 ± 50	-27.9	72–226 AD
2667	wood	65–80 cm	cellulose	1860 ± 60	-26.4	68–229 AD

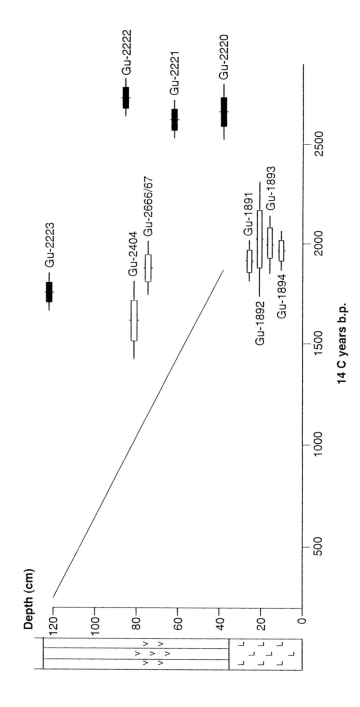

Figure 3: Plot of the ^{14}C dates obtained on the ditch fill sediments against depth (see Table 2).

late in the Iron Age, with a mean age of 1976 ± 40 ^{14}C BP. This estimate also agrees very well with the archaeological dating evidence and is considered to be secure. Calibration and statistical averaging of these calibrated dates yields a calibrated mean age of *c.* 80 cal. AD.

Four ^{14}C dates were obtained on the peats infilling the ditch (Table 2; Figure 3). Three of these assays, though stratigraphically younger are nevertheless older in ^{14}C age than the basal dates, and so are probably in error, and it is very likely that the assay GU-2223 is also 'too old'. It is most easily assumed that inwashed organic matter from the steep slopes above the ditch introduced errors in these ^{14}C dates, but there is no evidence for the inwashing of mineral matter into these peats. 'Old' carbon was presumably introduced as soluble fractions in water. These assays were obtained on heterogeneous organic components (Table 2), whereas assays GU-2404 and GU-2666 are humic acid extract dates on wood remains. GU-2667 is an assay on the cellulose fraction of the same wood dated for assay GU-2666, following exhaustive bleaching to remove all mobile organic acids which might have seeped into and contaminated the wood. This and GU-2666 strongly suggest that the wood dated is around 1820 cal. years old (Table 2), indeed close to the ages of the wood from the basal minerogenic sediments, yet slightly older than wood from the same unit dated by assay GU-2404. It may be that the lowermost peat, below 65–80 cm, accumulated very rapidly, but it is also possible that these wood remains slumped into the ditch some time after their death, and that these assays which seemingly securely fix the age of the wood remains themselves have little to do with the peat enclosing the wood.

A series of ^{210}Pb assays were obtained from the uppermost organic peats, and appear to indicate both that peat continued to form in the last *c.* 150–200 years, and that it did so at a rate close to that projected by the linear depth-time profile adopted in Figure 3 (Cook, G and Mackenzie A, pers. comm.), e.g. 14.4 cal. years/cm. This rate also agrees with an interpretation that palynological changes at *c.* 125 cm depth (Figure 2) are related to the agricultural improvements of the late eighteenth century (Findlater 1802). This is not good evidence that peat accumulated at this rate throughout the last 1900 years. Indeed, pollen concentration values (Figure 2b) are highly erratic, probably as much through differences in rates of peat growth as through differential compaction and changes in pollen productivity of local plants. Nevertheless the depth-time profile depicted in Figure 3 remains the best estimate of age for palynological events.

(b) palynology

Subsamples <0.5 cm thick were removed from three 50.0 cm monolith tins (Figure 2a – Sample Locations). These were treated by standard chemical procedures (Moore, Webb and Collinson 1991) with *Lycopodium* tablets used to assess pollen concentrations (Tipping 1987). Residues were stained with safranin, embedded in silicon oil and counted on a Vickers M15C microscope at mag. x400, and x1000 for problematic grains and all size measurements. Standard keys were employed in pollen identification; pollen morphological data for specific taxa are given in Table 3. Counts were continued to a sum of *c*. 500 total land pollen grains (e.g., inclusive of all those taxa in Figure 2a and 2b). These taxa also form the calculation base for the percentage changes depicted in Figure 2a and b (e.g. % tlp); fluctuations in aquatic and spore taxa (Figure 2c)

Table 3: Details of the pollen morphology of certain taxa recorded and the taxa employed in the construction of the cumulative curves for pastoral and arable indicators

Coryloid	includes both *Corylus* and *Myrica* (Figure 2a).	
Gramineae	grains >35 μm were tentatively assigned to one of Andersen's (1979) groups (Figure 2a); 1c – wild; II – *Hordeum* type; III – *Avena-Triticum*.	
Pre-Quaternary	trilete spores presumably derived from eroding Silurian strata or till.	
Pollen tetrads/clumps	commonly recorded (Figure 2), the fragility of these clumps of pollen probably indicate the local growth of parent plants.	
Pastoral and arable indicator herbs	the selection of individual pollen taxa as indicators of agricultural activity is difficult and contentious (Maguire 1983). The taxa employed here were derived from (i) previous studies, (ii) analyses of modern pollen/vegetation relations and (iii) descriptions of present plant communities. Against each taxon is a numbered source (see 'References'):	
Pastoral indicators	*Plantago lanceolata*	(Figure 2b) (1, 3, 4, 5, 6, 9, 10, 11)
	Plantago major/media	(Figure 2b) (1, 4, 10, 11)
	Rumex acetosa/acetosella	(Figure 2b) (1, 2, 3, 9)
	Ranunculus (non-batrachian)	(Figure 2b) (3, 5, 8)
	Trifolium type	(Figure 2a) (4, 5, 6)
	Medicago sativa	(Figure 2a) (13)
	Onobrychis type	(Figure 2a) (13)
	Umbelliferae	(Figure 2b) (1, 2)
	Linum catharticum	(Figure 2b) (4)
Arable indicators	Gramineae Group II	(Figure 2a) (1, 3, 10, 11, 12)
	Gramineae Group III	(Figure 2a) (1, 3, 10, 11, 12)
	Chenopodiaceae	(Figure 2a) (1, 10, 11)
	Cruciferae	(Figure 2a) (3, 7, 10, 11)

Sources
1. Behre (1981); 2. Caseldine (1981); 3. Donaldson and Turner (1977); 4. Greig (1984); 5. King and Nicholson (1964); 6. Putman (1986); 7. Reynolds (1981); 8. Roberts *et al.* (1973); 9. Tinsley and Smith (1974); 10. Turner (1964); 11. Vuorela (1972); 12. Vuorela (1973); 13. Spedding and Diekmahns (1972).

are expressed as % tlp plus these taxa. On Figure 2c are cumulative percentages for selected palynological indicators of both pasture and arable agricultural practices; these taxa are listed in Table 3.

(c) zonation

Significant percentage changes in major taxa form the basis of the subjective Local Pollen Assemblage (l.p.a.) zonation scheme (DU 6 zones A–G; Figure 2). Using the mean sediment accumulation rate of 14.4 cal. years/cm (above) the ages of l.p.a.z. boundaries within the peats (C–G inc.) are defined here, appropriately loosely:

l.p.a.z. boundary B/C = early-mid sixth century AD; l.p.a.z. boundary C/D = mid ninth century AD; l.p.a.z. boundary D/E = early eleventh century AD; l.p.a.z. boundary E/F = late thirteenth century AD; l.p.a.z. boundary F/G = mid eighteenth century AD.

The next section will use these age estimates to discuss the palynological changes in Figure 2 in chronological order. The sequence of changes is compared with the archaeological and documentary records for upper Eskdale only (Figure 1c). Correlation with adjacent dated pollen sites is not an aim of this chapter, partly because the pollen recruitment area of the Over Rig is very limited, and partly because this is dealt with elsewhere (Tipping, in prep.).

The historic palaeoecological record at Over Rig

The Romano-British Period

Interpretation of the palynological changes in the minerogenic sediments below *c.* 36 cm, prior to the mid-sixth century AD, is complex (Tipping, in prep.) but can be simplified to represent a fluctuating balance between pastoralism as the predominant agricultural undertaking and phases of hazel coppicing. There is no evidence for undisturbed native woodland at this time, and indeed woodland was already only a minor part of the vegetation in this upland valley. The composition and principal elements of the remaining woodland is reviewed from macrofossil and pollen data by Boyd (1988), who also produced tree-ring data to suggest hazel coppicing on the slopes above the site in this period (below).

Rare single cereal-type pollen grains (Gramineae >35 μm) are recorded in l.p.a.z. B, in possible support of Jobey's (1975) argument from his excavation at the late Iron Age site at Boonies, downvalley of Over Rig (Figure 1c) and *c.* 40 m lower, for crops to have been a component of the agricultural economy in the valley. Mercer (1981), however, considered that cereals were not grown around the contemporaneous site at Long Knowe, up-valley at *c.* 300 m OD (Figure 1c), and instead tentatively suggested that this site represented the upper end of a transhumant system. Extensive linear earthworks of late Iron and Romano-British age around Castle O'er, above Over Rig, are interpreted by Mercer (pers.

comm.) as related to a cattle-based economy, and there are suggestions in the Over Rig pollen record for species-rich mown meadow *(cf.* Lambrick and Robinson 1979; Greig 1984), perhaps on lowlying haughland by the river.

It is likely that at Over Rig this farming economy was maintained after the abandonment of Britain by Roman forces in the early fifth century, as argued by Turner (1979) for other areas of northern Britain, although apparently contrasting responses to Roman withdrawal at particular localities may imply her suggestion to have been too simplistic or general (Barber 1981; Dumayne 1993; Dumayne *et al.* 1994; Tipping 1995).

A 'Dark' Age

After the mid-sixth century AD the thriving agricultural economy in upper Eskdale underwent some contraction, seen in reductions in herbs and increases in proportions of *Betula* (birch) and *Alnus* (alder). A reduction in numbers of grazing domesticates may have been the primary cause, but this forest regeneration was only partial. Apparently contemporaneous phases of forest regeneration are seen at Fellend and Steng Mosses, on Hadrian's Wall (Davies and Turner 1979), although the ^{14}C dates do not allow confident temporal correlation. More widespread correlations with the agricultural recession recognised throughout northern Europe (Kristiansen 1984) are not confidently made, since there are a number of localities in northern Britain that do not provide evidence for a cessation, even partial, of agricultural activities, e.g. the northern Cheviots (Tipping, in prep.), or even economic recovery as at Kirkpatrick Fleming on the Solway Firth (Tipping 1995).

At Over Rig the sharply rising percentages of *Salix* (willow) pollen in l.p.a.z D, after the mid-ninth century AD, represents the on-site establishment of willow scrub, indicated by wood remains (Table 1) and frequent pollen clumps (Figure 2a). The very localised picture of the vegetation thus gained hinders interpretation. While the expansion of willow on the poorly drained terrace surface probably signifies a lack of grazing pressure there is no reason to assume the absence of agriculture from surrounding land.

Anglo-Norman Economic Recrudescence

At the beginning of l.p.a.z E, at around the beginning of the eleventh century, the willow scrub was in part cleared, somewhat abruptly although incompletely. Increased representation of alder and birch may be due solely to the ease of transfer of pollen to the peat following the removal of willows. Coryloid *(cf.* hazel) values in general rise erratically, a pattern suggested by Barber (1981) as perhaps implying the management of hazel. The same might be true at Over Rig, in which case the removal of willows could be seen as part of the reinstatement of formerly coppiced woodland abandoned in preceding centuries. The shrub pollen taxon *Prunus* type is recorded consistently. Wood tentatively assigned to *Prunus padus* (bird cherry), *P. spinosa* (sloe) and *P. avium* (wild cherry) was obtained from Romano-British deposits (Boyd 1988), although only *P. padus* and *P. spinosa*, together with *P. cerasus* (dwarf cherry) are now recorded from the region (Elliott 1896). Rosaceous taxa such as these and *Crataegus* have been suggested as representing hedges (Lambrick and Robinson 1979; Boyd 1984), perhaps to protect coppices from grazing animals.

Indicators of arable agriculture are not abundant, some of the grains of Gramineae >35 μm perhaps being derived from grasses such as *Glyceria fluitans* (seeds of this were recorded from ditch sediments; Robinson, D E, pers. comm.), although the evidence from the cumulative curve (Figure 2c) strongly suggests the re-establishment of a crop-raising economy. The intensity of grazing as indicated by pastoral palynological indicators is seemingly not heightened in this zone (Figure 2c), but the consistently rising record for *Rumex obtusifolius* suggests heavy grazing and trampling by stock (Hughes and Huntley 1988).

Particular grassland communities are further enhanced by the appearance of single grains at a number of levels of several distinctive legume species, particularly *Medicago* and *Onobrychis* type. The pollen taxon *Medicago* includes both *M. sativa* (lucerne) and *M. falcata* (sickle medick) (Moore *et al.* 1991). *M. sativa* is an introduction while *M. falcata* is native in restricted areas of eastern England (Clapham, Tutin and Warburg 1962; Fitter 1978); neither are native in southern Scotland (Elliott 1896; Milne-Redhead 1972; Martin 1985). *Onobrychis* type pollen is most likely to represent *Onobrychis viciifolia* (sainfoin) (Clapham *et al.* 1962; Moore *et al.* 1991). Again this is not native in southern Scotland, not presently winter-hardy north of Yorkshire (Spedding and Diekmahns 1972), and is restricted to calcareous soils in eastern England, although Turner *et al.* (1973) reported this pollen type from late prehistoric peats in upper Teesdale, suggesting it to have been a fodder crop. The occurrence of these two legumes is clearly not commonplace, particularly in medieval deposits from southern Scotland, and this raises many questions, reviewed fully below.

High and Late Medieval Upland Agrarian Practice

Towards the end of the thirteenth century, at the l.p.a.z E/F boundary (Figure 2), the rise in Coryloid *(cf.* hazel) percentages is considered to be local to the slopes above the peat, and does not signify a woodland regeneration phase. All other tree taxa decline or show no change. The steady increase in *Prunus* type values is abruptly curtailed at *c.* 100 cm depth, and while this may relate to alterations to hedged enclosures around Over Rig, there may be problems of core correlation between Monoliths 4 and 3 (Figure 2a) which render some interpretations problematic.

Nevertheless the appearance of *Ribes* pollen in this zone (Figure 2a) is unambiguous and noteworthy. *Ribes* (currant) pollen is very rare in British pollen diagrams (Godwin 1975). *Ribes rubrum* (redcurrant), the most likely species represented (Table 3) is thought to be native in southern Scotland (Milne-Redhead 1972; Martin 1975). Macrofossil finds of *Ribes* spp. in the British Isles include those by Boyd (1988) from Romano-British contexts at Over Rig, and from medieval contexts at Southampton (Dimbleby in Platt and Coleman-Smith 1975) and Worcester (Greig 1981), though the latter two are from urban contexts, as is the pollen evidence of *Ribes uva-crispa* type from seventeenth century Oxford (Greig 1994). The medieval finds may in any case represent wild fruits since Roach (1985) argued that cultivation commenced only in the sixteenth century. It is not known whether *Ribes* was planted or was growing wild at Over Rig. Its occurrence in both Romano-British and medieval times at Over Rig might indicate its persistence in natural scrub.

The fourteenth century showed a pronounced increase in arable palynological indicators (Figure 2c). Whilst this may relate to Cistercian monastic activity (below) it may also be linked to the demise of monastic control and the establishment in the later fourteenth century of tenanted farmsteads such as Lyneholm and Effgill (Figure 1c: Corsar 1982; Dodgshon 1983). Monastic control of the area was not formally ceded to private bailiffs, however, until 1484 (Armstrong 1883). Despite this, the planting of legumes does not appear to have persisted.

The economic stability apparent in the pollen record seems to have been maintained in the following centuries. The increasingly high percentages of Coryloid pollen (Figure 2a) distort the representation of other taxa, and induce declines in both pastoral and arable indicators (Figure 2c) but both practices were maintained. This picture can be mirrored in lowland areas at the foot of the Southern Uplands (Tipping 1995). This pattern differs from that at some other sites in the region (Turner 1970; Birks 1972a; Roberts *et al.* 1973; Davies and Turner 1979; Barber 1981; Dumayne 1992), which appear to depict agrarian recessions, though not necessarily synchronous nor sustained, renewed clearance seeming to occur at different times between the early fifteenth century (Barber 1981) and the sixteenth century (Davies and Turner 1979).

Discussion

The organic ditch fill that post-dates the late Iron Age complex at Over Rig presents many interpretative problems, not least being those related to chronology. Nevertheless, there are aspects of woodland history, and of medieval land management in particular, that merit further consideration.

The rich and diverse pollen assemblages from the site offer insights into past plant communities that are poorly represented at other sites. The prominence of tall shrubs in the pollen record, such as *Crataegus* type, *Prunus* type and *Ribes*, is unusual, and is only partly explained by the paucity of tree types. It is most likely that these grew very close to the site, possibly in natural scrubby woodland at times, but also at others possibly as components of managed landscapes, in hedgerows, for example, or in the case of *Ribes*, within garden plots or orchards. This diversity probably exists around most pollen sites but remains poorly discerned because most sites have much larger surface areas and markedly greater pollen recruitment areas than at Over Rig, with sampling points at considerable distances from sources of the dryland pollen that is normally of central interest. The ditch section at Over Rig was of course part of an archaeological site, and these commonly provide highly detailed palaeoecological reconstructions (e.g. Greig 1988, 1994; Lambrick and Robinson 1988) from pollen sites of very small spatial extent.

At Over Rig the ditch continued to receive sediment and pollen long after the archaeological site functioned, and the ditch behaved then as a 'natural' small woodland hollow. Such sites have been seen of most value in the reconstruction of wooded environments where the input of pollen is thought to come near-exclusively from trees immediately around the site. This has provided new insights into woodland composition and structure (Bradshaw 1981, 1988; Birks 1982; Mitchell 1988; Bradshaw and Hannon 1992). In partially deforested and open landscapes this relation breaks down as pollen sources become more disparate, but at Over Rig, and possibly many similar but unexamined sites the sensitivity of pollen recruitment to subtle natural and agrarian processes is maintained, and provides an enhanced palynological portrait of the 'cultural landscape'.

Boyd (1988) presented data on wood remains from the ditch fill at Over Rig which suggest a diverse woodland in the Romano-British period in upper Eskdale, containing alder, birch, hazel, poplar, ash, hawthorn, rowan, several species of cherry, ivy, holly, apple, and willow. Some of these were probably introduced to the site by people, and not being represented by pollen, need not have been local, but it is reasonable to assume that all these taxa were growing in upper Eskdale. Combining these data with the pollen analyses would suggest, however, that by the beginning of the historic period many trees were confined to localities protected from grazing, perhaps in ravines or behind fences. Indeed, Boyd assembled some evidence for woodland management in this period. This is in the form of the ages of cut branches, which suggest that around two-thirds of the assemblage was young, between five and twelve years old. This is tentatively suggestive of coppicing, although Boyd suggested that the age-range is not supportive of a highly organised system of even-aged clear-felling.

Another such subtle but significant element isolated at Over Rig is the possible introduction of legumes into grasslands, probably within the medieval period. Both *Medicago sativa* (lucerne) and *Onobrychis viciifolia* (sainfoin) have marked nitrogen fixing properties, and are associated with improved seeded grassland (Spedding and Diekmahns 1972), particularly for both grazing and hay production (Lane 1980). Could this have been the case at Over Rig in the early medieval period? Their appearance here at the beginning of the twelfth century AD is several hundred years earlier than conventionally assumed (de Candolle 1886; Franklin 1952; Kerridge 1967; Lane 1980; Overton 1985).

Contamination at Over Rig of these pollen grains from overlying sediments is unlikely given the sampling from a cleaned section, and it is considered that these legumes do date to the medieval period. The possibility that many agricultural advances conventionally dated to the early modern period occurred significantly earlier in key localities has recently been voiced by several historians (e.g. Campbell 1983; Outhwaite 1986; Williamson and Bellamy 1987). Attention focuses on the introduction of convertible or 'up-and-down' husbandry, with prolonged periods of fallow following ploughing, in which sowing of 'grass substitutes' (Overton 1985) would be seen as advantageous (Lane 1980), though not a necessary prerequisite (Searle 1974), greatly improving the quality and yield of pasture.

It may have been that lucerne was used as a fodder crop in prehistoric times (Lesins 1976), and also perhaps sainfoin (Turner *et al.* 1973). Spurr (1986) described the use in Italy during the fifth-sixth centuries AD of legumes as a means of shortening the fallow, and Lesins (1976) argued for its re-use in Spain in the eighth century, so that it is likely that this agricultural improvement had only to be re-discovered. Lane (1980) makes the same point, but argues for a late fifteenth century date for the development of convertible or 'ley' husbandry. Yet this type of farming regime is increasingly being seen as a medieval introduction in some parts of the country and in specific agrarian settings (Franklin 1952; Searle 1974; Williamson and Bellamy 1987).

Overton and Campbell (1992) argued that medieval stocking levels had the potential to be as high as those of the seventeenth century, 'since the technological means of increasing fodder supplies were available' (p. 392) – a view supported by Campbell (1972). But they also suggest that commercial incentives rather than ingenuity may have been lacking (see also Campbell 1988). In Norfolk, which Overton and Campbell studied, the demands on grazing imposed by intensive sheep farming, and their alleviation through convertible husbandry and ley crops, were delayed until the seventeenth century. In the uplands of southern Scotland this specialisation, and presumably the concomitant pressures on productivity, took place in the high medieval period (Dodgshon 1983), with many upland areas being given over to extensive sheep walks (Moffat, A 1985).

But who might have introduced this technique? David I granted Eskdale to Robert Avenel, an Anglo-Norman, prior to 1153 AD (Barrow, pers. comm.), but he had ceded part of this estate to the Cistercians at Melrose in 1165x1169 (Bannatyne Club 1837). In ceding the land Avenel agreed not to do 'damage... or injury to crops, meadows, hedged enclosures, cattle, beasts of work and burden and all other possessions of the monks' (Barrow, transl. and pers. comm.): cattle at that time were the principal stock. Avenel later converted part of his land in uppermost Eskdale to a hunting reserve (Gilbert 1979). The chronological controls on the date of introduction of these leguminous taxa are clearly insufficiently precise to determine which of these, Anglo-Norman lord or Cistercian monk, may have introduced forage crops like lucerne and sainfoin to this region. It is likely that both had sufficient energy, and the commitment to make major improvements to land quality, and both would have had connections with continental farming practice (Barrow 1980; Donkin 1963, 1978).

The evidence for sown 'grass substitutes' in upper Eskdale in the Middle Ages is inferential. It relies firstly on palynological identifications, which are unusual but not unique data sources for this period (Roberts *et al.* 1973; Moffat, B 1985). Greig (1994) records both *Medicago* type and *Onobrychis* from anthropogenic deposits, though from sixteenth and seventeenth century urban contexts at Tenby and Oxford respectively. These are equivocal in that neither lucerne or sainfoin can be identified to species, but comparison with authoritative floral lists allows the refining of the palynological record. Neither plant probably represented in the pollen record is native at present, and assuming this to be the case some 800 or so years ago (a reasonable assumption) then the taxa must have been introduced. And when the closely similar land management properties of these plants are appreciated then a clear reason for their introduction is established, and can be seen to fit within a picture of medieval entrepreneurial agrarian enterprise. The Southern Uplands may seem distant from the burgeoning resources and population pressures of East Anglia and the markets of south-east England, but the demands of the continental cloth trade and the export of wool through Berwick gave southern Scottish sheep-ranching very clear commercial incentives (Trow-Smith 1957; Lloyd 1977). It is argued here that these incentives led to the opportunity to discover anew farming methods not employed in the British Isles for several hundred years, and that the later collapse of the monastic economy meant that these techniques would not be re-discovered in other parts of the country for a few hundred years still.

References

Anderson, M L, *A History of Scottish Forestry* (Thomas Nelson, Edinburgh, 1967)

Armstrong, R B, *The History of Liddesdale, Eskdale, Ewesdale, Wauchopedale and the Debatable Land* (Douglas, Edinburgh, 1883)

Baillie, M G L, 'Suck-in and smear: two related chronological problems for the '90s', *Journal of Theoretical Archaeology*, 2 (1991), 12–16

Bannatyne Club, *Liber de Melros* (Bannatyne Club, Edinburgh, 1837)

Barber, K E, *Peat Stratigraphy and Climatic Change* (Balkema, Rotterdam, 1981)

Barrow, G W S, *The Anglo-Norman Era in Scottish History* (Clarendon Press, Oxford, 1980)

Bartley, D D and Chambers, C, 'A pollen diagram, radiocarbon ages and evidence of agriculture on Extwistle Moor, Lancashire', *New Phytologist*, 121 (1992), 311–20

Behre, K-E, 'The interpretation of anthropogenic indicators in pollen diagrams', *Pollen et Spores*, 23 (1981), 225–45

Belyea, L R and Warner, B G, 'Dating of the near-surface layer of a peatland in northwestern Ontario, Canada', *Boreas*, 23 (1994), 259–69

Birks, H H, 'Studies in the vegetational history of Scotland. II. Two pollen diagrams from the Galloway Hills, Kirkcudbrightshire', *Journal of Ecology*, 60 (1972), 183–217

Birks, H J B, 'The Flandrian forest history of Scotland: a preliminary synthesis', *British Quaternary Studies – Recent Advances,* ed. Shotton, F W (Clarendon Press, Oxford, 1977), pp. 119–36

Birks, H J B, 'Mid-Flandrian forest history of Roudsea Wood National Nature Reserve, Cumbria', *New Phytologist,* 90 (1982), 339–54

Boyd, W E, 'Environmental change and Iron Age land management in the area of the Antonine Wall, central Scotland: a summary', *Glasgow Archaeological Journal,* 11 (1984), 75–81

Boyd, W E, 'Methodological problems in the analysis of fossil non-artifactual wood assemblages from archaeological sites', *Journal of Archaeological Science,* 15 (1988), 603–19

Bradshaw, R H W, 'Quantitative reconstruction of local woodland vegetation using pollen analysis from a small basin in Norfolk, England', *Journal of Ecology,* 69 (1981), 941–55

Bradshaw, R H W, 'Spatially-precise studies of forest dynamics', *Vegetation History,* eds. Huntley, B and Webb III, T (Kluwer, Amsterdam, 1988), pp. 725–51

Bradshaw, R H W and Hannon, G, 'Climatic change, human influence and disturbance regime in the control of vegetation dynamics within Fiby Forest, Sweden', *Journal of Ecology,* 80 (1992), 625–32

Campbell, B M S, 'Agricultural progress in medieval England: some evidence from eastern Norfolk', *Economic History Review,* 36 (1983), 26–45

Campbell, B M S, 'The diffusion of vetches in medieval England', *Economic History Review,* 41 (1988), 193–208

Campbell, M H, 'Pasture establishment', *Intensive Pasture Production,* eds. Lazenby, A and Swain, F G (Angus and Robertson, Sydney, 1972), pp. 97–113

Candolle, de A, *Origin of Cultivated Plants* (Keegan, Paul and Trench, London, 1886)

Caseldine, C J, 'Surface pollen studies across Bankhead Moss, Fife', *Journal of Biogeography,* 8 (1981), 7–25

Clapham, A R, Tutin, W G and Warburg, E F, *Flora of the British Isles* (University Press, Cambridge, 1962)

Corsar, P, 'Platform-buildings: medieval and later settlements in Eskdale, Dumfriesshire', *Scottish Archaeological Review,* 1 (1982), 38–44

Davies, G and Turner, J, 'Pollen Diagrams from Northumberland', *New Phytologist,* 82 (1979), 783–804

Dodgshon, R A, 'Medieval rural Scotland', *An Historical Geography of Scotland,* eds. Whittington, G and Whyte, I D (Academic Press, London, 1983), pp. 47–72

Donaldson, A M and Turner, J, 'A pollen diagram from Hallowell Moss, near Durham City, UK', *Journal of Biogeography,* 4 (1977), 25–33

Donkin, R A, 'The Cistercian order in medieval England: some conclusions', *Transactions of the Institute of British Geographers,* 33 (1963), 181–98

Donkin, R A, *The Cistercians: Studies in the Geography of Medieval England and Wales* (Pontifical Institute of Medieval Studies, Toronto, 1978)

Dugmore, A J, 'Icelandic volcanic ash in Scotland', *Scottish Geographical Magazine,* 105 (1989), 168–72

Dumayne, L, 'Late Holocene palaeoecology and human impact on the environment of north Britain' (Ph.D. thesis, University of Southampton, 1992)

Dumayne, L, 'Iron Age and Roman vegetation clearance in northern Britain: further evidence', *Botanical Journal of Scotland,* 46 (1993), 385–92

Dumayne, L, Stoneman, R, Barber, K and Harkness, D, 'Problems associated with correlating calibrated radiocarbon-dated pollen diagrams with historical events', *The Holocene,* 5 (1994), 118–23

Elliott, G F, Scott, *The Flora of Dumfriesshire* (Maxwell and Sons, Dumfries, 1896)

Findlater, C, *General View of the Agriculture of the County of Peebles* (Constable, Edinburgh, 1802)

Fitter, A, *An Atlas of the Wild Flowers of Britain and Northern Europe* (Collins, London, 1978)

Franklin, T B, *A History of British Farming* (Nelson and Sons, Edinburgh, 1952)

Gilbert, J M, *Hunting and Hunting Reserves in Medieval Scotland* (John Donald, Edinburgh, 1979)

Godwin, H, *History of the British Flora* (University Press, Cambridge, 1975)

Greig, J, 'The investigation of a Medieval barrel latrine from Worcester', *Journal of Archaeological Science,* 8 (1981), 265–82

Greig, J, 'The palaeoecology of some British hay meadow types', *Plants and Ancient Man – Studies in Palaeoethnobotany,* eds. van Zeist, W and Casparie, W A (Balkema, Rotterdam, 1984), pp. 213–26

Greig, J, 'Some evidence of the development of grassland plant communities', *Archaeology and the British Flora,* ed. Jones, M (University Committee for Archaeology, Oxford, 1988), pp. 39–54

Greig, J, 'Pollen analyses of latrine fills from archaeological sites in Britain; results and future potential', *Aspects of Archaeological Palynology: Methodology and Applications,* ed. Davis, O M (American Association of Stratigraphic Palynologists Contributions Series 29, 1994), pp. 101–14

Hughes, J and Huntley, B, 'Upland hay meadows in Britain – their vegetation, management and future', *The Cultural Landscape – Past, Present and Future,* eds. Birks, H H, *et al.* (University Press, Cambridge, 1988), pp. 91–110

Jobey, G, 'Excavations at Boonies, Westerkirk and the nature of Romano-British settlement in eastern Dumfriesshire', *Proceedings of the Society of Antiquaries of Scotland,* 105 (1975), 119–40

Kerridge, E, *The Agricultural Revolution* (George Allen and Unwin, London, 1967)

King, J and Nicholson, I A, 'Grasslands of the forest and sub-alpine zones', *The Vegetation of Scotland,* ed. Burnett, J H (Oliver and Boyd, Edinburgh, 1964), pp. 168–231

Kristiansen, K, *Settlement and Economy in Later Scandinavian Prehistory* (British Archaeological Reports International Series 211, Oxford, 1984)

Lambrick, G and Robinson, M, *Iron Age Riverside Settlements at Farmoor, Oxfordshire* (Oxfordshire Archaeological Unit, Oxford, 1979)

Lambrick, G and Robinson, M, 'The development of floodplain grassland in the Upper Thames Valley', *Archaeology and the British Flora,* ed. Jones, M (University Committee for Archaeology, Oxford, 1988), pp. 55–74

Lane, C, 'The development of pastures and meadows during the Sixteenth and Seventeenth centuries', *Agricultural History Review,* 28 (1980), 18–30

Lesins, K, 'Alfalfa, lucerne', *Evolution of Crop Plants,* ed. Simmonds, N W (Longman, London, 1976), pp. 165–8

Lloyd, T H, *The English Wool Trade in the Middle Ages* (University Press, Cambridge, 1977)

Lowe, J J and Tipping, R, *A National Archive of Palaeoenvironmental Records from Scotland: A Pilot Study* (Scottish Natural Heritage, Edinburgh, 1994)

McVean, D N, 'Pre-history and ecological history', *The Vegetation of Scotland,* ed. Burnett, J H (Oliver and Boyd, Edinburgh, 1964), pp. 561–7

McVean, D N and Ratcliffe, D A, *Plant Communities of the Scottish Highlands* (HMSO, Edinburgh, 1962)

Mackay, A W and Tallis, J H, 'The recent vegetation history of the Forest of Bowland, Lancashire, UK', *New Phytologist,* 128 (1994), 571–84

Martin, M E R, 'Wild Plants of Dumfriesshire (V-C 72 Dumfries) 1985', *Transactions of the Dumfries and Galloway Natural History and Antiquarian Society,* 60 (1985), 21–42

Mercer, R J, 'The excavation of an earthwork enclosure at Long Knowe, Eskdale, Dumfriesshire 1976', *Transactions of the Dumfries and Galloway Natural History and Antiquarian Society,* 56 (1981), 38–72

Milne-Redhead, H, 'A check-list of the flowering plants, ferns and fern-allies of the Vice-counties of Dumfries, Kirkcudbright and Wigtown', *Transactions of the Dumfries and Galloway Natural History and Antiquarian Society,* 49 (1972), 1–19

Mitchell, F J G, 'The vegetational history of the Killarney oakwoods, SW Ireland: evidence from fine spatial resolution pollen analysis', *Journal of Ecology,* 76 (1988), 415–36

Moffat, A, *Kelsae. A History of Kelso from Earliest Times* (Mainstream Publishing, Edinburgh, 1985)

Moffat, B, 'The environment of Battle Abbey estates (East Sussex) in medieval times; a re-evaluation using analysis of pollen and sediments', *Landscape History,* 8 (1985), 77–94

Moore, P D, Webb, J A and Collinson, M E D, *Pollen Analysis* (Blackwell, Oxford, 1991)

Oldfield, F, 'Pollen analysis and man's role in the ecological history of the south-east Lake District', *Geografiska Annaler,* 45 (1963), 23–40

Oldfield, F, 'Pollen analysis and the history of land use', *Advancement in Science,* 1 (1969), 298–311

Oldfield, F, *et al.,* 'Geochronology of the last millennium', *Palaeoclimate of the Last Glacial/Interglacial Cycle,* eds. Funnell, B M and Kay, R L F (Special Publication No. 94/2 of the NERC Earth Sciences Directorate, Swindon, 1994), pp. 77–80

Oldfield, F, Richardson, N and Appleby, P G, 'Radiometric dating (^{210}Pb, ^{137}Cs, ^{241}Am) of recent ombrotrophic peat accumulation and evidence for changes in mass balance', *The Holocene,* 5 (1995), 141–8

Outhwaite, R B, 'Progress and backwardness in English agriculture, 1500–1650', *Economic History Review,* 39 (1986), 1–18

Overton, M, 'The diffusion of agricultural innovations in early modern England: turnips and clover in Norfolk and Suffolk, 1580–1740', *Transactions of the Institute of British Geographers,* NS 10 (1985), 205–21

Overton, M and Campbell, M S, 'Norfolk livestock farming 1250–1740: a comparative study of manorial accounts and probate inventories', *Journal of Historical Geography,* 18 (1992), 377–96

Platt, C and Coleman-Smith, R, *Excavations in Medieval Southampton 1953–1969* (University Press, Leicester, 1975)

Putman, R J, *Grazing in Temperate Ecosystems. Large Herbivores and the Ecology of the New Forest* (Croom Helm, Beckenham, 1986)

Reynolds, P J, *Iron-Age Farm. The Butser Experiment* (British Museum, London, 1981)

Roach, F A, *Cultivated Fruits of Britain: Their Origin and History* (Blackwell, Oxford, 1985)

Roberts, B K, Turner J and Ward, P F, 'Recent forest history and land use in Weardale, northern England', *Quaternary Plant Ecology,* eds. Birks, H J B and West, R G (Blackwell, Oxford, 1973), 207–21

RCAHMS, *Seventh report with inventory of monuments and constructions in the county of Dumfries* (HMSO, Edinburgh, 1920)

Searle, E, *Lordship and Community. Battle Abbey and its Banlieu 1066–1538* (Pontifical Institute of Medieval Studies, Toronto, 1974)

Spedding, R R W and Diekmahns, E C, *Grasses and Legumes in British Agriculture* (Commonwealth Agricultural Bureaux, Farnham, 1972)

Spurr, M S, *Arable Cultivation in Roman Italy* (Society for the Promotion of Roman Studies, London, 1986)

Tinsley, H M and Smith, R T, 'Surface pollen studies across a woodland/heath transition and their application to the interpretation of pollen diagrams', *New Phytologist*, 73 (1974), 547–65

Tipping, R, 'A note concerning possible increased pollen deterioration in sediments containing *Lycopodium* tablets', *Pollen et Spores*, 29 (1987), 323–8

Tipping, R, 'Holocene evolution of a lowland Scottish landscape: Kirkpatrick Fleming. II. Regional vegetation and land-use change', *The Holocene*, 5 (1995), 83–96

Tipping, R, 'The form and fate of Scottish woodlands', *Proceedings of the Society of Antiquaries of Scotland* (in press)

Trow-Smith, R, *A History of British Livestock Husbandry to 1700* (Routledge and Kegan Paul, London, 1957)

Turner, J, 'The anthropogenic factor in vegetational history. I. Tregaron and Whixall Mosses', *New Phytologist*, 63 (1964), 73–90

Turner, J, 'Post-neolithic disturbance of British vegetation', *Vegetational History of the British Isles*, eds. Walker, D and West, R G (University Press, Cambridge, 1970), pp. 97–116

Turner, J, 'The environment of north east England during Roman times as shown by pollen analysis', *Journal of Archaeological Science*, 6 (1979), pp. 285–90

Turner, J, *et al.*, 'The history of the vegetation and flora of Widdybank Fell and the Cow Green reservoir basin, upper Teesdale', *Philosophical Transactions of the Royal Society of London*, B265 (1973), 328–407

Vuorela, I, 'Human influence on the vegetation of Katinhanta bog, Vihti, S Finland', *Acta Botanica Fennica*, 98 (1972), 1–21

Vuorela, I, 'Relative pollen rain around cultivated fields', *Acta Botanica Fennica*, 102 (1973), 1–27

Walker, M J C, 'Pollen analysis and Quaternary research in Scotland', *Quaternary Science Reviews*, 3 (1984), 369–404

Williamson, T and Bellamy, L, *Property and Landscape* (George Philip, London, 1987)

Acknowledgements

Financial assistance for this project from Historic Scotland is much appreciated. Roger Mercer is thanked for inviting me to undertake the analyses, and he, Angela Wardell and Jane Webster assisted with fieldwork. My predecessors with palaeoenvironmental work at the site, Bill Boyd and David Robinson, generously gave information. Gordon Cook of the Scottish Universities Research and Reactor Centre provided the ^{14}C dates and much discussion.

Many thanks are accorded colleagues for discussing aspects of the work; Robin Andrew, Geoffrey Barrow, John Gilbert, James Greig, Jim Innes, Roger Mercer, Brian Moffat, Rob Scaife, Judith Turner and Graeme Whittington, and to Chris Smout for encouraging this publication.

6. Old Managed Oaks in the Glasgow Area

Martin Dougall and Jim Dickson

That ancient woodland can be found at all in the Glasgow area comes as a surprise to many. Roberts *et al.* (1992) calculate the area of Strathclyde Region covered by ancient woodland at 2.2%. While this is certainly only a very small part of the region it should be seen in the context of other parts of Scotland – 0.3% of Fife, 0.4% of Border Region (Roberts *et al.* 1992). Clearly the distribution of such woodland will vary widely within a large and diverse Region like Strathclyde, but the amount within the built up area around Glasgow compares favourably with these regions listed above – 0.7% of Glasgow District is ancient woodland.

This is only a small reduction from the time of Roy's map (1750) when approximately 4% of Scotland's land area was covered by woodland (Walker and Kirby 1989). The accuracy of their calculation based on Roy's map is discussed by Smout and Watson (this volume).

For our research two areas of woodland were studied in some detail – Garscadden Wood (NS 5272) and the Cadzow Oaks (NS 7353) (Dougall 1994) but a brief mention must also be made of Mugdock Wood (NS 5476). Located on the outskirts of Milngavie, near the start of the West Highland Way, this is a mixed deciduous wood. Much of the wood is on sloping ground, the land dropping gently from the ancient Mugdock Castle down to the Allander Water. On the steeper and therefore drier parts the vegetation is dominated by oak trees with some very large coppice stools. Large alder and birch coppice stools are found on the lower-lying and wetter parts of the wood.

These coppice stools are the most striking feature of the wood with some diameters well in excess of 2 m. Individual trunks are of no great age, around 90 years, showing that the last cut was fairly recent. It is the size of the individual stools which is significant, Stevenson (1990) and Rackham (pers. comm.) stating confidently that they indicate continuous tree cover for at least 400 years. There is the possibility that parts of the wood have been cleared at some stage, as indicated by pollen analysis of peat deposits within the wood, nonetheless this is seemingly not the case for the whole wood.

Documentary evidence that there was a wood present at Mugdock in past centuries can be found from the thirteenth century with further references from later medieval times (Smith 1886). This is followed by clear depiction of a wood on Blaeu's map (Blaeu 1654) and Roy's map (Roy 1747–55). Estate records document the practice of woodsmanship in the eighteenth and nineteenth centuries. This woodsmanship took the form of coppicing, the timber being advertised for sale and areas of the wood being let for grazing.

Mugdock Wood is now an SSSI and since 1981 has been within Mugdock Country Park. Aesthetically it is as pleasing and delightful as any wood with an unspoilt and natural feel. Its future currently seems secure.

For a fuller description see Stevenson (1990).

Cadzow Oaks

(see Figure 1)

The Cadzow Oaks are a remarkable area of wood pasture on the outskirts of Hamilton. There are now approximately 300 trees. Taxonomic analysis shows the typically confused situation discussed by Cousens (1962, 1963, 1965), Gardiner (1970), Wigginton and Graham (1981) and others. In an attempt to clarify the exact status of the Cadzow oaks a Hybrid Index was constructed in the manner described by Wigston (1974). Eight diagnostic features of the trees were selected, samples of the trees taken and then for each of these eight

Figure 1: General view of the Cadzow Oaks.

features individuals were scored depending on whether they show attributes of *Quercus robur, Q. petraea* or some intermediate condition.

For the Cadzow oaks some characteristics, e.g. leaf lobing and number, were almost always typical of *Q. robur*, but for others, e.g. leaf pubescence, there was a consistency of *Q. petraea* characteristics. Overall the trees showed more *Q. robur* characteristics although there is a clear influence from *Q. petraea*. This is despite some claims, e.g. Dengler (1941) that hybrids between these two species of oak rarely occur.

Cousens (1965) suggests that once an initial hybridisation does occur introgression with either parent species will then be common, resulting in the complicated assemblage of characters found in many trees like the Cadzow oaks.

As stated, the trees now stand within an area of pasture-land. Cattle, and occasionally sheep, graze freely among them. A few trees are within the grounds of Chatelherault Country Park and this has been very important for maintaining the trees in the public consciousness.

Several features of the trees are of note. One is their 'stagheadedness' – a term which describes the antler-like protrusions from the crown of trees such as these. Stagheadedness results from the dying back of parts of the crown, boughs often falling off the trees and then being replaced by fresh growth from below (see Figures 2 and 3).

Even more striking than their stagheadedness is the massive girth of many of the trees, allied in some cases with a pronounced epicormic growth. This results in massive burrs, ridges and other outgrowths mainly on the lower part of the trunks. It is unclear whether they have a genetic origin or whether they grow in response to repeated grazing of side shoots.

An important factor in the large girth of the trees is their considerable ages. Samples of timber removed for dendrochronology studies from living trees and from cut stumps date back to 1444 (Baillie, unpublished data, see also Baillie 1982). Some stumps are still present in the wood pasture and examination of these show their considerable antiquity, one stump possessing at least 440 annual rings.

It is possible that some of the living trees are even older than this stump. Attempts at coring trunks to ascertain their age proved unsuccessful, largely as a result of their hollowness, and therefore the ages of these trees can only be surmised. Some trees show a combination of massive girth and a small crown. This particular combination is of great interest since the large girth can only have been attained by slow growth over many years and so these trees are likely to be the oldest. By comparing their girth with that of cut stumps of slow growing trees – e.g. the cut stump with its 440 rings – it is possible to surmise that some trees may be approximately double the age of this stump. Certainly there is a local legend that the trees were planted by David I in the twelfth century and it is not inconceivable that they may date from such a time. Such ancient oaks have been documented before (Schadelin 1905).

The historical management of the trees is of enormous interest as it must, in some way, have contributed to their present growth habit if not their very survival to the present day. There are suggestions that the practice of pollarding was responsible for the trees acquiring their present shape (Hamilton District Council 1988, Kirby 1989) largely since this was a common method of

Figure 2: Stagheaded oak with massive epicormic outgrowth
and some lower bough dieback.

Figure 3: One of the most severe cases of dieback, revealing the hollow centre to the trunk. This tree is still alive.

managing trees in wood pasture systems. Our study of the Cadzow Oaks has shown that pollarding was not regularly carried out on these trees.

The evidence for this statement comes from several sources. Simple observation of the trees finds very few of them with the characteristic shape of a pollard: i.e. the boughs would be disproportionately small in proportion to the trunk. Approximately five of the trees have a shape that could be consistent with repeated pollarding, but most do not.

Documentary evidence provides confirmation. Old estate records (listed below as Manuscript Materials) and other historical documents (Gibson 1695, Statistical Accounts of Scotland) regularly mention these trees, notable as they were even in the eighteenth century. Yet no mention of any utilisation of the trees consistent with pollarding was ever found, despite a thorough study of old documents.

Most conclusive, however, is the interpretation of ring-width data from these trees. Rasmussen (1990) and Rackham (1975) show that when a tree is pollarded there is a marked decrease in the amount of growth possible until a new crown is formed. Consequently the ring-width increments show a pronounced decrease for a period of years followed by gradual recovery. Using the raw data collected by Baillie for his dendrochronology studies, more than 50 graphs of individual tree ring-width against time were plotted. No such pattern is discernible for the Cadzow Oaks.

So what is the history of the trees? They stand on ground that was formerly the hunting estate of the Dukes of Hamilton and the main reason for their survival seems to have been as an integral part of the 'chase'. Roaming among the trees in former centuries were wild white cattle and, to a certain extent, deer. It is our understanding that the trees have acquired their striking shapes simply as a result of their considerable age, periodically receiving severe setbacks and dieback occurring. Recovery then occurs and the trees soldier on.

The extent and number of the trees has decreased very considerably from the wide expanses of the sixteenth century to the present scattered remains. Aerial photographs show how significant the tree loss has been, even in the short time period since 1946 when these photographs first become available. Since then there has been at least a 50 percent decrease in the area covered by the oaks, although in some cases the fields cleared were quite sparsely populated by the oaks. It is essential that those which survive are now protected.

Garscadden Wood

The other area studied in detail is entirely different in nature – Garscadden Wood, sandwiched between Bearsden and Drumchapel, on the north of Glasgow. Its outward appearance is very deceptive and a casual glance fails to reveal the antiquity and importance of the wood.

The wood is approximately tadpole-shaped and some areas are of more interest than others (see map). In the eastern part of the wood – i.e. the tail of the tadpole – the wood consists of planted aliens and is of little interest. It is clear that this is a recent addition. It is the head of the tadpole where the interesting features are found – old earthworks and old trees. Yet they must be sought out, the canopy of much of this area being formed from maiden oaks, about 120 years old. Even this area, the head of the tadpole, is not homogeneous and it seems that there is an ancient core within this generally older part of the wood.

Historical documents and old maps provide less information about the history of Garscadden Wood than they do for the Cadzow Oaks, although they do show the increase in size of the wood as it encompassed areas of surrounding woodland in the late eighteenth century. Garscadden Wood appears on Roy's map of 1750 and subsequent maps show its increase in size as surrounding areas of farmland were included.

In Garscadden Wood old trees do not equate with large trees, so old trees are very easily overlooked. All are coppice stools with some fairly large stool diameters but their recent past means that all the existing trunks are small. This is not only in their overall height but also in their girths. None exceed 120 cm (girth measured at breast height) and it is likely that no individual trunk is older than 120 years. Moreover many of the trunks have been crudely hacked and vandalised.

In total there are nineteen clear examples of such oak rings, several of which have a stool diameter of more than 2 m. Oliver Rackham states (1980) that this typically results from 400 or more years of growth. All these oak rings are found in the area that has been identified as the ancient inner core of the wood, located within the head of the tadpole.

As this area is closest to the housing of Drumchapel it receives the most disturbance and vandalism. Fires occur regularly and trees are crudely hacked and chopped at. Despite this the old trees seem to survive, a modern form of coppicing occurring! Figure 4 shows part of the ancient area closest to the houses, its open nature being maintained since Drumchapel was built in the 1940s (as confirmed by aerial photographs). In contrast Figure 5 shows how attractive the wood is away from the houses – within the ancient core but north of the track that runs the length of the wood.

The other striking feature of Garscadden Wood is the presence of typically medieval earthworks, further reflecting a history of old woodsmanship. The array of earthworks in the wood was initially so complex and confusing that a full survey was undertaken for us by the Association of Certified Field Archaeologists, Glasgow University. The resulting map showed the presence of drainage ditches and possible runrig in parts of the wood, indicating that at one stage it had been cleared and used for agriculture. Significantly, no evidence of these past agricultural uses were found in the area of the old trees. Moreover the

Figure 4: View across part of the ancient inner core of Garscadden Wood with Drumchapel behind. Some of the small trees are ancient coppiced oaks.

Figure 5: Away from the houses but still within the ancient inner core of Garscadden Wood. The two trunks in the foreground are two outgrowths from one coppiced stool.

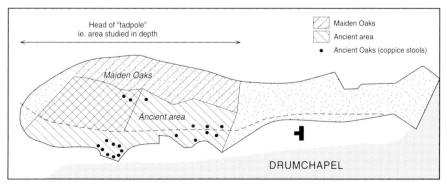

Figure 6: Garscadden Wood.

remains of an old woodbank can be deciphered on three sides of the old trees, confirming that there is an ancient inner core in the wood (see Figure 6).

The conclusion about Garscadden Wood then is that here there is a well preserved ancient wood with many of the classic features of an ancient wood as listed by Oliver Rackham in his accounts of ancient woodland in England (see references). The wood has proved remarkably resilient to the interference from nearby Drumchapel and, despite outward appearance, is a fascinating area. It is proposed that the wood should be set up as a local nature reserve.

More fully detailed accounts of these woods will be published elsewhere.

References

Baillie, M G L, *Tree-Ring Dating and Archaeology* (University of Chicago Press, Chicago, 1982)

Blaeu, J, *Le Grand Atlas* (Amsterdam, 1654)

Cousens, J E, 'Notes on the status of the sessile and pendunculate oaks in Scotland and their identification', *Scottish Forestry*, 16 (1962), 170–9

Cousens, J E, 'Variation of some diagnostic characteristics of the sessile and pendunculate oaks and their hybrids in Scotland', *Watsonia*, 5 (1963), 273–86

Cousens, J E, 'The status of the pendunculate and sessile oaks in Britain', *Watsonia*, 6 (1965), 161–76

Dengler, A, 'Bericht uber Kreuzungsversuche zwischen Trauben – und Stieleiche (*Quercus sessiliflora* Smith u. *Q.pendunculata* Ehrh. bzw *Robur* L.)', *Mitteilungen H. Goring – Akademie Deutsche Forstwissenschaft*, 1 (1941), 87–109

Dougall, N M E, 'The ancient oakwoods of Cadzow and Garscadden – their history, ecology and conservation' (unpublished MSc thesis, University of Glasgow)

Gardiner, A S, 'Pendunculate and sessile oak (*Quercus robur*, L. and *Q.petraea* (Mattuschka) Liebl.). A review of the controversy', *Forestry*, 43 (1970), 151–60

Gibson, E, *Camden's Brittania* (F Collins, London, 1695)

Hamilton District Council, *Chatelherault Country Park* (Hamilton District Council, Dept. of Leisure and Recreation, Hamilton, 1988)

Kirby, K J, 'Unpublished NCC report on Cadzow forest', (SNH Office, Balloch, 1989)

Rackham, O, *Hayley Wood – Its History and Ecology* (Cambridgeshire and Isle of Ely Naturalist's Trust Ltd., 1975), p. 221

Rackham, O, *Ancient Woodland* (Edward Arnold, 1980)

Rackham, O, *The History of the Countryside* (J M Dent and Sons, London, 1986)

Rackham, O, *Trees and woodland in the British Landscape* (revised edn. J M Dent and Sons Ltd., London, 1990)

Rasmussen, P, 'Pollarding of trees in the Neolithic: often presumed – difficult to prove', *Experimentation and Reconstruction in Environmental Archaeology*, Symposia of the Association for Environmental Archaeology No. 9, ed. Robinson, D E, Roskilde, Denmark 1988 (Oxbow Books, 1990)

Roberts, A J, Russell, C, Walker, G J and Kirby, K J, 'Regional Variation in the origin, extent and composition of Scottish Woodland', *Botanical Journal of Scotland*, 46 (1992), 167–89

Roy, Manuscript maps: *The Military Survey of Scotland* (1747–55). (Copies in National Library of Scotland.)

Schadelin, W, 'Von einem Grossen Eiche', *Schweize Zeitung Fortwissenschaft*, 56 (1905), 286–7

Smith, J G, *The parish of Strathblane and its inhabitants from early times* (James Maclehose and Sons, 1886)

Statistical Accounts of Scotland:

> *Old Statistical Account of Scotland* Vol. VII – Lanarkshire and Renfrewshire (E P Publishing Ltd., 1791–1799)
>
> *New Statistical Account of Scotland* (1845), pp. 251–94
>
> *The Third Statistical Account of Scotland,* Vol. 8: The County of Lanark (1960)

Stevenson, J F, 'How ancient is the woodland of Mugdock?' *Scottish Forestry,* 44 (1990), 161–72

Walker, G J and Kirby, K J, *Inventories of ancient long-established and Semi-Natural Woodland for Scotland* (NCC, 1989)

Wigginton, M J and Graham, G G, *Guide to the identification of some of the more difficult vascular plant species* (NCC, Peterborough, 1981)

Wigston, D L, 'The distribution of *Quercus robur* L., and *Q.petraea* (Matt.) Liebl., and their hybrids in south-western England. 1. The assessment of the taxonomic status of populations from leaf characters', *Watsonia,* 10 (1975), 345–69

Manuscript Materials

(Unpublished papers of the Hamilton Estate. These are mostly held in Hamilton Library; transcripts of many of these were consulted at Chatelherault Country Park).

Burrell, J, (1763) – (1801) Journals

Edward, Alexander, (1708) Plans and maps

Hutton, T, (1736) Letter dated Hamilton, 28 January 1736

Labourer's Account (1801–1802)

Ray, A, (1790) Journal 18 Feb 1790 to 12 March 1793

Wright, J P, (1740) Work Account for 9 June 1740 to 22 November 1740

7. Exploiting Semi-natural Woods, 1600–1800

Chris Smout and Fiona Watson

The central question in this chapter is how far the exploitation of Scottish woodland, 1600–1800, was, in modern terms, 'sustainable'. Some preliminary explanations are in order. Sustainability is essentially a twentieth-century term, the meaning of which has evolved gradually, beginning with the American Progressive notion of a 'maximum sustainable yield' applied to fisheries and forestry in the era of Theodore Roosevelt and Gifford Pinchot (McEvoy 1988), but more recently expressed by the Brundtland Report as a universal ideal of sustainable development which 'meets the needs of the present without compromising the ability of future generations to meet their own needs' (World Commission on Environment and Development 1987). This has subsequently been glossed as necessarily involving, firstly, the maintenance of biodiversity within ecosystems and secondly, the acceptance of such development by local societies (UNCED 1992).

The general ideal enunciated by Brundtland would have been immediately recognisable by early modern society. It is no more than a general notion of wise traditional use at peasant level 'adhered to because traditionally they were the only guarantee of survival' (Redclift 1987); or of 'good stewardship' at proprietorial level. It resonates, for example, with the laws of entail in England and Scotland which limited the rights of landed heirs to sell property acquired by their forefathers. The Earl of Lauderdale, political economist and Scottish landowner, knew all about sustainability when he wrote in 1804 that, 'the common sense of mankind would revolt at a proposal for augmenting wealth by creating a scarcity of any good generally useful and necessary for man' (Lauderdale 1819).

On the other hand the subsequent gloss would have been incomprehensible in an earlier Europe. The notion of preserving biodiversity was meaningless in a society which took it for granted that man had been given dominion over every growing plant and living creature, to use or to extirpate them at pleasure. Similarly, while the notion that change had to be socially acceptable might have worked in peasant cultures, it scarcely determined the behaviour of a Scottish landowning class in a country where the rights of property were wont to override the customs of their dependants to an exceptional degree (Smout 1989). We might therefore say that if early modern woodland management practices met the needs of the time without compromising those of future generations, that was probably an intended consequence, but if they happened to preserve biodiversity or to be socially acceptable to the commonality, that was an accidental by-product. Furthermore, to be realistic, it is perfectly possible and even likely that a management regime which maintained and increased the 'maximum sustainable yield' of timber products would, to some degree, both damage biodiversity and offend the local population. This was certainly true in late eighteenth-century Scotland.

What woods are we talking about? It has been estimated from Roy's military survey of *c.* 1750 that woodland at that time covered about four percent of the Scottish land surface (O'Dell 1953; Walker and Kirby 1989). Though the accuracy of such calculations has been questioned (Whittington and Gibson 1986), the character of this survey makes it unlikely to have been as much as 50 percent out in its depiction of woods. By its use of particular cartographic projection it may have exaggerated features of the valleys at the expense of the open hill, and thus to have overstated the extent of woods: conversely, it is also known to have overlooked some woods depicted on near-contemporary estate maps. Even if a slightly more generous figure than 4 percent was taken, it would still rank Scotland among the least wooded countries in Europe.

All of this wood would have been 'semi-natural', composed of native species growing by natural regeneration on their original sites, but modified by the pressure of human beings and their domestic stock over millennia – in many cases since the Neolithic (Dickson 1992; Tipping 1993, 1994). Timber scarcity appears in the Scottish Lowlands from the fourteenth and fifteenth centuries (Gilbert 1979) and thereafter became a talking point for outside travellers (Johnson 1773; Brown 1893). There was therefore a striking regional imbalance between the Lowlands and the Highlands, with most of the woodland in the latter region, and perhaps there covering about 8 percent of the land surface (Lindsay 1974).

The reasons for this imbalance were not simply that the Lowlands were more fertile, had a denser population, and more towns, so that ground that was bearing trees came to be required for cultivation. Southern England and France provide examples of much more extensive woods in more populated countries, and much of the Scottish Lowlands in fact consisted of bleak open moor perfectly capable of carrying a timber crop but unsuitable for cultivation. One better alternative explanation is the abundance in Scotland of alternative fuel and building material: peat was very widely available, and coal was noted as a common domestic fuel from the fifteenth century, initially dug in shallow bellpits or from outcrops that needed no more capital than a pick, a horse and a cart. Stone was everywhere present, an impediment to cultivation that could as well be put in the walls of a house as in a clearance dyke. There were certainly many things for which wood was indispensable, for example building crucks and rafters and most agricultural tools, but a community could make do with relatively less than in most parts of Europe. The second explanation is the relative importance of pastoral husbandry – especially in the Border counties, of extensive sheep farming. It has been calculated that the clip exported to Flanders in most years of the late thirteenth century was the produce of between 1,500,000 and 2,500,000 sheep mostly from the Border abbeys (Grant 1984). The same forces that kept the English Downs free of scrub kept the Southern Uplands of Scotland green and heathery. The effect of the rising profitability of sheep ranching was reflected in the manifest decline of woodland in the royal and baronial hunting 'forests' of the Borders, (Anderson 1967), and has been recently traced on monastic lands in Dumfries and Galloway between the Urr and the Nith, where grants of pannage before around 1180 (implying herds of pigs and cattle in oak forest) gave way abruptly to grants of pasture for sheep (Oram 1989, and pers. comm.).

Nevertheless, it would be quite wrong to imagine the south of Scotland as either completely devoid of woods or lacking a tradition of woodland management. The woods were simply more restricted in scale than in most parts of Europe. The main species in their composition were oak, with birch, willow, hazel and alder as important in most places, and elm, ash and sycamore as locally significant. The last-named was an exotic import from southern Europe, but planted in Scotland from the late middle ages both around houses and in woods: there is sycamore coppice in woodland in Fife that may well be 400 years old.

A native tradition of Scottish woodcraft analogous to that described for southern England (Rackham 1980) and France (Bechman 1990) emerges from a study of woodland contracts in the seventeenth and in the first half of the eighteenth centuries (SRO: Register of Deeds). The specialist terminology used suggests their antiquity: 'haggs', for divisions of a wood to be cut at any one time, derives from a Norse word for the hewing down of trees, shared with the north of England; 'rice' was from another Old English and Norse word for twigs and brushwood used as wattle on the fencing to exclude animals from the coppice; 'grain' was from a Norse word for branch; 'hain' was from the Norse to hedge or protect, and so on.

The main provisions in Lowland contracts embody three elements. Firstly, there was systematic use of coppicing (pollarding and shredding may well have been practised but are not mentioned in the deeds). The early rules of coppicing in Scotland included stipulations to cut the stool 'raised and smoothed as to prevent the diminishing thereof by water' (or alternatively not to be cut 'dished', or to be cut 'with ane ascent and descent' i.e. with an upward and downward stroke): other contracts stated it had to be cut four inches from the ground, and that the roots must not be damaged in any way. The cutting season was stipulated e.g. [he] 'binds himself not to cut any timber in the flee month which is called 15 days before Lammas and other 15 days after Lammas yearly' (i.e. between 16 July and 15 August). Often the season for oak began in April and ended in July. Other trees than oak might be called 'winter wood'. Small trees or withies were to be left, sometimes defined as those that could not be drilled by a small tool – could not bear a 'wormlick bore'. Very frequently it was a régime of coppice-and-standards, where a certain number of 'maiden' trees, growing straight from seed, were to be left: e.g. 'John and Alexander bind themselves... to leave in the several haggs of said woods as they cut the same yearly, 100 reserve or maiden trees proportionally, the most part whereof to be 8 inches round at 6 quarters high from the root'.

Secondly, the system of staggered cutting, and sometimes of cutting on a clear rotation, was established. Small woods might be felled in one season, or divided into a small number of haggs to be cut in turn, but the larger ones such as Branxholm and Mortoun near Langholm were on a ten-year fell. It does not of course follow that the woodcutters here would begin again after the ten years: the woods might well then rest another decade. The Wood of Kincardine on the Montrose estate, however, was sold in 1704 on a 24-year rotation basis, the 'wood to be divided in as many equal portions as there are years allowed to John and he to cut but one of these portions in a year', and in 1722 the same estate sold the 'third part of the woods of Monteith now ready to be cut... in seven years by equal divisions', suggesting a 21-year rotation. Arrangements were made for cleaning the haggs of brush and rubbish after cutting, for regulating the grazing of horses in the wood while work was continuing, for setting up wood-cutters' houses and so on. In the Torwood in 1740 the cutters were to 'thicken the haggs so cut with young trees from the nurseries in the yards of Torwoodhead' but this was exceptional: regeneration was the usual way of replenishing the felled divisions.

Thirdly, careful arrangements were frequently made for establishing and maintaining enclosures round the wood, and round the individual rotation haggs within the wood in order to exclude damage from animals. This was the most important provision of all. Thus at Innerkip in 1704 the woodmen had to 'build ane sufficient fencible chardyke of stake and ryce so as to keep out all horses, sheep or other cattle and that by 14 July yearly... and to keep up the same'; at the Wood of Kincardine in the same year they had to 'uphold the peallings [palings] within the wood during all the time of haining'; at Kippen in 1712 they had to 'give as much timber as will serve for pealling of the outside and indivisions of the said woods'; at Mortoun in 1722 they had to 'allow so much walling and top hedging as shall be found necessary and convenient for Sir Patrick for the feall [turf] dykes for inclosing the said woods and making cross dykes betwixt the haggs or faulds of the same'. There is a very strong impression in the Lowlands that grazing and woodland management were regarded as mutually antipathetic.

When management fell below standard, there was awareness of what to do. When in 1715 it was discovered that the woods on the Buccleuch estates in Ettrick forest were in poor shape, the chamberlain was instructed to make a particular inspection, to appoint proper foresters, to prosecute those who cut, stole or barked wood, and since:

> we are informed there is a good appearance of young springe in severall
> places... specially near Newark where wood grows naturally and every spring
> makes a pretty good show, but destroyed for want of incloseing,

the chamberlain was to mark out the places most proper to be enclosed with
fences, 'sufficient and sensible against beasts.' Three years later detailed
recommendations on the Ettrick woods called for the birch and alder to be
fenced and coppiced; the oak and ash to be thinned if kept for standards, or
coppiced with their stocks being carefully cut at the ground and the springing
thinned; and the hazel to be thinned, enclosed and coppiced or weeded out to
make room for more valuable wood (Smith, this volume).

As in the English and French systems, woods managed under these régimes
would perhaps have been indefinitely sustainable, though recently doubts have
been thrown on the long-term viability of coppicing, particularly under
conditions like those in the west of Scotland where continuous removal of
woody material combined with the effects on heavy rainfalls on acid soils might
have a deleterious effect (Hambler and Speight 1995). Besides, good woodland
management could also give way under other pressures on land use. The
monastic house of Coupar Angus in the fifteenth and sixteenth century managed
woodland at Campsie by dividing it into quarters, maintaining haining
regulations and appointing local tenants to have the responsibility of being
foresters. However, the demand for grazing land was such that animals were
allowed into the enclosures, and part of the wood was eventually reported as
'decayed' (Rogers 1879–80). Two centuries later, there was no trace of it: it is
not only good management, but continuity, that ensures sustainability.

The Highlands had retained appreciably more wood than the Lowlands, with
a different balance of trees. Birch was the most widespread species in most
regions, dominant particularly in Wester Ross and Sutherland. Oak dominated in
Argyll and Perthshire, but there were also often oakwoods, especially on south-
facing slopes, as far north as Sutherland and Wester Ross. Scots pine, which did
not occur naturally south of the Highland line, was dominant, generally in mixed
woods with birch, on poorer soils in two different habitats. The eastern
pinewoods comprised the relatively large forests of the Spey, the Dee and of the
Beauly catchment, along with a few straths to the north. The western pinewoods
ranged from near Ullapool to Glen Orchy in Argyll, but were more scattered and
normally on north-facing slopes. The main difference was that in the east the
pinewoods regenerated from seed relatively easily in a drier climate and on
more sparsely vegetated ground, whereas those in the west depended more on
catastrophe, such as fire or wind-throw, to create space in the deeply mossy or
peaty ground sufficient for seed to germinate. Other common trees in the
Highlands were hazel (generally coppiced), ash (where there was limey ground),
alder and willow (where it was wet), gean, rowan, holly and aspen. The last
three were probably much commoner than today, as they tend to be selectively

browsed by domestic stock and deer. It is not unusual to find early reference to woods of 'birk and hollyn'.

There are many problems in trying to ascertain the extent of woodland in the Highlands before the middle of the eighteenth century, when Roy's Military Survey gives a firmer basis for estimation. The first maps are those of Timothy Pont from the close of the sixteenth century; by and large they do not suggest that much more wood was present then than there was a century and a half later, but they are (for the most part) field sketches rather than finished productions (Stone 1989). Robert Gordon of Straloch also left unpublished rough manuscript maps; these have tree symbols over much wider areas than Pont, but there is some uncertainty about his first-hand knowledge of the ground. When Blaeu in Amsterdam published worked-up versions of the Pont maps and of others emanating from Gordon in 1654 they often had more woodland on than most of the Pont sketches, but less than the Gordon maps: this could have been as much for decorative as for cartographic reasons (Smout, this volume). Much more detailed manuscript maps of the upper Dee (*c.* 1703) and of parts of the Great Glen, Easter Ross and the Beauly catchment area (1725–30), suggest a distribution of woodland recognisably similar to that of later times, though not without some loss – on the Mar Lodge Estate, for example, woods in Glen Derry and Glen Lui are now much reduced (Avery 1725–30; RCAHMS 1995).

Some of the ambiguity may derive from uncertainty as to what to count as a wood, especially in the Highlands. Many of the early symbols seem to indicate scattered groupings rather than continuous wood, strikingly so in Pont's map of Glencoe and Mamore which is also annotated 'many fyrre woods here alongs', in an area that became almost totally denuded of Caledonian pine after 1750. Then there are several descriptions from the late eighteenth and early nineteenth centuries of hardwood scrub that appeared above the level of the heather in summer, only to be eaten back by domestic animals in winter when they came down from shielings on the hills (Williams 1784; Monteath 1827). Williams spoke of 'a great many thousand acres' of such land forming 'a rich stool of oak in a deep soil' between Speyside and the Atlantic sealochs; Monteath of 'many thousand acres of land that was formerly carrying Natural Woods [that] have of late years been left unenclosed and set aside for pasture land', particularly in Argyll. Perhaps these were the vestiges of much larger natural woods that had flourished in the Middle Ages but were now in their final stages of decay.

Examination of eighteenth-century woodland contracts often reveal differences in management practices between the Highlands and the Lowlands. Before 1750, there is generally a striking lack in the north of specific details to protect the wood by regulating coppicing, determining rotation and above all an absence of stipulations about fencing. Contracts may specify that certain trees (for example, the 'firs' or pines) should not be cut, or that trees below a certain size are not felled. Often the restrictions were in dangerously vague terms: e.g. 'Arthur and Roger bind themselves to cut down the trees according to the common and reasonable custom and at the proper times and seasons'. In this last case (relating to a contract between two Irish adventurers and the Earl of Breadalbane) the landlord later declared that the damage done by the contractors had been intolerable to the value of the estate and the interests of tenants, but he had no redress. The line between the detailed Lowland contracts and the looser Highland ones often follows the geographical line quite exactly, so that (for example) in Perthshire a contract relating to Innerpeffery on the Lowland side specifies coppice restrictions, haggs and fencing, but one relating to Logierait and another to Faskally on the Highland side specifies coppice regulation more vaguely, and haggs and fencing not at all. It is the absence of enclosure after cutting that is particularly striking, though in some areas, such as Lochtayside, oak woods were 'emparked', apparently from an early date.

The explanation is not that Highland woods were considered of no value. In cultural and aesthetic terms, woods ranked high even in the sixteenth and seventeenth centuries when (at least according to Thomas 1983) they were regarded poorly in England. The contrast is between epithets like 'delectable', 'fair', 'fair and tall', 'beautiful to look on', 'pleasing' in Scotland, and 'dreadful', 'gloomy', 'wild', 'desert', 'uncouth', 'melancholy' in England (Cheape 1993; Smout 1994). Woods were also regarded as extremely useful to the Highlanders in economic terms. Even stone buildings needed wooden crucks and cabers, and in the most forested areas the walls of entire houses were also made from wattle or planking. Occasionally large buildings such as a castle or a church were substantially wooden. All sorts of equipment from ploughs and harrows to mill machinery needed wood: temporary fencing demanded wattle frames of hazel: fish traps and creels were similarly constructed: holly boughs were occasionally cut for fodder: fir candles (the most resinous parts of pine trees) were used for light: bark was used for tanning leather and preserving fishing nets. The practical uses of wood in Highland society were infinite.

There are better explanations for the neglect of enclosure. Firstly, woodland was relatively much more plentiful in most places in the Highlands, the islands excepted, than it was in the Lowlands, so a need to husband the resource was not so clearly seen, and the physical difficulty of enclosure was much greater. Second, pine does not coppice and birch does so only weakly, so the full elaboration of Lowland practice was less applicable outwith the main oak-growing areas. Third, there was an important use of woodland as winter shelter for animals, the bottom end of a transhumance system that took them to the hill pastures, the shielings, in summertime. This last point holds the key to much of their ultimate decline, the failure, in fact, of sustainable use.

It is important here to distinguish between the proximate and the ultimate cause of deforestation. Some contemporaries, and most historians, were quick to blame a series of obvious culprits when they saw the forest felled. For the pine woods, chief among them were English speculators, beginning on the Spey at Abernethy with the lease of the woods to Captain John Mason in 1631. It is not known whether Mason actually cut any timber, but the York Buildings Company purchased 60,000 trees in the forest from the owner in 1726 and set about its exploitation with great vigour, floating the wood down to the sea in rafts for the first time, building an iron furnace that operated briefly, and erecting sawmills. The company came to grief through over-extravagance, but sales and felling continued. Higher up the Spey at Glenmore and at Rothiemurchus there was intensive felling late in the eighteenth and in the early nineteenth centuries, partly for ships' timbers and partly for deal planking: contemporaries by the 1830s spoke of 'devastation' in these ancient forests. But the fact remains that each of them are still there, possibly diminished in size (it is difficult to be sure) but undeniably sustained (Steven and Carlisle 1959). A similar point could be made about the Black Wood of Rannoch (Lindsay 1974), and the forests in the Beauly catchment area (Avery 1725–30), where we know of heavy exploitation, but also from pre-1760 maps, that they cover much the same ground now that they did 250 years ago. It could be cogently argued that the very value put on the timber gave the lairds the incentive to maintain them. Some of the baron court penalties for misuse of the wood were draconian on Speyside: for example, in 1693 burning heather too close to the woods was punishable by having the culprit's ear nailed to the gallows, and in 1722 reoffending by stealing wood three times was allegedly punishable by death (Steven and Carlisle 1959).

It is also true, however, that in these eastern pinewoods regeneration was very much easier, both under normal circumstances and either after fire or after disturbance of the ground, than it was in the west and north. It is easy to find, in the west, comparable acts of woodland exploitation, but many of the woods here are certainly now much smaller than formerly, and some have been reduced to small remnants. Examples of the latter are at Coigach in Wester Ross, sold to timber merchants in the 1720s, at Glen Orchy and Glen Kinglass in Argyll, sold to Irish speculators at about the same time, at Ardgour on Loch Linnhe and at Callart on the northern shore of Loch Leven. One major – though broken – stretch of pine, noted by Pont in the 1590s and still extant in the 1750s, was on the southern shore of Loch Leven from the mouth of Glen Coe. This is among the few large pine woods to have disappeared without trace in the last 500 years (though the Coille Mhor at the head of Strath Nairn is probably another and the pines inland of Gruinard a third). Natural woods like these were perfectly capable of regenerating vigorously, especially after fire, but could not do so if the seed trees had been removed – especially if the eighteenth-century form of removal, by horse, was insufficiently destructive of the thick western moss and heavy vegetation to allow fresh shed seed to come up through it. What was sustainable in the east might not be so in the west.

And of course it was always true that if heavy levels of browsing were allowed, whether by deer, sheep, goats or cattle, a pine wood, like any other wood, could not regenerate. A commentator in Argyll, speaking of remnant pine woods at high altitudes, said that:

> from the seed which they shed in winter, and which is driven to a distance by the storm, a beautiful plantation rises up in spring; but when the cattle are

driven up to the mountains in summer, this precious crop, the hope of future
forests, is for ever destroyed. (Smith 1798.)

In the east, fires in forests like Glentanar were usually followed by
regeneration, but in the early twentieth century 7000 sheep were pastured in it
and fires there were not then followed by new growth (Steven and Carlisle
1959).

The history of oak woodland in Argyll and elsewhere in the south and west
Highlands is comparable. Here the traditional villains are usually named as the
iron-masters, beginning with Sir George Hay in the early seventeenth century in
Wester Ross, and continuing with Irish and especially with English interests in
the eighteenth century in Invergarry, Loch Etive and Loch Fyne. Most accounts
stress the depredations that the charcoal burners are supposed to have wreaked
for this handful of furnaces, up and down the western sealochs (e.g. Darling
1947; Cheape 1993), though Lindsay has demonstrated the inherent
implausibility of such widespread damage, as well as showing that the longest-
surviving of the furnaces, in Lorn, was associated with stability in local
woodland, not decline (Lindsay 1975b). The exploitation of the oakwoods for
tan bark, however, was more prolonged, more widespread and heavier than the
cutting for industrial fuel. It was tanbark that brought Irish adventurers to the
woods – for example, of Locheil – even before the Act of Union (Spreull 1705)
and which continued to attract Scottish exploitation on a large scale well into the
nineteenth century (Nicol 1799; Monteath 1827). The explanation for the early
Irish interest lies in British legislation that forbade the export of Irish cattle to
mainland Britain: this drove the Irish to slaughter their animals at home, barrel
the beef for ships' provisions for the Transatlantic trade (English and French
ships used Cork as their main provisioning port) and tan the hides themselves.
By the end of the seventeenth century Irish supplies of oak bark were
insufficient.

In the early days – i.e. before the second half of the eighteenth century – the
cutting of the Highland oakwoods appears from contracts to have been largely
unregulated, but as the price of charcoal and bark increased all this changed. By
the time of the agricultural reports of the 1790s it was normal, in the main oak-
growing areas accessible to transport, to have coppice-management on 20–25
year rotation, followed by fencing to protect the regrowth for at least five years,
and sometimes permanently (Marshall 1794; Robson 1794; Robertson 1794;
Smith 1798; Lindsay 1975a). Further north – and more distant from the market –
there were still extensive patches of oak 'all shamefully abandoned, after every
cutting, in the same neglected condition', and even in Argyll critics in the early
nineteenth century still spoke of thousands of acres of oak regrowth abandoned
to grazing. (Robertson 1808; Monteath 1827). Although the biodiversity of the
woods must have been considerably modified as birch, hazel, willow, and holly
were discouraged in the interest of the more valuable oak (Monteath 1827), in
most respects and despite reservations this was the hey-day of sustainable
broadleaf forestry in the Highlands (Lindsay 1974).

All this was brought about by a management revolution. Until the middle of the eighteenth century, day-to-day exploitation of the Highland woods was loosely co-ordinated by the local baron courts, which fined the tenants for such offences as cutting greenwood without permission, for 'cutting high' on a coppice stool, for burning birch within a wood or practising muirburn too close to a wood: occasionally they suggested an interest in other good forest practice, such as systematically replanting native trees. The seventeenth-century baron court books of Glen Orchy provide a good illustration (Innes 1855). Local tenants were generally appointed to be foresters. They were not obviously concerned to regulate grazing (except occasionally that of goats), since a prime use of woodland was for winter shelter for stock (see also Watson, this volume).

When in the eighteenth century this system came under the critical eye of the agricultural improver and land steward, they were extremely critical of its effects: they found the regulations neglected, the woods pillaged for fuel, bark, and construction timber, and animals everywhere eating the regeneration (Williams 1784; Marshall 1794; Dickson 1975, 1976; Henderson and Dickson 1994). Their answer was to replace local control by a professional factor or specialised forester from the estate head office and then basically to introduce the Lowland system of wood management, with a particular emphasis on enclosure and on ending the former freedoms for the tenants to take what they needed from the wood. The reforms produced complaint of real hardship among tenants who found themselves deprived of critical pasture and shelter for their stock at the most difficult time of the year (Millar 1909). They also became short of timber for construction and everyday use: thus in Argyll where wood had been so freely available that farm houses were 'in some respects more commodious than in many other parts of the Highlands' (Robson 1794), a few years later the reservation of the woods for charcoal and tanbark production had created in many areas 'a great discouragement to the farmer', who then needed to buy his timber from Norway (Smith 1798). One serious consequence of the managerial change was that the link in much of the Scottish Highlands between woodcraft and farming was broken for ever. When the fences round these oakwoods again fell into decay, as the price for tanbark and charcoal collapsed in the second and third quarters of the nineteenth century, they were again used for pasture with very damaging results, and generally with little attention to any other value they might have to the farmer.

How far were the improvers' criticisms of the traditional looser controls justified, and, if so, why had an apparently unsustainable system of peasant husbandry been allowed to continue for so long? Consider, first how the traditional grazing system would have worked. Those modern enemies of natural regeneration in Scotland, deer and sheep, were a much smaller problem than now. Deer numbers were a fraction of what they are today, and in some areas where regeneration no longer occurs solely due to their browsing, their absence was a matter of concern to the landlord anxious for better sport (Watson 1983; Smith 1993). Sheep numbers similarly were low, and the size of the animal small: until the great invasion of the Highlands by Cheviot and Blackface sheep mainly in the first half of the nineteenth century, the Highland sheep was diminutive and kept by the tenants mainly for their own subsistence (Gray 1957).

The principal browsing animals of the traditional Highlands were horses, goats and cattle. Horses (though much more numerous than today) were probably not a problem as they are light feeders on trees: goats certainly were a problem, and, though also kept mainly for subsistence, were extremely numerous – 100,000 goat skins were sent from the Highlands to London in one year at the end of the seventeenth century (Smout 1963). The improvers were extremely critical of the damage they did, and most estates had effectively extirpated them from their tenants' flocks by the end of the eighteenth century. The greatest volume and weight of beasts, however, must have been the traditional Highland 'black cattle', which were kept both for the peasants' own use and to meet their rent obligations to the landlord. Cattle grazing had a plus and a minus side. On the plus side, the cow has heavy feet which punch holes in a mossy sward and thus favour regenerating trees, especially in the wetter west; it also feeds on grass with a tearing motion, which also disturbs the ground, and has runny dung that penetrates at once into the ground as fertiliser. Sheep and deer, by contrast, are too light to make much impact, nibble the sward closely like lawn mowers, and have hard dung, much of which dries and evaporates on the open hill. On the minus side, however, if cattle are too numerous they can create as much damage to the wood as any other animal simply by eating everything that comes up. In the eighteenth century, the complaints were of heavy and increasing grazing, and the observations numerous and damning.

One such was a very interesting comment in Sutherland in 1812, where the reporter told of a 'remarkable alteration on the face of this part of the country in the course of the last twenty years', the widespread decay of the natural broadleaf woods with which the straths were once covered (Henderson 1812). The reporter was torn between blaming climatic change and animal grazing. He said that 'naturalists aver' that severe frost and snow in April and May had caused the destruction: but as the main species was birch, which endures much colder climates than Sutherland, with some oak, which he reported as profitable where properly managed, the climatic explanation seems unlikely. More plausible culprits were the goats, since until very recently every farmer had kept a flock of 20 to 80, and 'the constant browsing of black cattle, [so that] it is not surprising that the [natural] oak is nearly gone'. At any rate:

> It is a well known fact, that in the straths where these woods have already decayed, the ground does not yield a quarter of the grass it did when the wood covered and sheltered it. Of course the inhabitants cannot rear the usual number of cattle, as they must now house them early in winter, and feed, or rather keep them just alive, on straw; whereas in former times their cattle remained in the woods all winter, in good condition, and were ready for the market early in summer. This accounts for the number of cattle which die

from starvation on these straths, whenever the spring continues more severe than usual; and this is one argument in favour of sheep farming in this country.

In a corroborative letter, the minister of Kildonan adds the details that formerly the animals were outwintered until January but must now be taken indoors in November, and that the replacement of the 'fine strong grass with which the woods abounded' by coarse heather had led to a 'degeneracy of black cattle in the parts that were formerly covered with wood'. It would be hard to find a better contemporary description of the knock-on effects on an ecosystem of unsustainable woodland management, but it was not the first hint in this direction. For example, as early as 1753 a tenant on the Mackenzie of Seaforth estates in Wester Ross had written:

> I hear from sensible honest men that other places in the country besides my tack have now less wood and more fern and heath than formerly, so that cattle want shelter in time of storm (as we never house any) and their pasture is growing more course and scarce. I know of severall burns that in time of a sudden thaw or heavy rain are so very rapid that they carry down from the mountains heaps of stone and rubbish which by overflowing their banks they leave upon the ground next them for a great way and by this means my tack and other are damaged and some others more now than formerly. (NLS.1359.100.)

Erosion and increased stream-flow are just what would be expected from deforestation, in addition to deterioration of the herbiage. We know of no external exploitation here to explain the losses. Interestingly, it was in these northern counties of Sutherland and Ross where most complaint came in the nineteenth century of deteriorating pastures, then attributed to sheep grazing (Hunter 1973). It may have longer and different roots.

The eighteenth century was marked by two novel features in the history of the Highlands – an unprecedented increase in human population, and an unprecedented increase in the numbers of black cattle as the external trade to the Lowlands and to England grew (Gray 1957). Human population of the five Highland counties grew by well over one half between 1755 and 1841, and Scottish cattle exports grew by at least fourfold between 1720 and 1814 – not all would be Highland animals, but unquestionably many were. Then in the first half of the nineteenth century cattle were largely replaced by even larger numbers of sheep. This pressure blew apart the balance between farming and woods. It could be argued that earlier practices of winter grazing at light levels had been at least semi-sustainable. Unfortunately, the eighteenth-century change was both subtle and insidious, and land management traditions were too inflexible to reduce the pressure of animals. This kind of thing must be common in the Third World today. The impact of all this on biodiversity extended beyond the trees themselves – the wolf was exterminated probably before 1700, and the largest woodland bird, the capercaillie, by 1780. But above all, the traditional ways of treating the Highland woods began to become much more damaging because there simply were too many people with too many animals.

An instructive example comes from Invercauld in Deeside in the 1740s, where a lawsuit relating to rights to cultivate on the edges of a forest were challenged by the feudal superior, who argued that it would prevent the regeneration of his pines which needed space outside the existing wood to seed successfully, as they would not do so within its bounds unless it was cut or blown over. The growth of farms in an area hitherto only lightly used by man and animal was depriving the woods of their natural means to change their boundaries by which they had traditionally survived (Michie 1901). Pressure of people meant that sustainability was threatened.

From this trap there were three ways out. The first was for local communities to resist the pressures and to continue to accord the traditional natural woods enough respect and value for them to survive. That this could at least occasionally happen is demonstrated in Assynt, west Sutherland, where the woods that were in existence around 1770 are virtually all in existence today, particularly those in the neighbourhood of settlements (Noble, this volume). A very similar situation pertains at Sleat on Skye (Alan MacDonald, pers. comm.). The second was for the eastern pine forests to come under commercial pressure and for their owners to respond by better management, including enclosure, as happened at Abernethy and eventually at Rothiemurchus. The third was for similar pressures to inspire the enclosure and care of the oakwoods of the southern Highlands, many of which became exceptionally well tended in the period 1780–1850. However, the last two remedies proved of short-term value when the price of Scottish wood products collapsed in the nineteenth century. Most even of the eastern pinewoods are now failing to regenerate due to pressure from deer numbers, and both oak and birch woods are generally under pressure from deer and sheep. That many semi-natural woodlands have survived over the last century and a half is due not so much to enlightened management, as to the ability of trees as organisms to endure for very long periods, providing they are not physically removed from the landscape. Even so, many semi-natural woods have been destroyed: we have lost 40 percent of Highland birchwoods since the Second World War. But just allowing them to survive, but not to regenerate, which is usually the extent of the most generous modern management over much of Scotland, is of course not a sustainable woodland policy in the long run.

References

Anderson, M L, *A History of Scottish Forestry* (Edinburgh, 1967)
Avery, J, MS map of the Moray Firth and Great Glen in Inverness Museum (1725–30)
Bechman, R, *Trees and Man: the forest in the Middle Ages* (New York, 1990)
Brown, P H, *Early Travellers in Scotland* (Edinburgh, 1891)
Cheape, H, 'Woodlands on the Clanranald estate: a case study', *Scotland since Prehistory:*

Natural Change and Human Impact, ed. Smout, T C (Aberdeen, 1993)

Darling, F F, *Natural History in the Highlands and Islands* (London, 1947)

Dickson, G A, 'William Lorimer on forestry in the Central Highlands in the early 1760s', *Scottish Forestry*, 29 (1975)

Dickson, G A, 'Forestry in Speyside in the 1760s', *Scottish Forestry*, 30 (1976)

Dickson, J H, 'Scottish woodlands: their ancient past and precarious future', *Botanical Journal of Scotland*, 26 (1992)

Forest Authority, *Caledonian Pinewood Inventory* (leaflet) (Glasgow, 1994)

Gilbert, J, *Hunting and Hunting Reserves in Medieval Scotland* (Edinburgh, 1979)

Grant, A, *Independence and Nationhood* (London, 1984)

Gray, M, *The Highland Economy, 1750–1850* (Edinburgh, 1957)

Hambler, C and Speight, M R, 'Biodiversity Conservation in Britain: Science replacing tradition', *British Wildlife*, 6 (1995), pp. 137–47

Henderson, D M and Dickson, J H (eds.), *A Naturalist in the Highlands: James Robertson, his Life and Travels in Scotland* (Edinburgh, 1994)

Henderson, J, *General View of the Agriculture of the county of Sutherland* (London, 1812)

Hunter, J, 'Sheep and deer: Highland sheep farming 1850–1900', *Northern Scotland*, 1 (1973), pp. 199–222

Innes, C (ed.), *The Black Book of Taymouth* (Bannantyne Club, Edinburgh, 1855)

Lauderdale, Earl of, *An Inquiry into the Nature and Origin of Public Wealth*, 2nd edn (Edinburgh, 1819)

Lindsay, J M, 'The Use of Woodland in Argyllshire and Perthshire between 1650 and 1850' (Ph.D. thesis, University of Edinburgh, 1974)

Lindsay, J M, 'Charcoal iron smelting and its fuel supply: the example of Lorn furnace, Argyllshire, 1753–1876', *Journal of Historical Geography*, 1 (1975a)

Lindsay, J M, 'The history of oak coppice in Scotland', *Scottish Forestry*, 29 (1975b)

McEvoy, A F, 'Towards an interactive theory of nature and culture: ecology, production, and cognition in the California fishing industry', *The Ends of the Earth: Perspective on Modern Environmental History*, ed. Worster, D (Cambridge, 1988)

Marshall, W, *General View of the Agriculture of the Central Highlands of Scotland* (London, 1794)

Michie, J G (ed.), *Records of Invercauld* (New Spalding Club, Aberdeen, 1901)

Millar, A H (ed.), *Scottish Forfeited Estate Papers, 1715: 1745* (Scottish History Society, Edinburgh, 1909)

Monteath, R, *Miscellaneous Reports on Woods and Plantations* (Dundee, 1827)

Nicol, W, *The Practical Planter, or a Treatise on Forest Planting* (Edinburgh, 1799)

O'Dell, A C, 'A view of Scotland in the middle of the eighteenth century', *Scottish Geographical Magazine*, 69 (1953)

Oram, R, 'The Lordship of Galloway, *c.* 1000 to *c.* 1250' (unpublished Ph.D. thesis, University of St Andrews, 1989)

Rackham, O, *Ancient Woodland: its History, Vegetation and Uses in England* (London, 1980)

RCAHMS, *Mar Lodge Estate Grampian: an Archaeological Survey* (Royal Commission on the Ancient and Historical Monuments of Scotland, Edinburgh, 1995)

Redclift, M, *Sustainable Development: exploring the contradictions* (London, 1987)

Robertson, J, *General View of the Agriculture in the Southern Districts of the County of Perth* (London, 1794)

Robertson, J, *General View of the Agriculture of the County of Inverness* (London, 1808)

Robson, J, *General View of the Agriculture of the County of Argyll* (London, 1794)

Rogers, C (ed.), *Rental Book of the Cistercian Abbey of Coupar Angus* (London, 1879–80)

Smith, J, *General View of the Agriculture of the County of Argyll* (Edinburgh, 1798)

Smith, J S, 'Changing deer numbers in the Scottish Highlands since 1780', *Scotland since Prehistory: Natural Change and Human Impact*, ed. Smout, T C (Aberdeen, 1993)

Smout, T C, *Scotish Trade on the Eve of Union, 1660–1707* (Edinburgh, 1963)

Smout, T C, 'Landowners in Scotland, Ireland and Denmark in the Age of Improvement', *Scandinavian Journal of History*, 12 (1989)

Smout, T C, 'Trees as historic landscapes: Wallace's oak to Reforesting Scotland', *Scottish Forestry*, 48 (1994)

Steven, H M and Carlisle, A, *The Native Pinewoods of Scotland* (Edinburgh, 1959)

Stone, J C, *The Pont Manuscript Maps of Scotland: Sixteenth-century Origins of a Blaeu Atlas* (Tring, 1989)

Tipping, R, 'A History of the Scottish Forests revisited', *Reforesting Scotland*, 8, 9 (1993)

Tipping, R, 'The form and fate of Scotland's woodlands', *Proceedings of the Society of Antiquaries of Scotland*, 124 (1994), 1–54

Thomas, K, *Man and the Natural World* (London, 1984)

UNCED, *United Nations Conference on Environment and Development: Agenda 21* (Rio, 1992)

Walker, G J and Kirby K J, *Inventories of Ancient, Long-established and Semi-natural Woodland for Scotland* (NCC, 1989)

Watson, A, 'Eighteenth-century deer numbers and pine regeneration near Braemar, Scotland', *Biological Conservation*, 25 (1983)

Whittington, G and Gibson, A J S, *The Military Survey of Scotland, a Critique* (Aberdeen, 1986)

Williams, J, 'Plans for a Royal forest of oak in the Highlands of Scotland', *Archaeologica Scotica*, 1 (1794)

World Commission on Environment and Development, *Our Common Future* (1987)

Acknowledgements

This is part of a study on 'Sustainability in the management of Scottish semi-natural woodlands 1600–1900', funded by the Economic and Social Research Council (grant no. L3202533166).

8. Rights and Responsibilities:

Wood-management as seen through Baron Court Records

Fiona Watson

In the historic period the relationship between people and woodlands has rarely been a direct one; rather, that relationship could be better described as triangular, involving the woods themselves, the people living and working in their neighbourhood, and those who own the land and/or the natural resources on it. While the landlord today (whoever or whatever that might be) can no longer maintain the degree of control over the local population experienced in previous centuries, the relationship between that population and neighbouring woodlands even in the late twentieth century is still governed by a set of rules prescribed by an external agent or agency. For those studying woodland history, this three-way relationship does not, therefore, merely engender questions relating to the comparative merits of these rules in relation to the trees themselves; we must also examine the relationship between the two groups of humans involved. This naturally revolves around the whole issue of *control*.

The baron courts of medieval and early modern Scotland, were, it could be argued, one of the most effective and influential legal institutions of that period, operating over much of the country and, most particularly, for the purposes of this paper, a large part of the Highlands. Their effect and influence was due to the fact that they gave the landlord an instrument of control over the *minutiae* of estate life, as well as the more general misdemeanours of the tenantry. Since these courts were concerned both to implement parliamentary statutes concerned with woodland management, and its own acts on the subject, surviving records therefore afford us a fascinating and detailed glimpse of the relationship between landlord, tenant and trees. It will perhaps already be objected that such evidence is by definition one-sided, exemplifying only the attitudes and aspirations of the landlord whose court it was. Certainly these records must not be taken at face value: the acts passed for the maintenance of woodlands, and the contravention of, or adherence to, these acts by the local populace, is only the starting-point for any discussion of the relationship of both groups with the trees themselves, as well as with each other. But it should be accepted from the start that neither side automatically occupied the moral high ground.

Some historians have dismissed the use of baron court records as requiring too much effort for too little return. However, research into just two sets of court books (SRO: GD 112/17; GD 50/136) – those for the Campbell lairds of Glenorchy (earls of Breadalbane from 1681) and the Menzies lairds of Weem and Rannoch – provides detailed information for an area stretching from Benderloch and Loch Awe in the west, across to Aberfeldy and the north shores of Loch Rannoch in the east, from the 1570s to the 1740s and the 1630s to the 1740s respectively. While not affording a definitive model (there can surely be no such thing), this evidence certainly provides us with a representative study of how landlords and tenants in the western and central Highlands regarded the semi-natural woodlands in their neighbourhood and the efforts expended by both groups to maintain them.

There would appear to have been variations in tree-management policies both between and within the two sets of land-holdings. This suggests a willingness on the part of landlords to accommodate the specific needs of each wood, and, more particularly, diverse forms of land-tenure and local custom; it also doubtless signifies their reactions to the varying degrees to which tenants accepted authority. For example, effective control over the remote lands of north Rannoch was not established by the Menzies of Weem until at least 1660, whereafter considerable effort was expended in training the tenants there in the basic rules of Menzies' wood management; this contrasted with the more established and sophisticated regulations governing the other Menzies' estate in the Appin of Dull, which was controlled more effectively from their castle at its centre (SRO: GD 50/136).

The lairds of Glenorchy operated a more homogeneous and intensively-managed administration over their vast estates, which comprised at least sixteen baronies with their individual courts: it is likely that they could only be matched in attempted effectiveness by the senior branch of the family, the Campbells of Argyll. The network of control operated by Glenorchy rested, in part, on the co-operation of a number of lesser lairds, such as Campbell of Glenfalloch, Campbell of Monzie and Campbell of Barcaldine, an option not open to smaller landlords such as Menzies. Its effectiveness is best illustrated by the astonishing regularity of court sittings, which ranged from at least once to three or four times a year; this compares most favourably with the Menzies' courts, which became almost annual only after 1700 in the Appin of Dull and were far less frequent in Rannoch. The problem of tenants absenting themselves from court on a regular basis, which was very much a feature of the Menzies' courts, was also a much rarer occurrence on the Glenorchy lands (SRO: GD 112/17; GD 50/136).

It might be expected that the care taken of any woodland, and the form of management which is implemented as a result, would be very much dependent on the commercial value placed on the trees themselves. The attention paid to woodland management by the Menzies of Weem, despite the lack of evidence for any commercial activity in the Appin of Dull woodlands in particular, and, indeed, the strong suspicion that these trees were not of any great commercial value, seems to challenge this view. By the 1630s, when the surviving records begin, the tenants had no rights in law to cut wood, even for the upkeep of their buildings, corresponding to the prevailing belief that all natural resources belonged unequivocally to the laird; if tenants did cut wood (and obviously they had to, since they required timber for most aspects of their lives), they were quite used to the idea that they should coppice, rather than lop branches off at will, and abstain from peeling bark and burning. This was not the case in Rannoch, where the tenants were usually prosecuted explicitly for 'cutting high', peeling and burning (SRO: GD 50/136).

The lairds of Weem made little profit directly from selling the Appin of Dull woods (except the oak wood of Caill, sold in 1740 for 2615 merks). Most of the woods seem to have comprised a basic mix of alder, ash, birch and hazel, (SRO: GD 50/138) and were thus better suited to local use than commercial exploitation. However, the woods did add a considerable sum to the laird's annual income in the form of fines imposed for the cutting of timber. Evidence for such fines unfortunately disappears after 1673 but in that year alone the total reached over £485 Scots (SRO: GD 50/136). Even if the larger individual fines, imposed for offences such as the destruction of planted pines, were held over the head of the offender as surety for future good behaviour, the lucrative nature of this system almost certainly dictated policy. In other words, the lairds of Weem permitted their tenants to cut, as carefully as possible, the wood on which their buildings and farm equipment depended, in return for a minimum charge, in the form of a fine, of 40s.; the more use made of the woods, the more profit. There can have been fewer more potent illustrations to the tenantry of the control exerted over their lives by the landowner; each and every single stick was required to be accounted for. The sustainability of such a policy nonetheless depended very much on the numbers of those living in the area, together with their accompanying stocks of animals, both of which placed pressure on the woods.

The population of the Appin of Dull before 1750 was high to modern eyes: 258 adult men were fined in 1719, implying a total population of at least 1000 people in the barony (SRO: GD 50/136). Yet it does not appear to have placed an intolerable pressure on these woodlands; most of the wood required was taken in a steady trickle, allowing for continual regeneration. Certainly, a comparison of today's Ordnance Survey maps with General Roy's maps of the 1750s indicates that the extent of the woodland in this area has remained more or less the same. However, this statement is extremely misleading: the 1750 levels have only been maintained through nineteenth-century planting, suggesting that the post-Improvement era, heralding the arrival of sheep and whole-scale enclosure, also brought about increasing pressure on these non-commercial woods.

The attitude of the Menzies' lairds to an increasing population, both human and animal, was therefore critical to the well-being of their trees. Since baron courts did not continue into the later eighteenth century, it is not possible to gain the same insight into that period; however, an example from earlier in the century provides us with some very powerful circumstantial evidence for the priorities of these particular lairds. During the 1720s a most obvious and staggering decrease in the number of convictions for wood-cutting took place (see Figures 1 and 2); this is almost certainly connected with the activities of one John McInnes, who was the only *salaried* forester appointed during the entire period covered by the court books. Foresters had been appointed before, but they had not been paid anything like the £13 that McInnes received. The use of unsalaried foresters occurred on both the Menzies and Glenorchy estates; however, the differing attitudes to wood management on the part of their respective lairds, as explained below, was crucial in determining the efficiency of the system. There is also evidence that the energetic McInnes sold wood to the tenants for their needs, a sensible policy which allows the landlord to control the use of wood, while, at the same time, acknowledging the needs of his tenants (SRO: GD 50/136). Astonishingly, however, when McInnes disappears from the records, no attempt was made to replace him and – surely no coincidence – wood-cutting immediately began to increase once more.

This episode suggests either that the Menzies found the loss of the income from fines unsatisfactory, or else that they just did not consider their woods to be worth McInnes's annual salary of £13 as the price for good order. Either way, it is clear that they were relying on the woods' natural powers of regeneration, which could prove unequal to the task if the human and animal population increased. Another landowner might well have decided that salaried foresters were worth spending money on if a significant income from timber was expected. In either case, basic economics, rather than a concern for the long-term future of the woodlands, is clearly a primary factor in determining policy. In this respect the laird differed little from his tenants, who were even more dependent on economic reality as a determinant of their actions. There is some evidence that the well-being of trees figured very low in the priorities of these eighteenth-century farmers and their cottars and servants. A sense of frustration can perhaps be detected in cases such as that of Ewen McInskellich, a servant of the minister of Weem, who was brought to court to explain why new timber had been cut for fencing around his master's corn yard. McInskellich replied that no-one had told him to cut the timber but he had done so because he had been 'ordered… to take care of the corn yard' (SRO: GD 50/136). In other words, those engaged in farming would make the best use of whatever resources were available, regardless of the bigger plan envisaged by the land's owner. Some tenants made an effort to avoid the detection of their tree-cutting activities, concealing their identity and operating 'under cloud of night' in order to avoid the inevitable fines. There is little evidence, however, to suggest that they regarded timber as a resource to be plundered at will, although they could have been more careful in adhering to the regulations regarding how timber should be cut. Wood was taken when and because it was required. Although the

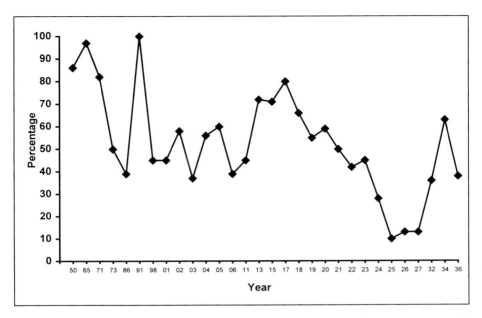

Figure 1: Incidence of wood-cutting in the Appin of Dull, expressed as a percentage of tenants summoned to court, 1650–1738.

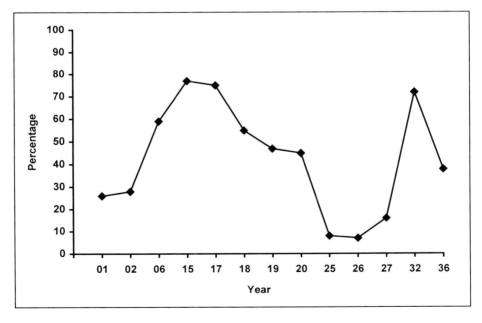

Figure 2: Incidence of wood-cutting in Rannoch, expressed as a percentage of tenants summoned to court, 1701–1736.

lairds did bemoan the continued cutting of green wood by their tenants, it is difficult to see what else the latter could have done in the absence of an alternative (SRO: GD 50/136). Equally, by emphatically excluding tenants from having any say in how the woods were managed, such a policy must surely have cultivated a lack of concern towards the future of those woods in those who lived and worked alongside them. Responsibilities should operate hand-in-hand with rights; neither we, nor their landlords, can seriously expect these early-modern farmers to have promoted a wider vision in which they would not be entitled to share.

The information to be found in the six volumes of the baron court records of Menzies and Rannoch is far more detailed and varied than the brief *resumé* given here. In particular, the fact that the tenants of the Appin of Dull were required to confess not only how much wood they had used since the last court, but also the uses to which that wood was put, enables us to build up an in-depth picture of the dependence of the rural population in western Perthshire in the late seventeenth and early eighteenth century on individual tree species. The detail and frequency of these confessions also suggests that the population as a whole was actively involved in facilitating the control mechanisms exerted by the court, both against themselves and their neighbours, however unwilling that involvement may have been. The principle was very much one of guilty until proved innocent: if charged, the onus lay with the accused to clear his or her name, rather than on the prosecution to prove guilt. Even the salaried forester, McInnes, was pulled up by his master for cutting more wood than he was given licence for (SRO: GD 50/136). However, if the degree of control exerted by the Menzies of Weem appears impressive, despite the likelihood that this was primarily intended to benefit the family's coffers rather than the trees themselves, this is but a pale imitation of the standards implemented by the Campbells of Glenorchy.

The evidence from the Glenorchy court books, which have survived from as early as 1571, provides even more detail as to the ways in which the community as a whole was involved in ensuring that use of the laird's woods was strictly controlled. The regulations printed in *The Black Book of Taymouth* in 1855 came from the 1620s but an examination of earlier court books shows that they were reiterations of previous acts.

Even in the earliest records of these courts, it is clear that control of each individual woodland, or even sections of the larger ones, relied on the effective-ness of tenant foresters, above whom were the estate ground officers. There is no direct evidence for the payment of these foresters, although some financial incentive, perhaps involving rent, was undoubtedly required to prompt the taking on and effective discharging of this considerable responsibility; the ground officers were certainly in receipt of fees (SRO: GD 112/17). The ideal of professional foresters was not to take root for over another hundred years; in this period they were the tacksmen and tenant farmers on whose lands the trees were situated.

Those of us accustomed to the ethos of professionalism in the modern world perhaps have a tendency to regard the effectiveness of such amateurs, however gifted, as limited. We should be very wary of transporting such values to the early modern world: professionals can lose their jobs and leave the area in search of another; the early-modern tenant farmers often had to stay and face the consequences of their inefficiency long after they had been demoted. Equally, the idea of professionalism in estate management from the eighteenth century is closely associated with the pre-eminent pursuit of profit and, as we shall see, the relationship between trees and profit is not necessarily a positive one.

This system of oversight depended, indeed, on the fact that the foresters lived *in situ*, and could therefore keep an eye on exactly what was happening in the wood and identify anyone attempting to perpetrate a misdemeanour. His (or her – there are instances of female foresters) more active role was to go with fellow tenants (or their cottars or servants) when they required wood and oversee the cutting. It is not clear whether or not a certain amount of wood was allowed to each tenant per annum for building and agricultural purposes, or whether payment was automatically required. It seems likely, as discussed below, that the norm changed from the former to the latter over time. What is clear, given the far fewer incidences of prosecution compared with the extremely high levels in evidence on the Menzies' lands, is that this system generally worked.

This success is all the more remarkable given that the rules governing cutting were extremely strict. Even when granted permission by the laird to take wood, prosecution could still follow if the tenant did not arrange for the forester, or the estate officer, to go with him. The laird would also prosecute if the wrong tree species was cut, indicating that the potential tree-cutter must know in advance exactly what the timber was to be used for. At each court hearing each forester was required to make a statement on oath regarding the condition of his wood. This statement appears to have been verified by the estate officer; woods which had not been 'sighted' in this way were held over for a verdict until the next court (SRO: GD 112/17).

This basic, sensible system of wood oversight, which, for all we know, might well have already been in existence for a considerable period of time, undoubtedly continued for centuries to come, and not just on Breadalbane lands: in 1774 the tenants of James Riddel of Ardnamurchan were still following this basic pattern, with the added restriction that tree-cutting could only take place in the months of February and June, presumably in order to give the trees as much chance to grow as possible (SRO: GD 112/10).

There was one other element of the 1774 conventions which was by no means standard two centuries earlier and that was the requirement to pay for timber. The whole vexed question of customary rights traditionally permitted to tenants and sub-tenants is too large a subject to cover in much depth here. However, it does seem . to be the case that some tenants on the Glenorchy/Breadalbane estates had the customary use of wood for the maintenance of their houses and farm buildings. A petition sent to the commissioners managing the estate for John, 2nd earl of Breadalbane, probably in the 1720s, asserted that the tenants of Ardradnaig, Claggan and Ardtallaig (in the barony of Ardtollony) were accustomed to having allowance for as much timber 'as would uphold the buildings and sheillings till of late that we were discharged by Robert Campbell, overseer of the woods of Breadalbane, from cutting any such timber...' They found this alleged innovation doubly unfair since they had recently increased their grassums in order to purchase tacks for eighteen years (SRO: GD 112/11). In 1593 three foresters in Benderloch were found guilty of wood cutting, having clearly believed that they had the right to cut sufficient amounts of timber for the use of their touns. The laird pointed to the fact that their tacks rendered them 'not free of wood in servicing the ground': these cases perhaps suggest that, even if the tacks had never explicitly mentioned such a right, tradition had, until now, permitted it (SRO: GD 112/17). A cursory examination of Breadalbane tacks has so far found mention of trees within them, except in those granted by Robert Campbell of Glenfalloch, a Glenorchy sub-tenant, to his own sub-tenants: in 1630, for example, his grant of lands within Benderloch included a stipulation both that the grantee should make his residence within the toun being granted and also that he should '...keip the wode thereof aftir the syting of tham at his entrie uncutit and undistroyit' (SRO: GD 112/10).

It should be noted, from the above, that the foresters themselves could be convicted for contraventions of the laird's regulations, although, as in the above case, such prosecutions may have come about through misunderstanding or a 're-interpretation' of the regulations. Despite such lapses, there is clear evidence for the emphasis placed by the laird on the responsibilities pertaining to the role of forester. Devotion to duty was actively encouraged by the fact that if the estate officers found even the smallest amount of wood cut without being accounted for, (i.e. not recorded as having been cut under the laird's licence), the foresters were held responsible for the fine unless they could find the real perpetrators. If this was not achieved before the holding of the next court or within forty days thereafter, then the forester would be forced to litigate against the offender himself in order to recoup his losses (SRO: GD 112/17). This responsibility could not be abrogated whatever the excuse: one forester explained that he could not find debtors (the real offenders) for unaccounted wood-cutting because he had been away on a hunt. Despite the fact that, as a tenant, he was bound to attend the hunt, he was not let off for the wood cutting and was left owing the fairly substantial sum of £4 Scots (SRO: GD 112/17). This seems to contrast with the situation on the Menzies' estates, where there were also a number of unsalaried tenant foresters appointed: there, as we have seen, a significant change in the pattern of wood-cutting occurred only when a salaried forester was at work, suggesting that the lairds generally did not provide the kind of encouragement noted above to their tenant foresters to act responsibly (SRO: GD 50/136).

There was obviously a temptation to accuse other tenants rather speculatively of wood offences, but any accused person could (and did) exonerate himself if he could find two 'famous persons unsuspect' to act as corroborating witnesses for his story. On the other hand, the claim of the laird's warrant for cutting was also not sufficient without corroboration (SRO: GD 112/17). It can only be presumed that the rewards for taking on such responsibilities were considerable; certainly, many foresters retained the office for considerable periods of time, although they could be replaced, presumably when they moved to another area, or else because either he or the laird wished to pass it on to someone else.

Despite the strictness of the rules and the effectiveness with which they appear to have been implemented, the emphasis remained nonetheless on the *actual*, rather than the *potential*, destruction of the woods. Thus, tenants who were accused of holding swine, against the laird's regulations, were absolved because no damage to the wood had actually been found; equally, evidence of insufficient park dykes was not enough to secure a conviction if the trees were found in good condition, although the tenants were nonetheless bound to maintain the dykes in future. Those found guilty of holding goats, which represented a particular menace to growing trees, could avoid the payment of the fine if they got rid of them (SRO: GD 112/17). However, the repeated prosecutions for the holding of goats suggests that it was difficult to persuade the tenantry in general of the need for their extirpation. The apparent success which the lairds of Glenorchy enjoyed in implementing their wood management policies should therefore be tempered with the realisation that the tenantry still weighed up the pros and cons, in economic rather than moral terms, of acquiescing in them. They thus shared a basic attitude with their contemporaries on the Menzies' estates; the main difference is that they usually concluded that it was not worthwhile ignoring Glenorchy's regulations, because the laird was determined to enforce obedience.

A number of baron court acts from 1576 make it clear that oak and pine were prized, in that order, even at that date. The £10 fine ordained for the peeling of oak bark was the only one to remain 'unforgiven', that is, not to be waived as surety for future good behaviour. The fine for the cutting of fir (pine), though not described in such menacing terms, was nonetheless set down at the same amount and other measures were taken to control what was obviously a thriving industry in the cutting and selling of pine wood at this time (SRO: GD 112/17). As an example of the extent of this industry, the justice court of Glenorchy and Lochawe, held in 1552, dealt with a most entrepreneurial McGregor, who was accused of cutting 100 fir (pine) and oak trees in Glenetive and Glenceitlein (at the head of Glenetive: NN 15 47), valued at 1000 merks Scots (SRO: GD 112/1). The 1576 acts suggest either that this problem had been finally noted as a serious one and attempts made to remedy it, or else, that the laird had become aware of the value of this particular timber and wished to conserve it for his own benefit. The acts appear to have been successful: most convictions for woodcutting in Glenorchy in the period after 1570 were secured only for the cutting of 'common wood', which probably meant alder, birch, willow and hazel, rather than oak, pine and ash, which were often specifically named (SRO: GD 112/17).

The woods belonging to the laird of Glenorchy were certainly more valuable than those enjoyed by the laird of Weem and it is tempting to attribute the former's greater success in keeping down the numbers of illegal cutters to this economic cause. The oak and pine woods of the Glenorchy's western estates were undoubtedly more lucrative in the long-term, but almost certainly not until the eighteenth century. The contracts made with Irish woodcutters in the 1720s and the subsequent problems surrounding the extraction of the timber seem to suggest that the trees being cut were extremely mature and are quite likely to have been previously untouched for commercial purposes. The potential for commercial exploitation does not therefore explain the successful management regime of the earlier period, especially since the Campbell woods along Loch Tay, which appear to have been similar in composition to those a few miles further east in the Menzies' lands of the Appin of Dull, were overseen in exactly the same way as the pine and oak woods of Glenorchy itself.

One of the biggest surprises contained within the court books is the clear evidence on Glenorchy lands for the existence of enclosed parks with dykes to protect the trees inside from the depredations of grazing animals, from at least the late sixteenth century. The time-honoured antipathy on the part of the local population towards enclosure is equally in evidence. In 1593 all the tenants of Benderloch were indicted by the laird for failing to uphold the park dykes 'in halding the guiddis (animals) fra eitting of the young oak' (SRO: GD 112/17). Three years later, in 1596, Glenorchy, as forester of the royal forest of Mamlorne, was given leave by the Privy Council to demolish shielings constructed by a number of individuals, including a laird, Colin Campbell of Glenlyon. It was claimed that they had been 'using the forest as pasture in the summer' and 'cutting and distroying in the meantyme the growand treis within the said forest', as well as proving harmful to the deer (SRO: GD 112/1). The forest of Mamlorne continued as a source of contention long after this, however: in the 1730s a long-running legal battle began between Breadalbane and the laird of Culdares, who also believed he had a long-established right to pasture his cattle in the forest. The numbers involved were considerable – 1200 beasts were mentioned in 1738. The dispute reached a climax in 1751 when tenants in Glenlyon (again) pulled down the house of the forester who was on the front line of the battle to expel the animals (Eg. SRO: GD 112/15).

The above examples show clearly that many tenants, including a number of lairds in their own right, were unwilling to countenance all aspects of woodland management imposed by the landowner. Their general acquiescence renders evidence of recalcitrance even more significant, suggesting that enclosure and the prohibition of certain animals was generally regarded as too great an interference with their economic situation and traditional ways of making a livelihood from the land. The problem of animals found grazing within enclosures, as a result of deliberate introduction or else negligence in the care of the dykes, continued, apparently unabated, not only throughout the pre-Improvement era but even into the nineteenth century: in 1808, Breadalbane was informed that cattle had been found in a wood enclosure within the Glenorchy and Lochaweside woods, as a result of which no wood could grow. The tenant had been upbraided for this on a number of occasions but, clearly, to no avail. The sympathy of the foresters themselves, in the earlier period at least, often lay with their fellow tenants, resulting in prosecutions for failing to remove animals and even for pasturing their own beasts in the parks (SRO: GD 112/11; GD 112/17).

There is further evidence to suggest that many of the laird of Glenorchy's tenants accepted his regulations only with the greatest of reluctance. One tenant was convicted not only for wood offences, but for swearing in court (using 'unreverent language'), presumably in response to the action taken against him. Another tenant was caught in the act of cutting by his more law-abiding neighbours and the timber found on him locked in the forester's barn (in this case, a woman); he came back later, however, broke the lock on the barn door and made off with the timber nonetheless. In 1619 two tenants were prosecuted for allowing their mares to pasture within Glenkinglass forest and for later freeing their animals from the barns in which they had been placed by the foresters, who had evicted them from the forest; the war over pasturing was far from over (SRO: GD 112/17).

Despite this evidence for a far from cowed and biddable population, there can be no doubt that the system upheld by the lairds of Glenorchy owed its success to the fact that the community as a whole was actively involved in it, both directly as foresters and also as 'sufficient witnesses' in any case requiring further investigation. The lairds of Glenorchy were also keen to intimate that their regulations were promulgated with the advice of the whole community, one of the very few landlords to behave in so parliamentarian a fashion (SRO: GD 112/17). This all implies that the community as a whole was versed in the details of woodcraft to a degree that we would doubtless find astonishing today. The cartographic evidence suggests that tree-cover within Glenorchy's estates was higher in the period prior to Improvement than subsequently; the pine woods of Glenorchy were noted in particular in Coronelli's map of Scotland, 1708, where they were described, most interestingly, as the Caledonian Forest (Coronelli, P, *Le Royaume d'Ecosse,* Paris, 1708). Despite the evidence for disagreement with some of their regulations, the lairds of Glenorchy appear to have maintained a sense of responsibility towards the needs of their tenantry, even at the potential expense of their own commercial interests: in 1725, only three years into a contract made with two Irish merchants, Breadalbane discovered that the agreement had been flawed and there was 'not one oak tree in the countrie for any use, so there will not be once they [are] done one fir tree' for building. He then added: 'I would not for double the value have the bargain hold. It is ane everlasting ruine to us, and 15 year old slaverie and the tenants get nothing by them…' (SRO: GD 112/11).

This particular earl (the 2nd) was very interested in estate management in general and forestry in particular, despite his frequent absences in London as befitted an important member of the British political establishment. He appears to have had first-hand experience of the wood-management policy practised on his estates, both in his own time and in that of his father. In 1726 he described to his chamberlain how young oak could be managed by setting fire to the enclosure, though unfortunately he gives no context to this practice, particularly in relation to coppicing (SRO: GD 112/14). Breadalbane advised that 'though the scrogs be cut, it is absolutely best to set fire to the whole enclosure immediately, before the young oak spring; it burns the rough course bottom of the oak and so the young oak comes soon and clean up. I saw the experience of it in Glenorchy, so pray you doe it immediatly a days time doeth the work'. The earl was a firm believer in the benefits of enclosure, having had cause to berate his officer a few years previously, because the latter had not yet made a dyke round a wood 'that is cutt that it be not eat', as had happened in his father's day. The officer was to engage upon this two-day job immediately 'or never see my face' (SRO: GD 112/15). There can be little doubt that the increase in the number of landlords who were truly 'absentee' (in the sense that – unlike the second earl – they did not regard their Scottish estates as their home even if they were often away) must have had an impact on the management of woodlands, as the estate came to be regarded primarily as a source of income, rather than an area of land held by the owner in trust for his own family *and* his tenants.

Interestingly, the second earl had a rather low opinion of the wood-management capabilities of the inhabitants of his lands. In 1722 he wrote disparagingly of Campbell of Glenfalloch's son who had taken a lease of the wood on the island of Innis Chonain in Loch Awe. The latter had complained about the difficulty in getting the bark off because of the density of bird droppings from the top of the tree. The earl declared this to be nonsense and attributed the cause of the problem to the fact that 'they are knavish and ignorant, for in England great old timber, the bark is best, but there is more pains in manadging it...' Glenfalloch was, of course, trying to engineer a reduction in the amount he owed for extracting the timber (SRO: GD 112/16). In the same year, Breadalbane expressed his concern about the difficulty in finding a chamberlain (the official at the top of the estate management hierarchy) of sufficient qualifications, requiring 'a person who understands woods, young and old', among other things. He certainly did not expect to find one on his own estates, remarking that '...no highland man [has] a notione of woods, so that to find a man for all these uses must be on Lochlomanside in Lus, or M'pharlans land...' (SRO: GD 112/16). The assertion that Lochlomondside and Arrochar (where the Macfarlanes owned land) were not in the Highlands does not conform to modern perceptions. It is, unfortunately, impossible to say whether or not Breadalbane, in this post-Union period, had fallen victim to a tendency to be impressed with English practices just because they were English, or whether this is indeed evidence for outdated practices in

Highland woodcraft. We can at least admit the possibility that either might be true.

The final test of Glenorchy wood-management must surely be the attitude towards fines. It is clear that the system of financial penalties for wood offences was quite different from that employed on the Menzies' estates, being based on the status (and therefore wealth) of the accused, as well as the gravity of the crime. The total sums brought in from fining could be significant (Benderloch, 1619, £234 Scots) but this was an unusually high figure; £20 Scots was a more usual income and this, together with the wood-management system as a whole, makes it clear that in the early modern period the lairds were more concerned with keeping a tight control of the amount of wood cut, whilst still allowing for the needs of their tenantry, rather than in making a profit from fines.

If such a system had continued indefinitely, there could surely have been little danger to the woods; even the effects of an increase of population and livestock could theoretically have been overcome because of the tight control over cutting already established. The reality, sadly, is different: the Glenorchy pine woods in particular have been reduced to a mere shadow of their former glory. The changing attitude towards trees – a result of increased commercialisation – is summed up well in a letter written to Lord Breadalbane by his Argyllshire factor in 1816, on the subject of a sale of woods in Glenorchy. The factor noted that it had been intended to reserve fifteen old oaks in the woods of Corryghoil; he now advised his employer '...that the fewer old oaks are reserved, the more desirable will the woods be to a purchaser'. Questions of aesthetics were not lost, however: he went on to note that '...as the old oaks are mostly out of sight of the Public Road, the appearance of this beautiful Glen will not in the smallest degree be hurt in the view of the many travellers who frequent Dalmally in the summer season, *though none be reserved*' (SRO: GD 112/14). It is unfortunate that we do not know Breadalbane's reaction to this advice; however, even if he rejected it, this is certainly evidence of a breed of factor with a rather narrow view of wood-management.

Conclusion

The evidence from both sets of baron court books make it clear that one of the primary functions of the court was to control the use made of the woodlands on each estate. Sections within the books were often entitled 'woods', but in fact covered all kinds of contraventions of baronial statue, indicating the pre-eminence of this aspect of estate management. In both the Menzies and Glenorchy estates, it is clear that the lairds operated an intricate system of control: in the one case, however, the primary purpose of the system was to engender an income; in the other, it was very much intended to limit the pressure placed on the woods. The levels of prosecutions for illegal cutting (high for Menzies; low for Glenorchy) corresponded to the respective policies.

The reaction of the tenantry to the respective wood management policies also appears to have been related to an understanding of their ultimate aim. The tenants on the Menzies' lands do seem to have exhibited a frustration with a financially-orientated policy which played on the legal rights of the lairds over the woods in the face of the regular timber requirements of the tenantry. The Glenorchy tenants perhaps more often saw the point of the lairds' regulations and generally adhered to them. This was not a blanket acceptance, however: there were clearly times when the lairds' interest (and, in the case of pasturing, the interest of the woods) was perceived to be in direct opposition to the requirements of the farmers. This is not, however, a tale of right and wrong: evidence for irresponsible behaviour towards trees can be found for both landlords and tenants. If there is a lesson to be learned from our predecessors in Weem, Rannoch and Glenorchy, it is surely that the local community is more likely to act responsibly if a direct relationship is maintained with the surrounding woods; no less important, however, is the need for a set of rules, and the means to enforce them, designed to maintain the trees in the face of changing fashion and economic circumstances to which both landlord and tenant farmer were, are, and no doubt always will be, subject.

References

SRO: GD 50. Scottish record Office, Menzies papers
SRO: GD 112. Scottish Record Office, Breadalbane muniments

Acknowledgements

Funding for the research was provided by ESRC grant L3202533166, part of the project on 'sustainability in the management of Scottish semi-natural woodlands, 1600–1900'.

9. Cutting into the Pine:

Loch Arkaig and Rothiemurchus in the Eighteenth Century

Chris Smout

How was the Caledonian pine exploited in the eighteenth century? Who was doing it, under what circumstances and with what consequences? Was the use sustainable? For this study we have chosen two contrasting woods, Rothiemurchus in Strathspey, on glacial soils, with relatively light cover on the ground, lower rainfall and (today) readier regeneration, and the Loch Arkaig group (including Glenmallie and Glen Loy) near Fort William, in peatier, more vegetated ground, with higher precipitation and currently little young growth. They are also contrasted in their ownership. Rothiemurchus belonged through that century, and subsequently, to one family, the Grants of Rothiemurchus, lairds of modest means who kept their political heads down but counted as Hanoverians. Loch Arkaig belonged to the charismatic Cameron chiefs, quintessentially and disastrously loyal to the Stewart cause until they finally forfeited their estates after Culloden: it then passed into Government management through the Commissioners of the Annexed Estates until 1784.

Both woods were comparatively large and, even in the seventeenth century, relatively well known. Rothiemurchus is referred to in notes probably made by Timothy Pont in the 1590s as the 'great and large firrwoods' in the vicinity of Loch an Eilean (Mitchell 1906, II, 577). The woods of Rothiemurchus, like those of Abernethy sheltered Montrose's army when pursued by the Earl of Argyle in 1644 (Fraser 1883, I, 275). An Aberdeen merchant named Benjamin Parsons, almost certainly an English immigrant in the wake of the Cromwellian armies, took a lease of the 'whole fir woods of Rothiemurchwes' in 1658 (Doune MSS 48; Munro 1988). Loch Arkaig around 1600 was described (probably again by Pont) as possessing 'a firrwood upon fourteen myles of length' along the south shore, and an oak wood on the north shore. John Speed in 1611 spoke of many of the pine trees there being very large (20 inches in diameter, 90 feet from the ground) and of interest to the Royal Navy, though again there is no indication that they were worked by outsiders at this stage (Steven and Carlisle 1959, 164–5).

Both woods are also of interest to conservationists, in the sense that they remain to this day as distinguished relics of the Caledonian pine. Loch Arkaig is considerably reduced from the dimensions as originally reported (if they were accurate) and to some extent from the dimensions as surveyed in the eighteenth century. Rothiemurchus is perhaps much the same in extent as it appears on eighteenth-century maps. On the other hand there are certain ways in which the woods are different between the eighteenth century and today.

Firstly, in the eighteenth century, though pine was dominant in both and they were described as 'firrwoods' (fir of course being the native Scottish word for pine), there was clearly a much greater admixture of other species. James Robertson the botanist, visiting Rothiemurchus, described the woods as containing 'abundance of excellent Fir and Birch, together with some Hazle and Poplar' (Henderson and Dickson 1994, 167). The impression of a great deal of birch in the woods round Loch an Eilean is confirmed by early nineteenth-century paintings. At Loch Arkaig, though pine was always to the fore in the minds of the woods' managers, quantities of birch, alder, hazel, rowan and oak are also mentioned. As a note of c. 1760 put it: 'NB the ffirr woods are so interspersed with the other woods that they cannot conveniently be cutt seperatly' (NLS, 17694, f.143). In a similar way, Joseph Avery's detailed early eighteenth-century map shows the main woods of Glen Affric, Glen Moriston and Glen Garry all as 'firrs and birch' (Avery MS 1725–30). The modern relative uniformity of most Caledonian pine relics is probably a function of nineteenth-century forestry practices.

Secondly, compared to the modern woods there was much readier regeneration. In Rothiemurchus it has perhaps never been a problem except sometimes in relation to excessive deer damage, and in the 1830s, following clear fell of much of the wood, the saplings were described as coming up again as straight and thick as trees in a nursery (Steven and Carlisle 1959, 121–2). In Loch Arkaig there has been little regeneration over the past 150 years, but an eighteenth-century traveller describes lavish regeneration at nearby Glen Garry after fire (Wight 1784, 139). There was also fire in the Loch Arkaig woods following the suppression of the 1745 rising, and in a detailed survey of 1756 it was estimated that, of 162,000 trees, 32,000 were immediately merchantable, 15,000 would become merchantable within twenty years, but upwards of 50,000 were 'young firr trees' that would take a longer time to mature (NLS, 17649, f.136). This suggests a healthy age structure in contrast to today.

Thirdly, there is the question of the size of the trees. It appears that they were in the eighteenth century on the small size compared to the present day. In Rothiemurchus, according to a law suit of 1742, English merchants had been persuaded by James Grant, son of the elderly laird, that his wood contained 300,000 large trees, measuring twelve inches square, six feet above ground. That should work out at a circumference of 54 inches minus the bark and whatever is lost in sawing – allowing three inches for these, the circumference of such trees would be between five and six feet. However, when they came to fell, they could not find 500 trees in the entire forest at or above that dimension, and not 2000 measuring even six inches square at ten feet above the ground. They felled 9000 trees altogether, but found them on the whole too small to be commercially valuable, and recommended that the estate allow them to grow larger before trying to sell them again. The laird retorted that all this was inaccurate, and the English company was just trying to squirm out of an unprofitable bargain (Doune MSS, 600). However, when Dr William Grant in the 1770s tried to sell Rothiemurchus logs for water pipes to the London water companies, the venture was again hampered by small size. There was a difficulty in finding timber of ten inches diameter (probably about three feet circumference with bark and waste): nevertheless, in three years they managed to cut 4000 such logs, 'good, bad and indifferent' twelve foot long and ten to eleven inches 'at the butt', before they gave up (Doune MSS, correspondence 1770–1774). There is no reason to believe the extent of the wood was either diminishing or growing: in its own terms, the exploitation was apparently sustainable.

The information on the size of the Loch Arkaig timber comes from two surveys carried out by professional wrights. That of 1756 identified 32,085 immediately merchantable trees, of which only 120 were as large as eleven inches square (with bark and waste perhaps five feet in circumference), and only about 5000 of even ten inches square. The rest were estimated at eight or nine inches square, say four feet in circumference. The usual point of measurement was five feet from the ground (NLS, 17694, f.136). The previous year the wrights had measured 726 trees that had (it was alleged) been illegally felled in the Loch Arkaig woods: the great majority were nine to ten inches square, with a very small number up to twelve inches. One tree in Glen Loy was fourteen inches square, but only 24 foot high in the trunk. The average was slightly larger than in the other survey, presumably because the bigger trees had been selected by the thieves (SRO: E768/44/20).

It is of course not at all difficult to find evidence of larger trees than these in some other eighteenth-century Scottish pinewoods, though when the evidence is closely inspected, there are signs that they are exceptional. The forest of Glenmore, further from a floating river than Rothiemurchus, was generally recognised as containing bigger timber, and Dr William Grant recommended buying 3000 trees from their neighbour the Duke of Gordon to make water pipes just because their own were so small (Doune MSS, correspondence 1771). In upper Deeside, Thomas Pennant found trees at Invercauld ten, eleven and even twelve feet in circumference, though the standard size of plank manufactured there, eleven inches broad, suggests an average circumference of about five feet. He considered the Dalmore woods 'the finest natural pines in Europe both in respect of their size and the quality of their timber', speaking of seeing trees 80 to 90 feet high and ten feet in circumference (Pennant 1774, 109, 115). James Robertson said of the Abernethy pines, 'none of the trees are large. I saw only one which measured 13 feet in circumference and 50 feet in height', and he described those near Amat in Sutherland as 'the finest I have seen in Scotland',

with a single tree of 30 to 40 foot of uninterrupted trunk and eight and a half feet
in circumference (Henderson and Dickson 1994, ff.166–7). A visit to the latter
wood today reveals several at least of these dimensions, which suggests that
larger trees are more numerous today than they were in the third quarter of the
eighteenth century.

Steven and Carlisle in their accounts of individual woods several times
mention individual trees of twelve foot girth and more, but more significantly
state that the average circumference of Caledonian pine in the remnant Scottish
woods in the twentieth century 'usually lies between five and six feet', at breast
height, while 'girths up to about nine feet are not infrequent' (Steven and
Carlisle 1959, 77). These are certainly much larger than most trees described in
eighteenth-century Rothiemurchus or Loch Arkaig, and barely equal the
standard cut for plank at Invercauld. If, as has been suggested, the capercaillie
needs much large old pine for its survival, its extinction around 1770 may have
had as much to do with habitat decline as with the pressures of hunting for food.

There are two likely explanations for the small size of the trees in these
woods. The first could be a prior history of continuous exploitation, so that the
woods were being constantly harvested before they attained maturity. Secondly,
there may have been a previous history of cutting episodes that concentrated on
the large trees, and the regenerating trees (as measured, 1740–1770) had not had
time to grow to a greater size.

In Rothiemurchus we can be fairly confident that the latter did not happen in
the seventeenth and eighteenth centuries: the Grants on several occasions tried
to interest outsiders in the wood, but every venture ended in failure or at least in
a limited impact. Benjamin Parsons from 1658, apparently cut some wood in
Rothiemurchus, Abernethy, Kincardine and Glencalvie, and floated it to
Garmouth, where he had a sawmill and built at least one ship, but he did not
prosper and was in financial trouble by 1671 (Munro 1988). In 1710 part of the
woods were leased for ten years to a merchant from Banff in partnership with a
merchant from London; they were still operating after five years but also seem
to have abandoned the tack before its conclusion (Doune MSS, 82, correspondence 1720). In 1738, the English merchants from Hull, Perrott and Field, were
persuaded through a third party to offer for a lease to cut 40,000 trees, but
abandoned it after they had cut 9000 because, as explained, the trees were too
small. The Hull partners alleged in court that Grant had hood-winked the experts
that Perrott and Field sent from England to judge the woods. They said they had
'good reason to believe that their servants were carried twice or thrice through
the same places of purpose to make them believe there was a great abundance of
large trees in the wood' (a tale the Grants rejected as 'false and calumnious').
They had also been informed that the woods were too big to see in their entirety,
and had been taken to a knoll (probably Ord Bain above Loch an Eilean) to
view them, being told that all the rest were just as large. In any event, Perrott
and Field withdrew from operations after two years after paying Patrick Grant
£1000 (Doune MSS, 600). And the pipe works that the laird's brother instituted

in 1771 also only lasted a short time – in this case under four years.

The fragmentary estate accounts at the Doune hold clues as to where the timber was really going, and of its true value to the estate's prosperity. The main exploiters were not men from London or Hull, or even from Aberdeen and Banff. In 1766, for example, there were 106 buyers of wood 'at the back of Lochinellan', all local men apart from one from Cromarty. In the three years 1769–1771, wood sales fetched £370 per annum, which compares very well with the £400 raised by two years' operations from Perrott and Field in 1740–1, and, indeed with the £175 which was the rental of the farms of Rothiemurchus in 1771 and 1772. In these three years, two-thirds of the value of the wood cut came from nearly 14,000 pieces of 'sparwood', relatively small trees sold as logs, and the rest from sawn deals of somewhat larger trees (Doune MSS, 143). It was a constant cropping of timber of a handy size for local tools to fell and trim, and the markets were no doubt also predominantly local. Clearly a good deal of Strathspey wood was floated down the river for ultimate use in the burghs of the Moray plain, or taken by pony to Inverness, Forres or Nairn, but owners probably varied as to where they first sold the wood. Sir James Grant, the owner of Abernethy, was told in 1778 that 'your wood sells cheaper at Inverness, after being floated down to Garmouth, than Rothiemurchus's wood sells at Rothiemurchus, notwithstanding the quality of your wood is greatly better than Rothiemurchus's' (Fraser 1883, II, 459). Since the timber was presumably intended mainly for building small houses, there was no point whatever in allowing trees to grow to any greater size than necessary.

The position in Loch Arkaig is more obscure, but has features in common with Rothiemurchus, especially the attempt to interest external buyers, their lack of success where known, and the manifest importance of local uses. The first unequivocal reference to external interests in Lochiel's woods is a contract of 1674 with John Davidson and William Munro, concerning their bargain for erecting an iron mill at Achnacarry: six years later Lochiel sold to John Davidson and one Thomas Richaby from County Antrim, 'his heal woods excepting his firwoods within Glenlui and Locharkick', and in 1688 Mathew Riccaby assigned half the iron mill to Lochiel until his debts and those of another Irishman called James Stammie or Tammie were cleared: a gentleman of that name had given an obligation for a loan from Sir Ewen Cameron as early as 1626. Nothing more is heard of this iron works, but in 1701 John Cameron of Lochiel sold oakwoods to another Irish adventurer, Henry Fullartoun in Balliknock in County Down, and again in 1714 he sold 'the oak bark from the foot of Arkick joyning Loch Lochy on the north side to the head of Locharkick' (among other stretches) to two tanners from County Meath: yet another contract is signed for 'the oaken wood on the south side of Locharkick' with a merchant of Drogheda in 1721, and in 1723 Donald Cameron of Lochiel sold to Roger Murphy of Enniskillen, birch, ash and oak timber on the estate: the following year it was apparently extended to him and two partners to include 'his heal woods lying within the bounds of Lochiel, Glenlui and Locharkick', with certain restrictions which probably (though not certainly) excluded the fir woods from exploitation. In all this activity, there appears to be little or no interest in the pine, though a great deal in charcoal and especially in tanbark from the hardwoods (SRO: GD 1/658/1). The Jacobite lairds were obviously keenly involved in the timber market with outsiders, primarily in Ireland: as has recently been emphasised, the supporters of the Stewarts were no less interested in making money than the supporters of the house of Hanover (Macinnes 1996).

Some time before the Jacobite rising of 1745 the Camerons do appear to have involved an English company in the Loch Arkaig fir woods. Thanks to the apparent loss of their archives after Culloden we have no details apart from passing references in later documents. One of 1755 claims that 'Lochzield sold 3100 fir trees (a small part of the woods) with some decayed and fallen timber to an English Company anno 1739 for £2000 sterling' – an extremely high price, if correct (NLS, 17694, f.69). The next is in a letter of 1760 from a merchant offering to buy the fir woods 'upon the left side of Loch Arkick... the best part of which was cut down in the time of the late Mr Cameron of Lochiel' (SRO: E768/35/1). Another witness spoke of 'vast numbers' of discarded tops of trees left in the wood by the English Company (SRO: E768/14). A further reference in a history of the rising by a Whitehaven man said that Cameron of Lochiel had been engaged in 'large dealings with some of our merchants for timber', but that they had fallen out over payment of £1200–£1400: it was feared after the fall of Carlisle in November 1745 that the Jacobite army would turn and plunder Whitehaven to 'take by force what the law would not give him a just title to' (Ray 1752).

Surely there is a parallel here to the Hull merchants in Rothiemurchus: another English firm drawn into Scottish timber speculations only to find that the wood did not live up to expectations, and pulling out without completing the bargain. Very interestingly, there is a third venture of a similar date and scale, relating to the Chisholm woods in the Beauly catchment area. In this case a 'wood surveyor', one John Lummis 'late of Sheriff Haillss in the county of Salop, now of Preston in the county of Lancaster', who was also the third party involved in the deal between Perrott and Field and the Grants, and who further-more had interests in timber on the estate of Callart on Loch Leven to be sold as cordwood to an ironworks near Fort William, engaged the interests of a partner-ship mainly of Preston and Liverpool merchants. There was, he affirmed 'about 100,000 of the said [fir] trees which are in measure 4 feet to 12 feet in circum-ference and 40 to 80 feet in length' which Roderick Chisholm of Strathglass was willing either to sell in bulk at 1s. 4d. each, or to allow the purchasers to choose 10,000 of the best trees at 5s. each (SRO: RD2/15). In the event, Chisholm, who claimed already to have had 30,000 trees cut on the ground and left lying by the York Buildings Company by whom he had not been paid, in 1742 sold to the Preston Company £50,000 trees at 1s. a tree, to be extracted over twenty years: within a year the bargain was declared null and void because the first 300 trees could not be floated out. Lummis (called Summis in the writ) was involved in negotiations with Lord Lovat to float the timber through his estate (Munro, ed., 1992). It was another timber speculators' fiasco.

Such are the similarities that it would be surprising if Lummis was not involved in the Loch Arkaig bargain as he had been in those with the Grants and with Chisholm. There was a war on, supplies of timber from the usual sources in Scandinavia were scarce and expensive, which no doubt made all the Scottish pine woods more attractive. Indeed, when Prince Charles Edward sent John Murray of Broughton to contact Lochiel in 1745 he went under an assumed name, pretending to be 'come from England to buy wood' (Gibson 1995, 59). It is vexing that we know nothing more in detail about the 1739 bargain, because, just possibly, it swept out most of the really big trees that had caught John Speed's attention in 1611. But that is speculation.

The later involvement of outsiders, at least in the eighteenth century, all seem to have had very limited success or impact. When the woods came under the management of the Commissioners for the Annexed Estates they were anxious to put a stop to petty local pilfering (as we shall see) and regarded the pine as an asset of great value. However, when it came to attracting outside capital, it proved more difficult. In 1764, the Commissioners agreed to sell 2000 tons of pine wood (probably about 10,000 trees) over a three-year period to a local sawmill owner, who undertook to sell it all on to a Glasgow partnership (including Provost George Murdoch) after processing: but he illegally sold some of it to local shipbuilders and then went bankrupt (SRO: E768/35/3). The Glasgow partnership took over the agreement but found that they could not cut so much within the stipulated period, partly because in order to do so they had had to construct floating canals in the wood, and had the 'aqueducts broke down by the country people'. They also objected to having to take all trees of eight inches square – 'its now found from experience that this size is rather too small'. They continued: 'its now a pretty well established fact from experiments that a tree of sixty years is near double the measurement... of what that same tree would have been at fifty' – which at least establishes that contemporaries thought of 50–60 year-old pines as suitable for harvesting (SRO: E768/35/4).

The lease was then taken over by a local partnership formed by Ewen Cameron of Glenevis and a colleague, who undertook to cut 200 tons a year of wood 9 inches square and upwards. Then they in turn got into trouble, failing to find good markets locally, on the Clyde, at Campbeltown or in Ireland, and could not fulfil the bargain. 'It will be necessary for the preservation of the woods', they concluded in 1772, 'that no more of it should be cut for some years' (SRO: E768/35/5). After that the Commissioners seem to have placed a moratorium on external sales for the rest of the century. Interestingly, the Grants of Rothiemurchus put a similar stop to harvesting their woods between 1787 and 1809, presumably also to allow them time to recover. Indeed, no-one with distant markets in view seems to have made any profit from the Loch Arkaig woods in the eighteenth century, and the total number of trees felled in this way is unlikely to have exceeded 12,000 in the entire century. In view of the estimated size of the wood in 1756 (162,200 trees) these seem inconsiderable inroads.

However just as at Rothiemurchus, this may not at all be the whole story. What about local people cutting for local use? Coille Phuisteachain in Glen Loy was traditionally reserved for local use, for Cameron tenants to take what they needed for their own purposes for building, but this was stopped at the forfeiture in 1746 (SRO: E768/44/19.4). However, a startling state of affairs on the entire estate was revealed six years later, when John McPhee, former Bunarkaig innkeeper currently employed by the Town Guard in Edinburgh, came to the officers of the Commissioners of Annexed Estates and asked for payment for acting as forest guard to the Loch Arkaig woods. His story was that Patrick Campbell, the government factor, had armed him with a gun in return for his promise to deter wood thieves and to report on any removal of wood that he could not himself prevent, but the factor never paid him a penny, or attended to any of his reports, but rather abused him and called him a 'Bitch and whore's son' when he reported thefts until McPhee became so unpopular through his vigilance and refusal of bribery that he was forced to flee to Edinburgh without his family. He claimed that general 'havoc' had been made of the wood with Campbell's connivance. His testimony was backed by a skilfully phrased letter from his wife, complaining of harassment by local people and ending 'take me out of this before they make an end of me, for God's sake endeavour to send some money to relive your poor children' (SRO: E768/27).

All the accusations the factor indignantly denied, but they triggered a prolonged judicial enquiry generating hundreds of pages of evidence (SRO: E768/27 and 44). From this it became clear that just about everyone locally had been helping themselves to wood, including the original informant, who had also regularly allowed peculation by the tenants of neighbouring estates in exchange for a little whisky. The list of apparent thieves included the local customs officer, who defended himself stoutly, claiming that the 'enemies of public tranquillity' always regarded those who held his office with an 'evil eye', and that he himself was an 'Eyesore and Beacon of the envy and malice of numbers of the inhabitants'. His claims that he had only taken (with the factor's knowledge and permission) a little burnt wood to repair his house and warehouse devastated in the wars, were nevertheless rather undermined by testimony that he removed 40 horse loads, some of it 'under cloud of night'. Soldiers built an officer's house and a barracks for themselves out of the timber. A pier and a gallows at Inverlochy were made from it. Tenants also rebuilt substantial houses from it, and John Cameron of Fassifern built a brewhouse as well: a wright in Maryburgh reported that for the last he had cut eight or ten trees 'of the very best firr, some of them being 26 foot long and 18 inches square' – that would probably have been trees getting on for six feet in circumference. The minister himself was involved: he got 36 planks which the factor told him to say was for the use of the kirk, but he (being a man of the cloth) deponed under oath that it was really for himself. The Sheriff Depute of

Inverness was shown to be involved – embarrassingly for himself, since on conducting the initial preliminary enquiry he had tried to fob off the Commissioners with the verdict that there had indeed been thefts, but that the folk who had done them were so simple it was impossible to estimate what the damage had been. Ewen Cameron, tenant in Glenevis, took 82 horse loads, and sometimes 60 horses were employed at a time in the woods on his behalf: he used it to build a bridge and to repair a house, mill and other property. Glenevis is about twenty miles from the main woods, ten miles from the nearest ones, Fassifern a little further. Cameron of Fassifern could at least claim some cutting rights under a wadset that went back to 1675 (SRO: GD 1/736/4), but there is little sign that the other culprits had a legal leg to stand on.

It is indeed impossible in the end to be certain of the full extent of what was taken, though expert wrights in 1755 traced 776 trees that were either still lying in the woods or had been transported to Fort William. The point rather is that the woods were seen as immediately useful to the people in and around the foot of the Great Glen, that they had some traditional customary (though not legal) rights to them under the old lairds, and for a time after the forfeiture just helped themselves without much restraint. We must assume that after 1755 the Commissioners had greater success in putting a stop to such practices, but on the other hand they palpably also found it very difficult to put the forests to anything except local use. The parallels with Rothiemurchus – vigorous local demand, sluggish external demand – seem very close.

The main problem that outside entrepreneurs had, apart from the difficulty of extraction and the need to clear obstructions in the floating rivers, was competition from Norway, both for price and, perhaps, for quality. The first point was expressed by a customer who in 1763 wanted to use Loch Arkaig timber on Lewis: 'the prime cost, the charge of manufacturing it and floating it to Fort William together with the freight of carrying it from that place to Stornoway will make it come as high as wood could be brought from Noroway' (SRO: E768/15/4). The second point is illustrated by a man in Fort William in 1752 who wanted to borrow a little wood from Loch Arkaig to finish a wash-house for the garrison: he had expected to use timber sent from Irvine (that was bound to have been Scandinavian) but it failed to arrive. If he could use local wood immediately, he promised to 'return you in kind when the next coal ship comes from Irwin which will be better timber and better seasoned than yours' (SRO: E768/44/7.16). One recalls that when Inveraray Castle was being built the demand generated by it for Scandinavian timber was so great that skippers of boats from Norway were sometimes advised to divert to Loch Fyne to see if they could sell their cargoes there, rather than in the Clyde (Lindsay and Cosh 1973). Only when Norway and the Baltic were cut off by hostilities or hampered by post-Napoleonic tariff policy did the market for home-grown Caledonian pine thrive a little more – witness the heavy cutting in Rothiemurchus and elsewhere in Strathspey during and after the Napoleonic Wars, and the revival of interest in the Loch Arkaig woods in the first decades of the nineteenth century (Steven and Carlisle 1959, 113, 166). Otherwise it did not bear the expense of carrying very far. On the other hand, within a certain local radius it was cheap and available, liable to be increasingly exploited since both population and economic activity were growing in the eighteenth-century Highlands all the time. It is hard to draw a firm conclusion about the sustainability of use in Loch Arkaig woods in the eighteenth century, but at the end of the day the woods at least survived, though perhaps only because management responsibility was exerted again in the nick of time.

Finally, and by way of a postscript, it is worth saying a word about how the woods were formally controlled. At Rothiemurchus, control was traditional and minimal, through local tenants appointed as foresters, and baron courts that enforced fines for such offences as cutting young wood, and that regulated burning in or near the woods (Doune MSS, 149). There was no enclosure before the mid-nineteenth century. At Loch Arkaig in Lochiel's time we know nothing about regulation except that the old laird appointed Dugald Cameron, one of his tenants at Invermallie, as forester, and the same individual was re-appointed there by the first forfeited estates factor (SRO: E768/44/7/1). After the scandal of the wood thefts, however, the Commissioners thought again. General Churchill recommended to them a certain Alexander Cameron, who, he said, would make a good forester because 'he had acquired him so many enemies in the Highlands that it makes it intirely in his interest to discharge any trust reposed in him under the government'. True, he had stolen a little Lochiel wood but that was 'very trifling' (SRO: E768/15/1). The Commissioners sensibly ignored the advice. A new factor, Henry Butter, took over and directed wood management himself. In 1773 the famous improver Sir Archibald Grant of Monymusk produced a plan to plant trees – apparently mainly oak – on five farms on the Lochiel Estate, and the factor responded by suggesting suitably restricted areas for planting 'for the beauty and ornament of the country': he was obviously concerned least the planting be so extensive that it intruded on the tenants' cattle pasture. The 'possessors of the farms above mentioned are honest and industrious', he said, his nervousness exacerbated by the fact that one of the farms in question was Corpach, his own (SRO: E768/66).

The following year, the factor reported with much less hesitation on the virtues of enclosing the fir woods of Loch Arkaig. This proposal was ambitious – there were to be six and a half miles of dyke along the south shore of the loch, and the enclosure was to be three quarters of a mile in depth, encompassing about 3000 acres of the wood called the Guisach, much of which was currently bare of trees. The heather in these areas was to be burned and fir seed sown in it, so that they and: 'the natural seedlings may grow to great advantage, when preserved in this inclosure, as had been experienced in a similar case lately upon the annexed estate of Barisdale' (SRO: E768/73/3). The experiments had mixed success, but as far as we know at present, these were substantially in advance of any similar attempts to preserve and extend the natural reserves of any of the Caledonian pine in private hands. The Annexed Estate Commissioners were ambitious: traces of their dyke were still visible, two centuries later, as monuments to their pioneering intentions to take positive initiatives in favour of sustainable woodland management, rather than merely to go with old custom and hope for the best.

References

Avery, 1725–30: Joseph Avery's manuscript 'Plan of the Murray Firth', in Inverness Museum.

Doune MSS, records relating to Rothiemurchus Estate kept at the Doune, National Register of Archives (Scotland), survey 102. I am most grateful for permission from John Grant of Rothiemurchus to examine these.

Fraser, W, *The Chiefs of Grant* (2 vols., Edinburgh, 1883)

Gibson, J S, *Lochiel of the '45: the Jacobite Chief and the Prince* (Edinburgh University Press, 1994)

Henderson, D M and Dickson, J H (eds.), *A Naturalist in the Highlands: James Robertson: His Life and Travels in Scotland, 1767–1771* (Scottish Academic Press, Edinburgh, 1994)

Lindsay, I G and Cosh, M, *Inveraray and the Dukes of Argyll* (Edinburgh University Press, 1973)

Macinnes, A I, *Clanship, Commerce and the House of Stuart, 1603–1788* (Edinburgh, 1996)

Mitchell, A (ed.), *Geographical Collections Relating to Scotland Made by Walter Macfarlane* (3 vols., Edinburgh, Scottish History Society, 1906)

Munro, J, 'The golden groves of Abernethy: the cutting and extraction of timber before the Union', *A Sense of Place: Studies in Scottish Local History*, ed. Cruickshank, G (Scotland's Cultural Heritage, Edinburgh, 1988), pp. 152–62

Munro, J (ed.), *The Inventory of Chisholm Writs, 1456–1810* (Scottish Record Society New Series, 18, Edinburgh, 1992)

NLS 17694, National Library of Scotland MS, papers relating to the forfeited estates of Lochiel, Kinlochmoidart and Ardshiel.

Pennant, T, *A Tour in Scotland, 1769*, 3rd edn (Warrington, 1774)

Ray, J, *A Compleat History of the Rebellion* (Bristol, 1752)

SRO: RD = Scottish Record Office, Register of Deeds.

SRO: E768 = Scottish Record Office Exchequer papers relating to the forfeited estates, Lochiel.

SRO: GD 1/658/1. = Scottish Record Office, inventory of the charters and other writs contained in the charter chest of Cameron of Lochiel, 1472–1727. The actual charters and writs were burned by government troops in 1746 when they sacked Achnacarry, so some important details remain obscure.

Steven, H M and Carlisle, A, *The Native Pinewoods of Scotland* (Oliver and Boyd, Edinburgh, 1959)

Wight, A, *Present State of Husbandry in Scotland* (Edinburgh, 1784), vol. 4

N.B. A more extended account of Rothiemurchus appears as T C Smout, 'The history of the Rothiemurchus woods in the eighteenth century' in *Northern Scotland*, 1995, pp. 20–31.

Acknowledgements

This is part of a study on 'Sustainability in the management of Scottish semi-natural woodlands', funded by the Economic and Social Research Council (grant no. L3202533166).

10. Changes in Native Woodland in Assynt, Sutherland, since 1774

Robin Noble

Background

The Parish of Assynt, centred now on Lochinver, might be described as typical of the West Coast of Scotland. Much of it is a highly dissected plateau of Lewisian Gneiss, which may appear to the outsider as inhospitable in the extreme, largely characterised by bare rock. Much of the rest might be said to be watery, being either fresh-water loch or bog, but despite this, there are in some parts quite notable areas of native woodland. These areas of woodland are the subject of this chapter.

In 1774, Assynt was thoroughly surveyed for the Sutherland Estates who then owned it, by John Home, a surveyor from Edinburgh. He worked in Assynt from early June that year until 16 September and, under some pressure, had produced the final maps by the following March. John Home's survey of Assynt, edited by R J Adam, was published by the Scottish History Society in 1960. The original survey listed and mapped, farm by farm, the areas of 'Infield, Sheelings, Natural Woods, Hills, Moss and rocky Muirish Pasture, and Lochs' and these were mapped in the 1960 volume by K M MacIver, although strict accuracy of scale was not claimed (Adam 1960).

The present writer spent a significant part of each year from 1959 to 1972 in the middle of what is now seen to be one of the largest areas of native woodland in the Parish. He then lived at Elphin, part of the Assynt parish surveyed by Home, from 1974 to 1980, and has continued to make frequent visits to the area. He also has an archive of photographs of the Parish going back over 30 years.

The Study

The study summarised in the present chapter is a comparison of the location of native woodland as mapped by Home in 1774, with its present distribution as revealed on the various Ordnance Survey maps, and in the *Inventory of Ancient,*

Long-established and Semi-natural Woodlands of Sutherland (G J Walker 1985). The map exercise has been supported by innumerable field visits over a long period. It should be emphasised that what follows is not a quantitative comparison of mapped areas of woodland, although such a mathematical exercise could probably be undertaken given the information provided by Home. This chapter is rather a general look at the changes in the distribution of native woodland in Assynt over the period from 1774 to the present.

The pattern is summarised in Figure 1. What is immediately apparent is that the distribution of woodland in Assynt does not at first sight seem to have changed much from 1774 to the present. Then, as now, a large section of the coast of Assynt, from Achmelvich, round Stoer Point and almost as far as Oldany Island, was quite devoid of woodland. South of Achmelvich, woodland reached the edge of the sea only at the head of Loch Roe – which is well-wooded now – while the shores of Loch Inver were almost bare. East of Oldany Island, along the shore of Eddrachillis Bay, the amount of woodland increased, as it does now, reaching its maximum along the south-west shore of Loch a' Chairn Bhain, then fading out along the shore of Loch Glencoul.

Inland, then as now, native woodland followed the lines of the many rivers, burns and lochs that seam the dissected plateau. There were and are notable areas of woodland along the Loch Roe–Torbreck–Manse Loch system, along the Kirkaig River, around the western end of Loch Assynt, and in Glen Leraig. The hinterland from Achmelvich Bay to Clashnessie Bay was, however, as bare of trees in 1774 as it is now. Further inland, much of the higher ground was also bare, as now, with one significant exception; around Elphin, especially from Cam Loch to Loch Urigill, the 1774 survey shows a considerable area of woodland – little is to be seen there now.

After the initial mapping was done, it was decided to look at two areas in more detail, one coastal (Drumbeg–Ardvar) and the other well inland, centred on Elphin.

In Drumbeg–Ardvar, the car-borne visitor cannot but notice how much native, largely birch woodland there is in this area. The topography is very irregular, and the many rocky ridges and hummocks are largely devoid of trees. From Oldany eastwards the road winds through narrow glens and hollows, and these contain considerable areas of birchwood. Some of the available maps do not give an adequate indication of the area covered by this woodland, but the reasons for the discrepancies are not clear. O.S. 1" Sheet 13, for instance, did note that the headland in Loch Drumbeg called An Abha was covered by native woodland (with the addition of a few pines which were presumably planted). However O.S. 1:25000 Second Series and the NCC Inventory both fail to note that this woodland is still very much in evidence.

The Inventory lists the woodland, on the shores of Loch Nedd and in Glen Leraig, by Loch Ardvar, and on the south-west shores of Loch a' Chairn Bhain, as a number of discrete units, but this approach is in a way misleading – these areas, particularly Nedd–Glen Leraig and Loch a' Chairn Bhain, are basically

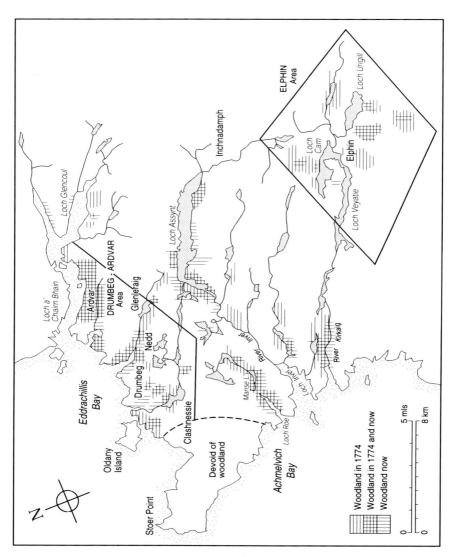

Figure 1: Changes in native woodland in Assynt.

wooded, with some clearings carved out of them, and other open spaces largely caused by the presence of wetland or exposed ridges. Speaking generally, these are areas of healthy woodland: 'semi-natural' or not, they have a *natural* structure, with areas of regeneration, areas of maturity and decline, and fallow areas. Parts of these woods are much frequented by sheep, there are certainly roe deer, and there have been red deer living in the woodland in Glen Leraig nearly all year round, since at least the 1960s, to the writer's certain knowledge. Despite that pressure, the general impression is one of healthy woodland.

There has in fact been quite significant growth since the 1960s; certain photographic viewpoints, much used in the 1960s, are now virtually impossible to use, as the outlook is largely obscured by trees. There are still views from Nedd over the loch 'to the beautiful bank of wood of Glenlirag along the opposite side, hanging over the Bay' which in 1774 John Home thought 'truely romantick, and adds greatly to the rural beauty of this Farmstead', but it is not as easy to photograph now as in the 1960s.

In addition to this (vertical) growth since the 1960s, it is quite clear that native woodland has invaded areas which in 1774 were bare of trees. The western shore of Loch Nedd is now almost as well wooded as the eastern upon which Home remarked. The in-by croft land in Nedd is now virtually surrounded by woodland, with fine trees growing on the rocky 'baulks' described by Home. In Glen Leraig itself, Home did remark that there were many trees growing on the rocky baulks, but the arable 'haugh along the burn, close ground with a rich black soil', particularly on the west side of the burn, had almost completely disappeared under trees by the 1960s. At that period, the parallel ditches and raised ridges of feannagan or 'lazy-beds' were quite obvious to the optimistic fisherman who was prepared to follow the rough path through the thick press of trees. (Some of the evidence and all of the romance has been destroyed by the building here of a fish-farm and its approach road in the 1980s.)

There have been some changes in the composition of the woodland, however – the 'mostly oakwood' of Home has largely gone, although its name remains, and it has been replaced with a fine mixed birchwood, with rowans and a number of aspens on the shore of the loch. It is quite possible that the oakwood was at some stage felled; if this is so, it was replaced by natural regeneration of birch and other hardwoods, despite the grazing animals.

Prior to the Clearances, Glen Leraig supported a total population of ninety. Afterwards, there was one shepherd's house (the old cottage that may still be seen) and the whole area occupied by the former community was given over to sheep. The present writer has no information about the number of sheep carried in Glen Leraig at any one time, and figures for the sheep farm of this century are not helpful, as by this time it was run together with neighbouring Ardvar. Whatever the numbers of sheep (and it is important to note that it was actively shepherded and well-stocked until the 1980s), the grazing pressure was not sufficient to restrict or eat into the area of woodland. As we have seen, the close black soil of the burnside haugh disappeared under trees, and if the oakwood was felled, its place was taken by a dense growth of birch.

When shepherding was at its most active, both in the sheep-run of Glen Leraig and in the neighbouring crofting community of Nedd, there was an attempt to ensure that sheep did utilise the summer grazing on the higher ground. As the working population of Nedd declined and aged through the 1960s, 1970s and 1980s, there was much less active day-to-day shepherding and the sheep spent a greater part of their time down near the coast, around the crofts and in the woods. Despite this, and the presence already alluded to of roe and red deer, let alone the inevitable cutting of trees for fuel, the woodlands do not seem to have suffered.

By Loch Ardvar, again the story is much the same. In 1774, Home remarked on the extensive natural woods, and they exist now where they did then, notably on Meallard, at the head of Loch Ardvar, in Glen Ardvar, and in an extensive belt from Lochan na Dubh Leitir (near Kerrachar) along the shore of Loch a' Chairn Bhain as far as Torgawn. The steep offshore island of Eilean a' Ghamhna, which was probably never inhabited, appears strangely to be both well-drained, devoid of grazing animals and of trees, despite its proximity to a substantial area of woodland. All these areas of woodland appear healthy, and their future should now be assured as sheep have been taken off Ardvar, and stalking has been resumed.

The situation in the Elphin area is in real contrast; the only remaining significant area of native woodland by the 1970s was on the south side of Loch Urigill, and when visited then it consisted only of aged trees, many of them recumbent, with no young growth. Of all the other areas mapped by Home, only the faintest traces remain. Of the wood on the north and east side of the hill of Elphin, there is nothing to be seen except for a few trees in the steep-sided bed of the burn that flows from Urigill to Loch Cam. Eilean na Gartaig in Loch Cam and a small strip on the peninsula between Lochs Cam and Veyatie are still wooded, but of those mapped by Home north of Loch Cam, only a small fragment remains. The wood to the west of Loch Awe has totally disappeared, although a few fragments remain on the islands in the loch (again there are a few pines, which are probably planted). Home did in fact note that this woodland had been lately much reduced by cutting, and it certainly did not survive this process.

The same story can be told of most of the former farms in this inland area: Lyne had no woods in 1774, and still has none; Ledmore had woodland on the edge of Loch Borralan, which has completely disappeared. Home noted that there was here one area of 'sweet green swairded grass growing upon the remains of a natural wood' – this has also gone. Knochan has lost virtually all of its woodland.

As described above, there is clearly a contrast in the changes in woodlands of the coastal zone of Drumbeg–Ardvar and the inland zone centred on Elphin. It does not seem possible to guess what numbers of sheep might have been put on the sheep-runs of Glen Leraig or Ardvar, as opposed to Lyne and Ledmore, or how many sheep the crofting communities of Nedd or the inland communities of Elphin and Knockan may have had at their peak. There is however a marked tendency for the woodland in the upland areas to have suffered quite severely since 1774, in contrast to those on the coast. This cannot be ascribed to significant differences in the pressure being exerted on the different areas, at least in terms of population. Indeed, by 1774, the coast was regarded as congested, and one can only assume that this heavy population would one way or another place quite a strain on the existing woodland.

One would not wish to suggest that all the coastal woodland extant in 1774 has survived; the south side of Loch Glencoul, steep and remote from habitation though it always has been, has lost nearly all its woodland. Nor has the inland area around Elphin quite lost all it must have possessed in Home's time; along the steep south shore of Loch Veyatie, under Cul Mor, there yet remains an appreciable area of native woodland, although officially it is in Coigach and was not mapped by Home. Despite these exceptions, the general contrast in survival between coastal and inland area remains, and it is this surviving patch of woodland under Cul Mor which may point to a factor relevant in the search for an explanation.

Discussion

Loch Veyatie is a long, narrow loch running roughly north west to south east, and so what has been described as its south shore is in fact protected from the prevailing south-west winds by the bulk of the mountain of Cul Mor and its foothills. The areas of woodland are to be found on these foothills where they descend steeply to the loch – they face roughly north east. Also facing north east, and somewhat sheltered by the much less significant bulk of Druim na Doire Duibhe, is the moribund area of woodland beside Loch Urigill. It is noteworthy that these then are the only surviving areas of native woodland around Elphin. In addition, the steep southern shores of Loch Assynt are sheltered from the south west by the bulk of Beinn Gharbh, and here too significant woods remain at Garbh Doire and An Coimhleum. In each case, the opposite side of the loch is more exposed and virtually devoid of woodland. There are, for instance, almost no trees at all on the northern shore of Loch Veyatie, and it is hard to see that this area which is particularly isolated geographically, could ever have been subject to heavy grazing.

Much of Assynt in fact has this north east to south west 'grain', and the extensive area of woodland on the south side of Loch a' Chairn Bhain already referred to, is also very sheltered from the prevailing wind, being protected by the bulk of Quinag. It is certainly noticeable that the opposite shore of the loch has no woodland at all. Woodland also remains on the southern shore of Loch Glendhu, but not on the north. In the very narrow sheltered glens, this effect is not noticeable and there is woodland on both sides. This is true of Glen Leraig, the Loch Roe–Manse–Loch Torbreck system, and on the Kirkaig.

The view that shelter or general exposure is significant could be confirmed by the fact that by 1774 that section of the coast that runs from Achmelvich Bay round Stoer Point to Oldany Island was already devoid of trees. This is by far the most exposed section of the Assynt coast, and the effect is exacerbated by the fact that Stoer Point (which has a different geology) is comparatively smooth in its topography – there is little shelter to be found. The lack of shelter and the different geological structure of Stoer Point (it is composed of Torridonian Sandstone) are the major differences between this section of the coast and the Drumbeg–Ardvar section. There certainly cannot have been any real difference in the pressures exerted on these different sections of the coast by their populations. In 1774, the whole coastline was regarded, as has been said, as somewhat congested, Drumbeg–Unapool as much as Stoer.

A general look at the distribution of the present native woodland in Assynt suggests that much of it is found below the 300 foot contour. Where it exists at a greater height, it is often found on a relatively steep slope facing north east, away from the prevailing south-west winds. Some support for this general observation may be found by looking elsewhere on the West Coast.

The neighbouring Parish of Coigach has something of the same 'grain', and the patches of relatively healthy woodland on the south-west shores of Lochs Osgaig, Bada na-h-Achlaise, Lurgainn, Doire na h'Airbhe and an Doire Duibh are in contrast to their generally bare north-easterly shores.

Other, relatively low-lying parts of the north-west Highland coast support areas of healthy native woodland. Along the coast of the Scoraig peninsula, from Allt na h'Airbe westwards, the steep, north-east facing slope contains some small areas of young woodland, and there is significantly more further up Loch Broom. On Little Loch Broom, native woodland is to be found along the north-east facing shore below Badluarach, and on Rubha Reidh there is a significant area by Loch an Draing, again facing north east. The sheltered area from Gairloch to Badachro supports a considerable area of healthy woodland; one nameless wood (OS 1:50,000, Sheet 19, GR 8227714) when visited in 1993, proved to be healthy in structure, despite having sheep, red and roe deer at the time of the visit. Substantial sections of the shores and islands of Loch Maree still retain healthy native woodlands, mostly below the 300 ft. contour. It only reaches a significantly greater height on the steep north-east facing slopes of Coille ne Glas Leitire, protected by the foothills of Beinn Eighe. The surroundings of Loch Torridon might not generally be considered to be wooded, but Beinn Shieldaig itself has, most interestingly, two discrete areas of native woodland, a large birchwood on the steep slopes facing north over Ob Mheallaidh and the better-known Caledonian pine on its south-west face, and around Loch Shieldaig. Further out, steep slopes hold healthy woodland at Lower Diabaig, Kenmore, and Arinacrinachd. Much of the long, exposed coastline of Applecross is completely bare of trees, with the marked exception of healthy woodland on the sheltered shore of Loch Toscaig. What might be termed Glen Kishorn, by Rassall, shows instructively, the well-known ashwood surviving (however marginally) on the limestone, in contrast to the bare Torridonian on the other side of the glen. The limestone side of the glen, being more fertile, must always have been used most heavily by man, sheep and deer, but it is exactly there that the woodland survives.

Conclusions

The evidence from Assynt makes it clear that the view that much of the decline in our native woodland occurred in the last 200 years, is, at least for Assynt, a major over-simplification. Broadly speaking, it is native woodland inland and over a height of about 300 feet, that has seen the most serious decline since 1774. This is in complete contrast to the coastal zone, where much healthy woodland remains, and where the area of native woodland has remained roughly constant, indeed has, in places increased since 1774. Furthermore, the evidence from Assynt suggests that exposure may be at least as potent a factor as grazing animals or human exploitation in determining where such woodland will or will not flourish.

The geomorphological factors which encourage the retention of woodland in the generally wet conditions of the West Coast have long been known (Pearsall 1950). This present and very brief study suggests that in addition there is a climatic or exposure factor, which has resulted in loss of woodland on exposed coasts and hills, and over extensive areas inland. To some extent, this is self-evident; areas in the path of westerly rain-bearing winds are obviously prone both to damage by salt spray (with which anyone who has tried to grow trees in Orkney is well-acquainted!), and to water-logging.

It should at least by now be clear that there is no simple answer to the question; 'What caused the loss of Scotland's native woodlands?' The answer is not simply man and his grazing animals, but a whole range of factors, some of which have been briefly considered above. There are others which would also have to be taken into account – climatic change, and the effects of major volcanic eruptions in Iceland throughout pre-history and history. The impact of individual factors will have varied from place to place and from time to time; the Highlands and Islands of Scotland are remarkable for the diversity of their geology, and that geology and its subsequent history is fundamental in determining the evolution of the landscape we see today.

Implications

If the above tentative conclusions are accepted, it could be suggested that in some instances, conditions for the growth of healthy native woodlands on the

West Coast of Scotland are at present marginal. In the light of the predicted climatic deterioration that may follow global warming, for instance, it is now suggested that some time should be spent in assessing more precisely the climatic conditions currently pertaining at a number of woodland sites, ranging from healthy coastal sites to moribund and declining inland sites. Such information might allow new woodland and regeneration schemes to be located in those places where they would be best placed to survive future changes in climate.

References

Adam, R J (ed.), *John Home's Survey of Assynt* (Scottish History Society, 1960)
Pearsall, W H, *Mountains and Moorlands* (Fontana New Naturalist, London, 1950)
Walker, G J, *Inventory of Ancient, Long-established and Semi-Natural Woodlands of Sutherland* (Nature Conservancy Council, 1985)

11. Birchwoods in a Deeside Parish

Neil A MacKenzie and Robin F Callander

Introduction

The purpose of this chapter is to illustrate how a knowledge of local woodland history can provide insight into the dynamic relationship that can exist between the pattern of self-sown native birchwoods at a landscape scale and other competing land-uses, and so contribute to the birchwood resource's sustainable management and development.

After a long history of neglect and decline, the conservation and expansion of native woodlands has recently become central to the delivery of National Forestry Policy (UK Government 1994) and is likely to be given increasing priority (Worrell and Callander 1996).

The management of native birchwoods is an important part of this. They account for over half the surviving area of native woodland in Scotland and are particularly widespread in the Highlands, where they have been a dominant component of the natural forest cover for over 8000 years (MacKenzie and Callander 1995).

This chapter reviews the findings of investigations into the woodland history of the Highland Deeside parish of Finzean. While the principal research was carried out some time ago as part of wider studies (Callander 1981–85; MacKenzie 1985), the results have become increasingly relevant as interest has grown in the management of native woodlands at a landscape or catchment scale, rather than just a site by site basis. Important examples of this recent interest are the proposed forests of Deeside and Strathspey (Scottish Office 1994) and Scottish Natural Heritage's proposals for a Forest Habitat Network for Scotland (Peterken *et al.* 1995).

In this chapter, after a brief description of Finzean parish, some of the main aspects of the parish's woodland history are outlined, including the destruction in the sixteenth and seventeenth centuries of the extensive native forest in the western half of the parish, which was considered to have been of equal quality to the adjoining forest of Glen Tanar (Dinnie 1865); and the development of plantation forestry in the eastern half of the parish from the eighteenth century and the continuing influence of this type of forestry on the destruction and regeneration of birchwoods locally.

The historical information presented is drawn from Callander (1981–85) and MacKenzie (1985) and unless otherwise given, the original sources for that information can be referenced in those studies.

The final part of the chapter considers the significance of the results from this and related woodland history research for the types of landscape scale proposals identified above.

Finzean Parish

The parish of Finzean was created in 1903 as a quoad-sacra parish covering the southern half of the traditional Aberdeenshire parish of Birse. The boundaries of Finzean parish coincide with the upper half of the catchment of the River Feugh, the first main tributary of the Dee west of Aberdeen.

Finzean parish with the rest of Birse forms the eastern edge of Highland Deeside (Figure 1) and is representative of it, with an extensive landscape of heather moorland, self-sown birch and pine woodlands, commercial plantations of Scots pine, relatively smallscale mixed farming and a scattered settlement pattern (Callander and MacKenzie 1991). The parish's land use and social history also reflects its Highland character (Callander 1981–85).

Finzean parish has an area of approximately 7000 ha (17,000 acres) (Figure 2). The western half of this area is the Forest of Birse, covering *c.* 3750 ha of largely uninhabited heather moorland which has a long and distinctive history as a commonty or area of common land. In the eastern half of the parish (3250 ha), the valley opens out into farmland and settlement and for over 200 years, more or less all this area has been owned by Finzean Estate.

The Forest of Birse

The designation of this part of the parish as a 'forest' results from its early feudal status as a Royal Hunting Reserve. In the twelfth century, the Forest and all the other lands of Birse were granted to the Bishops of Aberdeen and this has contributed to the survival of records about the medieval use and management of the Forest, as well as its ecological character. The Bishops' rent rolls indicate, for example, that the native pinewood contained significant quantities of oak and hazel (Browne 1923).

Under the Bishops, the Forest was used in common by all the inhabitants of Birse for a traditional pattern of shielings and a diverse range of natural materials. As part of this, they were allowed to take wood from the Forest for use on their holdings and tenants also had to supply the Bishops with wood from the Forest as part of their rents. However, throughout the fourteenth and

Scale 1 : 625,000

━━ Kincardine & Deeside District boundary

Figure 1: Location map of Highland Deeside and the Parish of Finzean.

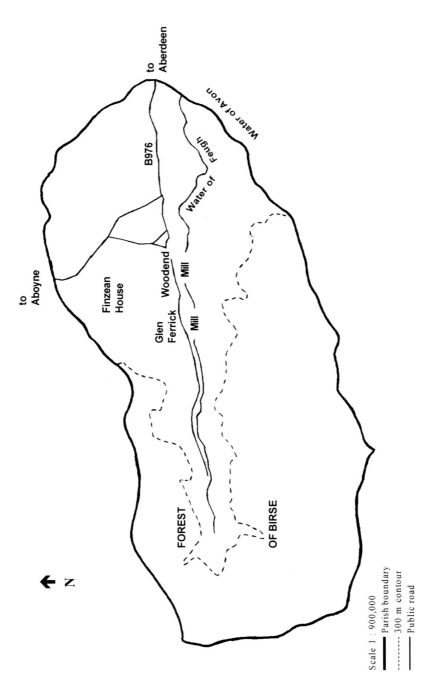

Figure 2: The Parish of Finzean.

fifteenth centuries, there were disputes about the illegal use and exploitation of the Forest, including some by the powerful barons appointed by the Bishops to enforce the rules governing its use.

The situation deteriorated further during the sixteenth century, when the break up and disposal of the Bishop's land in Birse exemplified the corrupt dissipation of the Church's resources at that time. By the beginning of the seventeenth century, the use of the Forest of Birse as a commonty was being literally fought out between the Earl of Aboyne and the parish's other new landowners. Over-exploitation during these times resulted in the diminishing forest on the commonty becoming dominated by birch rather than pine, with local tradition recalling fire as one of the causes.

Blaeu's 1650s map shows the Forest of Birse commonty as still well-wooded, but Gordon of Straloch recorded at the same time that this extensive birchwood had been recently cut down (MacFarlane 1908). He also reported it as growing up again and some timber continued to be extracted from the commonty into the early eighteenth century. However, by the 1750s, when the continuing disputes over the use of the Forest as a commonty reached the Court of Session, the area had no timber left of any value (Browne 1923; Callander 1981–85).

The fate of the commonty's woodland can be contrasted with the survival of part of the same original forest across the eastern edge of the commonty of the individually held private lands of Finzean Estate. These woodlands of Glen Ferrick and Woodend are shown clearly on Roy's map of 1755 and are still there today as Scotland's tenth largest and most easterly surviving genuinely native pinewood.

The first documentary record of Woodend is not until 1549 and its English name also suggests it had only recently been established as a new township. Its name and its location within the start of the narrow upper part of the Feugh valley that forms the forest of Birse, also suggest it may have been an encroachment into the original commonty.

The 1755 Court Session judgement, while recognising there were no longer any woods of value on the commonty, took the precaution of specifying the arrangements that would govern the use of any woods that should happen to grow upon the commonty in the future (Browne 1923). During this century that has gradually started to happen and there is now extensive pine natural regeneration over much of the north side of the commonty (MacKenzie 1992). This is spreading from several sources and is now more or less continuous across the Forest of Birse between the native pinewoods of Glen Ferrick in the east and Glen Tanar in the west, a distance of 6 km. At some time in the future a pinewood in the Forest of Birse may yet once again come to be considered of equal quality to that in Glen Tanar.

Finzean Estate

During the break up of the Bishop's lands in the sixteenth century, a branch of the Farquharsons acquired the township of Finzean in the part of Birse to the east of the commonty. By 1760, they had acquired the whole of that part of the parish and consolidated it into a single estate. This area is still owned by the Farquharsons as Finzean Estate.

The Estate started to develop systematic plantation forestry from the mid-eighteenth century. Extensive estate records, good map sources and surviving field evidence allow the history of that enterprise and the individual plantations on the Estate to be traced and analysed in detail right through to the present time.

By the start of the nineteenth century, there were just over 400 ha of 'plantations' on the Estate. While these were all referred to at the time as 'plantations' many were initially established simply by enclosing and protecting natural regeneration of pine and birch which had arisen from existing native woodlands. In some instances gaps were planted up, particularly with larch (Callander 1986). These estate 'plantations' were all managed for pine timber and, up to this time, harvesting was all for local consumption: building materials for the reconstruction of farm steadings and houses, bridges, fencing and other estate purposes as well as sales to tenants. It was not until 1808 that, following a large windblow, timber also started to be sold to outside timber merchants.

The area of 'plantation' continued to be expanded, reaching over 600 ha by 1825 and 750 ha by 1850. An increasing number of these were established by planting rather than natural regeneration. However, during this period, the established 'plantations' were heavily over-exploited to meet the debts of the then laird, so that there was virtually no marketable pine on the Estate by 1850.

The 'plantation' resource was built up again by re-stocking and new planting during the second half of the nineteenth century to a new peak of extent and maturity. However, this resource was then in turn over-exploited during the first half of this century. A combination of family circumstances, wider economic conditions and two bouts of war-time fellings, meant that by 1950 many of the nineteenth century plantations had been felled and not re-stocked, while no new plantings had been undertaken. The final devastation came with the great gale of 1953.

The Estate started replanting in the 1950s, still largely relying on Scots pine, and in the last few years the plantation area has again reached the same extent as at the start of the century.

Local Birch Dynamics

Historical records show that the inhabitants of Birse, with others in the Highlands, made considerable use of birch prior to the eighteenth century for a wide variety of agricultural implements, domestic articles and construction purposes. The evidence from a legal dispute in the adjoining parish of Glen Tanar also indicates at least some attempts locally by that time to manage birchwoods on a systematic basis (Ross 1995).

The pattern of local use appears to have diminished rapidly during the eighteenth century as a result of major changes in farm structure and leases and the local economy generally. There is also no evidence from the mid-eighteenth century until recently of management by Finzean Estate to perpetuate the local birch resource. However, the development at that time of the Estate's forestry plantation enterprise based on Scots pine and its subsequent management, has been the dominant influence on the pattern of birch survival on the Estate over the last 200 years. This influence can be demonstrated from the sequence of map sources available, detailed records on the history of individual plantations and existing field evidence.

The pattern of birch survival follows the pattern of troughs and peaks in the extent and maturity of Finzean Estate's plantation resource, which had troughs in the mid-eighteenth, nineteenth and twentieth centuries and peaks at the end of each one. However, the troughs and peaks in the extent of local birch have been offset from those for plantations due to the nature of the interaction between the two resources.

This interaction or cyclical relationship has two main components. The first relates to the plantation establishment phase and has two aspects to it. Firstly, following each pine trough, the setting up of enclosures to protect new or restocked plantations has also encouraged birch regeneration and survival. Secondly, however, each time the area of plantations has increased towards a peak, the extent of local birchwoods has decreased because the expansion has been concentrated disproportionately on existing birchwood sites. In these latter instances and throughout the period, the birchwood has been felled except for the retention of a nurse stock.

The second main component relates to the thinning and final felling of plantations. As the plantation resource has matured towards each peak, the retained or invasive birch regeneration has tended to be either selectively felled to favour the pine or else shaded out as the pine closed canopy over them. Then, it has only been towards the end of the traditional 100–120 year pine rotation that thinning has opened the canopy sufficiently for any new birch regeneration, with final felling starting the whole cycle again.

Surveys in 1947 and 1985 that recorded the birch resource on Finzean Estate illustrate the nature of its relationship with the plantations. At both these dates the extent of birch was very similar at around 150 ha. However, there was a marked change in distribution with approximately 50 percent of the birchwood present in 1947 having disappeared by 1985 due to site clearance to expand the plantation resource (Figure 3). These losses were compensated for by new areas of birch regenerating within the plantation enclosures and by the colonisation of some other ground on the Estate by birch.

By 1985, the selective removal of plantation birch was already leading to a

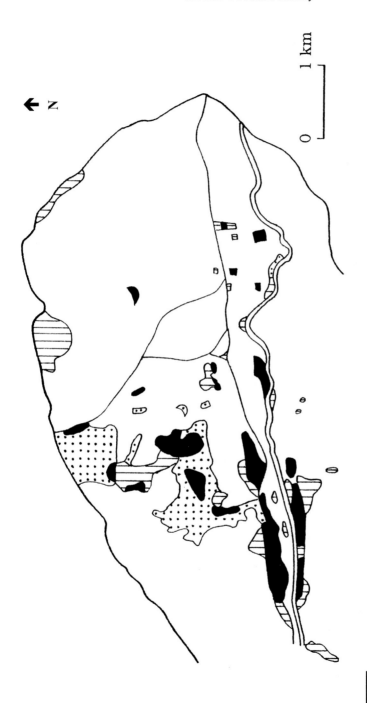

Figure 3: Birch woodland in Finzean parish, 1947–1985.
(The Forest of Birse and the southern part of the parish have been excluded.)

Birchwood present in 1947 and 1985

Birchwood lost since 1947

New Birchwood since 1947

rapid reduction in the overall birch resource. While some of these birch were being felled to waste, the Estate was harvesting over 300 tonnes a year and substantial quantities were removed on several occasions by contractors as part of their plantation thinning contracts.

Thus, during the 1980s, when the plantation resource was continuing to mature and expand towards its current peak, the birch resource was already declining from its peak. This repeats the conspicuous trends of previous centuries, even though many other factors have always also influenced local birch survival. One such factor was myxomatosis in the 1950s, which reduced browsing pressure sufficiently for birch regeneration to become established in several areas. There may have been similar transitory episodes in the past, for example, during 'the ill years' of the 1690s (Smout 1979) when a reduction in people and their stock may have favoured regeneration.

Despite such other considerations, the results outlined here show that, although birch may not 'officially' have been part of Estate forestry, it has consistently been involved with it for more than 200 years. The results, by showing the impending decline of the local birch resource, have also contributed with other factors to changes to more sustainable birch management on Finzean Estate during the last ten years.

Discussion

The natural tendency of birch and pine in the boreal forest environment of the Highlands is to regenerate outside their existing canopy. This is dependent on the availability of ground to colonise which, in turn, is determined by the character of the surrounding land uses.

This interaction means that an historical approach is important to understand the origins and current composition and structure of many individual native birch and pine woods, and thus a crucial element in determining appropriate management (Callander 1986). Research can reveal a complex ebb and flow of the boundaries of individual woodland boundaries, as they have expanded and contracted over time under different land use influences (Peterken 1986).

Historical studies have been an important influence on the management of individual woodland sites in Finzean, most notably in determining that Glen Ferrick is a genuinely native pinewood. The findings reported here show how historical studies can also reveal the dynamic relationship between native birch and other land uses at a multi-site landscape scale. The patterns and trends that emerge again have important implications for management if the intention is to perpetuate or expand the local birch resource.

The same type of dynamic relationship has also been shown to be operating over Deeside as a whole by a study for the period 1947–85 (Brown and Wightman 1988). As in Finzean, while the total area of birch was similar at both dates, 50 percent of the area of birch in 1947 had been lost by 1985. Forestry was again the main influence and the total birch area was only maintained by birch colonisation at particular sites in mid Deeside compensating for losses elsewhere in the valley.

The fluid situation shown by these studies is a crucial factor to be considered as part of current proposals to establish the Forests of Deeside and Strathspey (Scottish Office 1994). The intention of these designations is to ensure the woodlands in each catchment are managed on a co-ordinated basis to perpetuate and develop their existing character. The Forest areas are both over 1300 sq. kms. and both contain substantial native woodland resources that are very similar in scale and character. In addition to around 9000 ha of self-sown birchwoods, they also contain over 22,000 ha of self-sown native pinewoods (Callander and MacKenzie 1994). These pinewoods, like the birchwoods, reflect their own dynamic relationship with other land use influences.

To achieve the woodland objectives for Deeside and Strathspey Forests requires understanding the patterns, timescales, trends and influences underlying the current dynamic woodland environment and part of this understanding can only come from an historical perspective. While this may appear ambitious on such a scale, much of the information needed has already been collected or is relatively easily available. Inventories exist, for example, of all the existing woodland in each Forest area with the data computerised, including the maps of their distribution. Details exist from contemporary studies of the age structures and origins of many individual woodlands and this allows their development over time to be 'stripped back'. This information can then be linked with the historical studies that already exist for a number of the main woodlands in each Forest area and so provide a picture of the changing patterns and trends.

A clear perspective on the dynamic of the overall woodland resource and its different components is also necessary to implement Scottish Natural Heritage's environmental strategy of a Forest Habitat Network (Peterken et al. 1995). The Forests of Deeside and Strathspey have been identified as core areas within this overall network. Within them, the focus is on maintaining or improving the interconnectedness of both woodland and non-woodland habitats, as well as different species and types of woodland.

Contrast between areas can also provide an empirical laboratory. A major example is between the western and eastern halves of Highland Deeside. An historical understanding of the woodland expansion that has occurred in the eastern half this century and the influence on this of the various competing land uses, may provide valuable insights into the scales, patterns and rates of natural regeneration that may now be achieved in the western half of Highland Deeside.

The contribution of historical studies to the Cairngorms Forests, and to related landscape scale proposals, is not just environmental and silvicultural but also social and cultural. As the Finzean studies showed the parish's woodland history is closely related to its social history and this is very much the case throughout Highland Deeside. Finzean is also not unusual in the quality of its historical sources. Highland Deeside is, for example, owned by a small number of large estates which have typically been with the same family for centuries and have extensive estate records. Forests have always been vital to the area's economy and there are still unusual vestiges of woodland culture. These include the two water-powered wood working mills in Finzean, both of which still operate as traditional local businesses.

Highland Deeside has a wealth of sources, from the old estate papers to the detailed information on the existing woodlands, from which to build a thorough forest history. This could make a major contribution to establishing the identity of the proposed Deeside Forest and the socio-economic and environmental benefits that are anticipated to flow from this (Rural Forum 1995). The exercise of compiling Highland Deeside's woodland history, rather than just the results, could also be a useful tool in local community development.

Conclusion

The Finzean studies reviewed in this chapter have illustrated the important relationship between native birchwoods, forestry and other land uses at a parish scale. This type of dynamic interaction is repeated across the rest of the Highland Deeside catchment, and potentially Strathspey given its similarity.

The studies highlight the need to incorporate an historical approach as part of achieving co-ordinated and targeted management of the exceptional native woodland resources in the proposed Deeside and Strathspey Forests. The current woodland patterns are trends with which a new set of management ambitions will need to be integrated.

The use of woodland history to inform forestry and related land use management can also be linked to its potential contribution locally to community development.

References

Brown, I R and Wightman, A D, 'The birchwoods of Deeside 1947–1987: a declining resource?' *Scottish Forestry,* 42 (1988), pp. 93–103

Browne, G F, *Echt-Forbes family charters, 1345–1727* (W and R Chambers, 1923)

Callander, R F, *History in Birse* (Robin Callander, Finzean, 1981–1985), nos. 1–4

Callander, R F 'The history of native woodlands in the Scottish Highlands', *Trees and wildlife in the Scottish uplands,* ed. Jenkins, D (Institute of Terrestrial Ecology, Banchory, 1986), symposium no. 17

Callander, R F and MacKenzie, N A, *The native pine woodlands of Highland Deeside,* a report for the Nature Conservancy Council (NE Region) (Aberdeen, 1991)

Callander, R F and MacKenzie, N A, *The native woodlands of Highland Deeside,* a report for Scottish Natural Heritage (Aberdeen, 1994)

Dinnie, R, *An account of the Parish of Birse* (Aberdeen, 1865)

MacFarlane, W, *Geographical collections relating to Scotland,* eds. Mitchell, Sir A and Clark, J T (Edinburgh, 1908)

MacKenzie, N A, 'The management and utilisation of birch in an upland Aberdeenshire parish', (M.Sc. thesis, University of Edinburgh, 1985)

MacKenzie, N A, 'An inventory and survey of seven native pine woodlands on Highland Deeside', (unpublished report for the Nature Conservancy Council for Scotland (NE Region), Aberdeen, 1992)

MacKenzie, N A and Callander, R F, *The native woodland resource in the Scottish Highlands* (Forestry Commission, Edinburgh, 1995), technical paper 12

Peterken, G F, 'The status of native woods in the Scottish Highlands', *Trees and wildlife in the Scottish uplands*, ed. Jenkins, D (Institute of Terrestrial Ecology, Banchory, 1986), symposium no. 17

Peterken, G F, Baldock, D and Hampson, A, *A forest habitat network for Scotland,* (Scottish Natural Heritage, Edinburgh, 1995), research, survey and monitoring report 44

Ross, I, 'A historic appraisal of the silviculture, management and economics of the Deeside forests', *Our pinewood heritage*, ed. Aldhous, J R (Forestry Commission/RSPB/SNH, 1995)

Rural Forum, *Forests and people in rural Scotland* (Rural Forum, 1995)

Scottish Office, *Cairngorms partnership*, (HMSO, 1994)

Smout, T C, *A history of the Scottish people, 1560–1830* (Fontana, 1979)

UK Government, *Sustainable forestry – the UK programme* (HMSO, 1994)

Worrell, R and Callander, R F, *Native woodlands and forest policy in Scotland* (WWF Scotland, 1996)

12. A History of two Border Woodlands

A H H Smith

Introduction

> For a country like Scotland... it is not merely fascinating, but economically important, that the history of the fate of the natural forests be traced... To look back over the centuries is essential... to the forester... if he is to have a proper understanding of the part played by the forest in the past and of its future potentialities. Something that was stolen from the forest in the past must be returned to it now and in the future: the mistakes of the past must be paid for by the present so that the future may benefit. (Anderson 1967, pp. ix–xii.)

The growth of interest in the history of forest development and clearance, foreshadowed by Anderson (1967), has led to a continuing reappraisal of woodland history in Scotland. This process is occurring over a range of temporal and spatial scales (e.g. Dickson 1993; Dumayne 1993). Historical woodland ecology has been developed primarily through the work of Rackham (1986, 1993) and Peterken (1993), whose use of field observations, maps, documents and associated material has led to detailed accounts of particular woodlands. Such techniques have been applied in Scotland (e.g. Tittensor 1970; Gilbert 1979; Stevenson 1990; Dickson 1993) but to a more limited extent.

The two woodlands studied here are of different characters. Black Andrew [NT 402295] is an 88 ha plantation of introduced conifers with a few scattered broadleaves along the Yarrow Water, defined as long-established woodland of plantation origin. Tinnis Stiel [NT 391293] is categorised as ancient woodland as defined in Walker and Kirby (1987). It is 14.5 ha, of which 3 ha is thought to be semi-natural woodland and the remainder introduced conifers (Walker and Badenoch 1989).

Overview of the woodland history of the Yarrow Valley to 1650

The original forest composition in the Yarrow Valley was of oak–elm–ash–

hazel woods at lower levels, merging upwards into birch–hazel woods, with birch-willow scrub at higher elevations (Birks 1989; Anderson 1967). Associated species included rowan, alder, holly, juniper, willow and hawthorn. Evidence of Mesolithic occupation comes from microliths, which may date from 6000 BC, from the Yarrow and Ettrick valleys (Elliot 1985). Contemporaneous anthropogenic effects on the forest are uncertain; one result may have been the spread of hazel (Anderson 1967). Predomestication stock management, by periodic and repeated burning to increase deer productivity and control annual herd movements (Morrison 1983), provided an essential stage in the cultural development which resulted in woodland becoming progressively marginalised through both attrition and direct clearance. However, agricultural crises in prehistoric times were serious enough to have major social and demographic effects (Morrison 1983), with the potential for pulses of woodland expansion. The general caution, '...not to guess at facile explanations of changes in prehistory...' (Rackham 1986, 106) applies.

The identification of numerous sites of cord rig cultivation in the Tyne–Forth area provides evidence that, during the Iron Age and Romano–British periods, indigenous communities were, '...accomplished farmers and cultivators who exploited a range of habitats using previously unsuspected technological innovations' (Topping 1989, 162). Although the majority of settlements did not cover extensive areas – arguing for widespread small-scale forest clearance – continued occupation over a long period with woodland exploited for building timber, fuel and fodder, and with grazing affecting regeneration, would have had a cumulative effect (Hanson and McInnes 1980). A local example of such a settlement, which shows evidence of multi-period occupation, is that of Lewenshope Rig [NT 386305] adjacent to Tinnis Stiel (RCAHMS 1983).

Anderson (1967) concluded that at the time of the Roman incursion man had made little impression upon the heavily wooded valley floors and lower slopes in the Lowlands. This analysis has been re-evaluated, with extensive clearances before the Roman invasion proposed (Dickson 1993). Paleoecological reconstruction emphasises the spatial and temporal variability of clearance and the complexity of local variation (Dumayne 1993). While no firm conclusions can be drawn, it seems likely, given the evidence of the nature and density of settlement, that deforestation was well advanced. Renewed pulses of clearance at this time possibly related to military activity (Dumayne 1993), the nucleation of settlements and the introduction by the Romans of improved agricultural technology in order to increase local corn production (Piggott 1982). Nevertheless, the intensity and date of clearance at precise locations remains problematic, particularly as localised depopulation may have led to phases of regeneration.

Evidence in post-Roman and Dark Age Selkirkshire is scarce. Anglo-Saxon occupation and settlement of Lothian and the Borders accelerated from about 600 AD. This is now considered to have been a small scale affair with settlement by a warrior aristocracy who exercised power by taking over existing structures of authority and administration (Dodgshon 1981). In the Yarrow valley, this process can be seen in the Anglian settlement names of Lewenshope (from the name, *Leofurne*) and Fastheugh (*faest*, strongly defended and *hoh*, hill). There is a further possible connection between the Anglian Edibnedschell and the site later known as Auld Wark (Elliot 1985), in turn replaced by Newark, from which centre planting was to radiate in the eighteenth century. This continuity of settlement indicates sustained pressure on the existing woodland; much of the remaining woodland in densely colonised areas may already have been largely confined to the steep banks of rivers and streams (Anderson 1967).

Feudalism followed the introduction to Scotland of powerful Anglo–Norman families in the twelfth century and the progressive integration of independent lordships into a single domain under the Scottish king, combined with the territorial and institutional delegation of this authority. Many of the land grants of this time were located in the waste (Barrow 1980). Evidence of such settlement in Yarrow can be seen in the name, Mountberger Law [NT 315275], originally Montbergeris, Norman-French for 'hill of the shepherd' (Elliot and Gilbert 1985); from its location at the head of the valley, it is reasonable to infer a well-defined pattern of land holding further down the valley at this time.

The establishment of forests as hunting reserves is attributed to David I (1124–1153). His charter to Melrose Abbey, probably dating from 1136, grants the monks rights of pannage in the forest of Selkirk and Traquair (Gilbert 1979), the area that came to be known as Ettrick Forest and which incorporated the Yarrow Valley. The designation of forest did not imply continuous, dense woodland, '…a forest is a certain territory of Woody Grounds and Fruitful Pastures, privileged for wild Beasts and Fowls of the Forest, Chase and Warren… A forest doth lie open and not enclosed.' (Manwood 1598, in Anderson 1967, vol. 1, 91). It need not imply the absence of settlement as proposed by Dodgshon (1981). Indeed, from a reading of the first Forest law, it is suggested that during the time of David I pasture, except during time of pannage, was free in royal forests; subsequent laws, probably dating from the reign of William I (1165–1214), requiring all animals to have permission to enter the Forest record the first major disputes between hunting and other economic activities (Gilbert 1979).

The administrative development of Ettrick Forest reflects these increasingly conflicting demands. Initially, the ability to exercise control was often limited by English claims. Nevertheless, the forest remained under grant to the Douglases from 1324 until their forfeiture in 1455 when it was annexed to the crown. The Scotts of Buccleuch had possessions within the forest at an early period, before 1398, with their power and possessions increasing after the Douglas forfeiture.

Throughout this period, the most important development was the establishment of sheep farming. Relaxation on pasturing is evident in the thirteenth century, with the appearance of tolls of foggage and herbage payable for grazing permits in the forest. In the fourteenth century ploughing in the

Ettrick was only permitted on previously ploughed land, a restriction that was maintained until the early sixteenth century, but freedom from this limitation could be granted to tenants (Gilbert 1979). The establishment of shielings in the fifteenth century indicates an increase in grazing pressure. James I (1406–1437) kept sheep in Ettrick Forest and the holders of the 'stedes' (holdings) also kept domestic stock. Anderson (1967, vol. 1, 167) envisaged the valley bottoms as carrying, '...quite a dense stand of oak, ash, elm, birch and hazel...' and although some such stands probably remained, it is likely that they were already discontinuous.

By 1455 the structure of Ettrick Forest had coalesced into the three wards of Tweed (47 stedes), Yarrow (26 stedes) and Ettrick (47 stedes). Records of illegal fellings can be found, though the assumption that wood was cut on the stedes from which the offenders came, given that the location is not specified, is not accepted by Gilbert (1979). The relevant holdings are Tynneis, Fastheuche, Auldwark and Newark (Black Andrew was subsequently established on parts of the latter three). The duties of the forester tenants to keep the forest in wood and deer were set out in the statutes of 1499; after this date, tenants were allowed to take timber for their own needs from their own stede.

By 1484, sheep farming had expanded to the extent that some stedes were classed as sheep stedes and by 1502 the king had sheep on twenty holdings, including Tinnis (Anderson 1967). Following rent increases in 1501, the king began to set Ettrick in heritable feu-ferme. This gave rights to improve the holding and was established in conjunction with longer leases and freedom to plough, sow and sublet. On some stedes this represented a considerable reduction in restrictions on farming (Gilbert 1979), and provided the incentive for the building of substantial farmsteads (Dodgshon 1981). This process was not uniform and hunting rights were still reserved. The extent of the remaining woodland is unclear, although some certainly existed at Tinnis as it was let with woods in 1520 (Anderson 1967).

The rapid pacification of the Borders following the Union of the Crowns (1603) allowed commercial sheep farming to flourish (Whyte 1983). This intensification put yet more pressure on whatever woodland remained. The splitting of townships imposed additional pressure (Dodgshon 1981; Whyte 1983), a process that was common in Ettrick from the fifteenth to the seventeenth centuries. Subsequent re-amalgamation and the adoption of single tenancies proceeded swiftly in the eighteenth century (Whyte and Whyte, 1991); with the majority of Ettrick in single tenancy by the 1760s (Dodgshon 1981). An account of 1649 (Elliot and Scott) mentions woods at Newark, with a later description of '...a gret deall of wood above and below the castle...' (Hodge 1722, 359). The holding of New Wark and Old Wark were in the possession of the Scotts of Buccleuch by 1622 (Anderson 1967) and Tinnis from 1619 (Innes 1850). It is from this period that more direct evidence relating to Tinnis Stiel and the area over which Black Andrew was subsequently to be established is to be found.

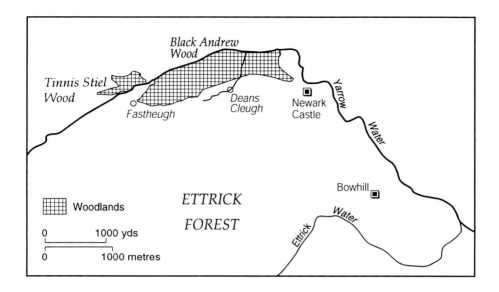

Figure 1: The location of Tinnis Stiel and Black Andrew Woods.

Tinnis Stiel and Black Andrew

The evidence on which the history of the woods is based is both cartographic and documentary. The sparse cartographic evidence is briefly reviewed; this is followed by evidence from the more extensive documentary sources. The plans of the Buccleuch lands by Ladd (1718) represent one of the earliest estate surveys in Scotland (Dodgshon 1981). The survey shows clearly the location of the woods and there are also comments on species and structure. Annotations on the map for Tinnis state that, '…here is some young thriveing wood,' for New Wark that, '…here is some large timber trees of Oke Ash and Sycamore and abundance of young wood as burch and ash.' At Old Wark there is stated to be, '…some young wood by the river,' and at Fastheugh, '…some old decaying trees and wood.'

Roy's Military Survey (1749–55) shows Black Andrew as bare ground, with only a fringe of trees along the Yarrow. The remnants shown by Ladd may have disappeared or, alternatively, been too insignificant with respect to the purpose of the survey to have been included. Tinnis Stiel is shown. Ainslie's map of 1773 shows Black Andrew as far as Deans Cleugh [NT 349297], not to its current eastern boundary. Tinnis Stiel is less well represented than on the Military Survey. An estate plan by Crawford (1810) is a more detailed representation, showing Black Andrew fully established and Tinnis Stiel with a water meadow on its southern boundary. This is an accurate reproduction of what actually existed, not a plan of proposed improvements, although with a subsequent addition. Thomson, in 1824, shows that the water meadow at Tinnis Stiel has been abandoned while the Ordnance Survey 6" First Edition of 1858 has Tinnis Stiel as open, mixed broadleaves with regeneration on the water meadow and Black Andrew, with a cleared area at the eastern end, as dense mixed woodland.

Documentary evidence for woodland management is available for 1638 with payment to, '...ane man for keeping the woods at Newark, Fastheugh and Aldwark.' (SRO: GD 224/943/2). Such payments may exist for 1625–29 (SRO: GD 224/943/1), but they could not be deciphered, and management may date back to a late sixteenth century enclosure at Newark (Blaeu 1654). Records of payments to a '...forester of the woods...' (SRO: GD 224/399/4) continue throughout the seventeenth century (SRO: GD 224/399/4: /285/13: /403/2: /403/5). The designation of wood forester is significant as the title relates specifically to woodland management rather than being purely nominal. The valuation of the woods at Newark and Fastheugh in 1695 (SRO: GD 224/253/5) is indicative of commercial interest. There are no records of payments for plants or planting during the seventeenth century; management activity presumably being directed towards the conservation of existing remnants through managing natural regeneration, restricting access and prosecuting illegal felling.

The early decades of the eighteenth century were characterised by an increase in management intensity, attributable to the personal interest of Duchess Anna, (b.1651, succeeded 1661, d.1732). In 1707, a note by the Commissioners in the margin of the Chamberlain's accounts refers to the forester's wages as, 'Allowed for this year; but hereafter must give an Account of all the Timber that is cut in the Wood and for whose use and if any be stolen to give... the particular circumstance of it before he get payment of this allowance.' (SRO: GD 224/253/9). A direction to the chamberlain by her Commissioners in 1715 clearly indicates the growing involvement:

> Her Graces woods in the Forest being very much wasted and destroyed, you will take particular inspection of the woods that remain... and appoint proper foresters to look after and preserve them from further damage, and such persons as you can discover to have been guilty of cutting, stealing or imbarking of wood... be prosecute and punished with the utmost rigour... And whereas we are informed there is a good appearance of Young Springe, in severall places..., specially near Newark where wood grows naturally and every Spring makes a pretty good show, Butt destroyed for want of incloseing, Wee therefore recommend you to... mark out the severall places... most proper to be inclosed... And that you make a distinct report of the whole and likewise of the charge and expense that shall be judged necessary to make inclosures sufficient and fencible agains beasts...' (SRO: GD 224/935/4).

This communication encapsulates the problems and formally initiates the development of the enclosure and planting program. The report that the

Chamberlain, Pringle, proposed in 1716 (SRO: GD 224/935/4) was not found. However, a survey of Liddesdale was undertaken in that year by Pringle and his successor in Ettrick in 1718, William Scott, in which they give a detailed account of location, area, state of growth and proposed treatment. Each location was considered in detail:

> There is a very great spring of Birch and Allar which after due felling in a few years rises to a good height growing very thick... (it)... should be well fenced and would yield most profit by copes. There are some Oaks and Ashes if reserved for standards would come to a good perfection, if it be not felled copes ways, it must of necessity be weed because being too thick they cannot come to a body... Upon the whole it would be of great use that all old high cut stocks were carefully cut at the ground for their better springing and that some persons were appointed to cut up shots where they are so thick that they eat one another out. The great number of Heasels that are growing everywher if wedd and hained... would yield hoops and the like otherwise (they) should be kept down for the checking of more useful timber. It would be proper to turn them all into copes, when once put in order... they would much answer and yield much profit for the supplying the work, the Oaks and Ash if preserved will soon be valuable forest... (SRO: GD 224/935/4).

The extent of silvicultural understanding and commercial intent is evident and it is reasonable to assume this level of expertise in Ettrick, given that the same individuals controlled the woods. The report outlines the reasoning behind the silvicultural operations carried out at Newark and Tinnis Steil. In the accounts of 1699 (SRO: GD 224/253/6) Newark and Fastheugh continue to be mentioned but, more significantly, there are payments for, '...weeding, cutting the bramble and training up the young Timber in Tinnis Steell...' Payments to two foresters, at Newark and Tinnis respectively, continue until 1719 when the forester at Tinnis was discharged and his duties taken over by the remaining forester at Newark (SRO: GD 224/253/21). The tending of Tinnis Stiel was therefore intensive during this period with some control over grazing as the, presumed, natural regeneration became established. Paying off the forester at Tinnis is perhaps explicable in terms of the establishment phase being completed and the woodland requiring less protection and maintenance.

The site of Black Andrew was scarcely wooded at this time, as Ladd's survey of 1718 illustrates, the dereliction of the Fastheugh woods mitigating against their early enclosure. The exact date of the Ladd survey is unclear; his instructions date from 1714 (SRO: GD 224/935/4): on the flyleaf of the volume of plans there is the inscription, 'It is informed that these measurements were made in the year 1718 by one of the name of Laud from England'; payment is made in the accounts of 1722 for measuring in Ettrick in 1721 (SRO: GD 224/253/23). As well as payments for silvicultural operations and enclosing – building stone and 'faill' (turf) dykes – there are records of compensation for the loss of grazing that enclosure entailed. These payments were made for between four and six years depending on the length of time that exclusion was maintained.

A further development in 1719 was the employment of a gardener, paid for '…preparing… severall nurseries of Barren planting, gathering seeds, sowing, weeding and transplanting and for setting seven hundred young Ash and Elm trees…' (SRO: GD 224/253/21). This is the first direct record of planting and, as the nursery was only then being established, the trees were bought in from a nearby estate. The cost of the plants was met by selling, '…peices of Wood lying scattered and rotting on the ground at Foullshiells…' (SRO: GD 224/253/21) and planted on 'corn ground' within the enclosures at Newark. Foulshiels lies opposite Newark on the North of the Yarrow. The early plantings used locally collected seed and it was not until the establishment of commercial nurseries that native species from outwith the locality were used.

In 1720, the Chamberlain is directed to give tenants timber for their houses and, '…upon his own view… (to) cutt Wood where best to be had…' (SRO: GD 224/253/20). In the accounts for that year (SRO: GD 224/253/22) there are many records of wood also being purchased for this purpose, local availability not meeting demand; timber is also recorded as being salvaged from ruins (SRO: GD 224/253/24). In 1720 James Wilson and George Moffat, the forester and gardener respectively, made a submission for a pay-rise for looking after, '…inclosures, which contain above two hundred thousand buds or young trees…,' and so that they can, '…be encouraged to propagate Timber in the Forest where it is now very much wanted and also to oversee and notice that no damage be done by cutting and stealing of what remains of the old Woods or the young Spring…' (SRO: GD 224/253/24). In addition, Hugh Wilson was paid for, '…pruning the young Alder and Birch trees growing in Tinnies burn and on the waterside of Yarrow near Tinnies bank, which were sned in winter 1720…' The presence of sycamore at Newark in 1720 is recorded in an invoice for dyking to protect, '…a young spring of Plaintrees and Allars…' The next stage of development can be seen in a change in the gardener's contract; from 1722 he is paid for, '…training up the nurseries of Barren planting and setting out the same in the Tenants yairds and other proper places…' He receives additional payments for, '…making holes to plant young Ashes…', including, '…248 at Tunnies… and for layeing the stones on the ground round the roots of the tree to preserve them from the scythe…' (SRO: GD 224/253/24).

The early planting and enclosures follow the pattern, characteristic of the period, of radiating out from the main house. There is increasing activity with enclosures expanding to protect thriving natural regeneration, the more permanent of these enclosures being made around Newark. It was in these permanently protected areas that planting was initiated, with some reclamation of agricultural land. The cost of enclosure and the vulnerability of new plantings to destruction were a factor in their location, as landowners sought to promote estate profitability and tenants were often suspicious of planting activity (Anderson 1967; Whyte 1979).

Planting expanded in the following years, with 'firrs' first recorded in 1724. In the same year there are records of the collection of haws for the establishment of a nursery of thorns, to be used for hedging and planting on top of the faill dykes (SRO: GD 224/253/26). The weedings (thinnings) were initially sold for firewood but, over the years, as their size increases they begin to be used for house repairs. The pattern established in the first three decades of the eighteenth century appears to continue, with the slow spread of enclosure, planting on the tenanted farms and maintenance of tending operations. The omission from this period is any significant income from wood sales, indicative of a period of woodland re-establishment. The woods in Ettrick Forest were valued for sale in 1735 (SRO: GD 224/253/38) but as there is no record of any income from sales in the accounts of the following year, it is unlikely that any sale occurred. There was a wood sale in 1743 as there is a payment for, '...valuing and intimating the roup of the old oaks at Newark.' (SRO: GD 224/253/46) Fraser (1878 in Anderson 1967) maintained that much wood was cut at the direction of Francis, 2nd Duke of Buccleuch (1695–1751); these accounts provide little support for this assertion. In 1749, the form of the accounts changes, with the introduction of generalised headings, and there is therefore no detailed information from this source for the following ten years; the vouchers do not indicate any major developments.

There are two reports on the woods in 1760; the first made to the Chamberlain, the second his report to the Commissioners. In the first report the woods at Tinnis are mentioned,

> ...having also viewed and inspected the Wood upon the farm of Tunnies (we) are of the opinion that it is come to its full growth and might be sold... that (it) is also overthick and should be thinned if not immediately sold and if Tunnies Wood be sold it will take about £30 to enclose the stock shoots... (SRO: GD 224/83/2).

The Chamberlain's account states that:

> The wood upon Yarrow is of no great extent and consists mostly of Ash Birch, and Alder with some Oaks... The Tenants... have been served mostly out of the Weedings of it for building and repairing their houses for a Great many years, part of that wood is at its full growth for country uses and might be sold... (SRO: GD 224/83/2).

The first report relates to Tinnis Stiel, there being no other wood at Tinnis, and it is not yet permanently enclosed. The distinction between large timber and that fit for 'country' uses is important, as the many country uses contributed to the commercial viability of the woodlands while providing locally useful and valuable materials. There are also comments which illustrate the antipathy of farmers to forestry operations, with reference to complaints about grass being spoilt when, '...leading away... Timber...' (SRO: GD 224/1005/2/6).

The site of Black Andrew is shown on the Military Survey of the 1750s as essentially bare ground. The extent to which its detail can be trusted is uncertain, though some analyses consider that woodland, a potential impediment to troop movements and cover for enemies, was carefully defined (O'Dell 1957; Skelton 1967). The establishment of extensive woodland at Black Andrew may have been prompted by a neighbour.

The following was written as part of an exchange of letters:

> That the farm of Fastheugh… as it is a very barren part of the estate incapable of any improvement but from planting and is situated directly opposite to Hangingshaw, the seat of Mr. Murray, which renders the prospect from thence disagreeable, Mr. Murray would be extremely obliged to His Grace if he would do him the favour to let him have that farm… for another of equal value… (SRO: GD 224/85/12).

No exchange took place but work began in 1762, 'Incloseing that part of Fastheugh hill called Black Andrew… about 150 aikers to be planted… the dyke consisting of 488 roods…' (SRO: GD 224/253/65). The dyke included a guarantee of maintenance for ten years, and in 1763 a house for the park keeper was built (SRO: GD 224/253/66). The plants were supplied and the planting carried out by Dickson's nursery, a common procedure (Anderson 1967). The planting density was to be 2800 trees per acre, comprising 800 seedbed ash and elm, 250 transplanted firs and 1750 seedling firs. Direct seeding was used for some areas, Dickson's invoice including an amount for, '…planting tree seeds on the stony places…' (SRO: GD 224/253/67). The use of Scots pine as a nurse for broadleaves was widely practised, although sometimes used on inappropriate sites with heavier and more fertile soils (Anderson 1967). The planting on this site was made with this awareness. The original estimate had proposed 500 transplanted firs but a note on the back reads, 'I have taken only 250 transplanted firs… because I suppose that there is not above the half of the hill where the soil is proper for them…' (SRO: GD 224/253/67). Planting took place in 1764 and 1765; a report of 1766 says that the plantation is thriving but, '…wants 20,000 Transplanted firs to fill up the gaps… transplanted (firs) because by cattle being prevented from going upon it, the grass and fairns are grown so luxuriant that seedbed firs… would be choaked from growing.' (SRO: GD 224/253/67). As will be explained later, Black Andrew was planted in two stages, this first stage from the current western boundary to Deans Cleugh [NT 408296].

No extensive felling was carried out at Tinnis Stiel up to 1766, as the income from the timber sales would certainly have been recorded. Tinnis Stiel was finally enclosed in 1772, the accounts recording the, '…inclosing of Tinnis Wood with a stone wall…' (SRO: GD 224/5222/1/5). The thinning proposed in the report of 1760 may have taken place, advice in 1769 being that in areas, '…such as Ettrick fforest where the Woods are of much smaller extent, the Haggs be so disposed as to admit of cutting by a rotation of three or four years.' (SRO: GD 224/459), temporary paling being used to enclose the cut areas. Felling probably occurred in 1773 as there is an invoice from Dickson covering March 1774 and January 1775 for pit planting at Tinnis with ash, elm, oak and beech and also with ten spruce firs, ten silver firs, ten larch and ten 'Balm of Gilead' firs; in all a total of 4200 trees. Peterken (1985) remarks on the impression gained from Anderson (1967) that while planting in broadleaved woods in Scotland has been a longstanding practice, it has affected the policies rather than the woods now regarded as semi-natural; this example belies that impression.

In the wood accounts for the late eighteenth and early nineteenth century there are numerous entries for the sale of 'small firs', many of which must have been the product of thinnings at Black Andrew. The increasing productivity of Black Andrew is reflected in an invoice for putting in a road in 1803 (SRO: GD 224/564/18). A report of 1802 on agricultural improvements, while not mentioning woods directly, says in relation to Tinnis that, 'A considerable portion of the land lying between the publick road and the river, is already inclosed with stone dykes and a water meadow...has already been laid out.' (SRO: GD 224/590/1) More detailed accounts for the early decades of the eighteenth century were not found. A water-powered sawmill, built between Black Andrew and Bowhill in 1818 (SRO: GD 224/590/2), is further evidence of increasing activity with earlier planting fuelling increased commercial activity. No other direct information for the first three decades of the nineteenth century was found.

A report of 1833 (SRO: GD 224/502/7) is a useful summary:

> Tinnis Stiel Plantation. Planted in 1775. Consists of Oak, Ash, Elm and Larch fir, was thinned in 1825. In good order.
> Black Andrew Old Plantation. Planted 1764–5 and again 1818. Consists of old Scotch fir and Spruce ditto. Proposed to prune Oak and plant vacancies.
> Black Andrew Plantation Addition. Planted in 1813, consists of Oak, Spruce and Scotch fir. Part was thinned last year. Proposed to thin remaining part and prune hardwood.

The dates on this report are believed to be accurate, as the Black Andrew planting of 1764/5 and the planting at Tinnis Stiel in 1775 are independently corroborated. An element of conflict – the Black Andrew addition of 1813 – exists between this report and the Crawford survey of 1810 which shows the whole plantation established. The boundary of the original planting has not been ascertained with complete certainty but, working from the final invoice and the current records, a reasonable estimation can be made. The invoice is for planting 143 acres (SRO: GD 224/253/67), the current total area of Black Andrew is 217 acres (Compartment records, Bowhill), with the area to the west of Deans Cleugh [NT 408296] being 159 acres. It is proposed that the planting of 1764/5 was confined to the west of the burn; although the original dyke crossed the burn as there is reference to, '...making and putting up paleing on the Braehead at each end above the water where a stone dyke would not stand...' (SRO: GD 224/253/66). The discrepancy in area can be accounted for by the fringe of trees along the Yarrow and measurement errors.

The reason for the whole area not being planted originally may lie in a report of 1791 which refers to, '...a small stripe of land belonging to Fastheugh on the south and east sides of Black Andrew plantation (that) should be added to Newark...' (SRO: GD 224/459), this rationalisation being needed before the rest could be enclosed and planted. The Ainslie map of 1773 supports this interpretation, showing Black Andrew only as far east as Deans Cleugh. This explanation appears to call into question the accuracy of the Crawford (1810) survey, the probable solution is that the eastern end was redrawn at a later date. A difference in colouring on the original plan, the alignment of Hangingshaw and the practice of establishing foresters' cottages on the edge of plantations (Anderson 1967), rather than in the middle where it is now situated, support this interpretation.

The OS 6" First Edition (1858) shows an unplanted area with a few scattered trees, broadleaves and conifers, in the north-east corner of Black Andrew; no direct information about this was found. It is shown as being planted on Crawford (1810) and on a second survey dated to about 1830 (Crawford and Brooke c. 1830). One possible explanation is that the area was planted as part of the addition to Black Andrew but failed, it being a frost pocket (G Booth pers. comm.), and was perhaps further cleared when the north lodge was built sometime before 1858.

Developments after this time are not well documented in detail. The accounts for the forester's department mention all the expected operations but with few references to locations (SRO: GD 224/618/619). There is cutting of dead firs, brush and shooting tracks in Black Andrew in 1835/6 (SRO: GD 224/503/7), and rooting and levering out blown trees in Black Andrew birch plantation in 1839 (SRO: GD 224/1105) – Anderson (1967) notes that the use of birch dwindled as it seeded too freely – and cutting and peeling larch bark in 1876 (SRO: GD 224/1117). Bark cutting is recorded in Tinnis Stiel in 1838 and felling in 1875 (SRO: GD 224/510/9/12). Income from bark is recorded throughout the nineteenth century, with the final record in 1885 (SRO: GD 224/1112). Extensive sales were made from Black Andrew in 1885–87, these were thought locally to have been caused by extensive windblow (G Booth pers. comm.). This is borne out by the accounts with payments for, '...pruning blown up trees at Black Andrew...' (SRO: GD 224/1118), from March 1885 through to January 1888; there is no specific mention of the replanting that is likely to have occurred. Developments in the twentieth century are not included here but there is information available, including personal recollections, from which the story could be continued.

Conclusion

Tracing the history of individual woodlands requires the coalescence of evidence from disparate sources. A full explanation should explore the archaeological evidence and consider relict features as well as the fragmentary, and often temporally and spatially discontinuous, information available from documents, maps and estate plans. This use of estate records indicates that information about specific locations over time is available. Details of plantation establishment, silvicultural operations and other events such as enclosure, which are significant in terms of the history of a woodland, were recorded. The degree of detail depends on the type of records and the form in which they were kept. In this case, increasing activity led to successive reorganisations of the estate administration, which resulted in less detail being available from the estate accounts: no adequate substitute source was found.

References

Anderson, M L, *A History of Scottish Forestry,* ed. Taylor, C J (2 vols., T Nelson & Sons Ltd., London, 1967)

Barrow, G W S, *The Anglo-Norman Era in Scottish History* (Clarendon, Oxford, 1980)

Birks, H J B, 'Holocene Isochrone Maps and patterns of Tree Spreading in the British Isles', *Journal of Biogeography,* 16:6 (1989), 503–40

Dickson, J H, 'Scottish Woodlands: Their Ancient Past and Precarious Present', *Scottish Forestry,* 47:3 (1993), 73–8

Dodgshon, R A, *Land and Society in Early Scotland* (Clarendon Press, Oxford, 1981)

Dumayne, L, 'Iron Age and Roman Vegetation Clearance in Northern Britain: Further Evidence', *Botanical Journal of Scotland,* 46:3 (1993), 385–92

Elliot, W, 'Prehistoric, Roman and Dark Age Selkirkshire', *Flower of the Forest: Selkirk: A New History,* ed. Gilbert, J M (Byway Books, Galashiels, 1985), ch. 1, pp. 9–18

Elliot, W and Gilbert, J M, 'The Early Middle Ages', *Flower of the Forest: Selkirk: A New History,* ed. Gilbert, J M (Byway Books, Galashiels, 1985), ch. 2, pp. 19–29

Elliot, W and Scott, W, (1649), 'Description of the Shiredom of Selkirk', in Macfarlane, W, *Geographical Collections Relating to Scotland,* ed. Mitchell A (Scottish History Society, 1908), Vol. II, 138–9

Gilbert, J M, *Hunting and Hunting Reserves in Medieval Scotland,* (John Donald, Edinburgh, 1979)

Hanson, W S and McInnes, L, 'Forests, Forts and Fields: A Discussion', *Scottish Archaeological Forum,* 12 (1980), 98–113

Hodge, J, (1722), 'An Account of the Remarkable Places and Parish Churches in the Shire of Selkirk', in McFarlane, W (1908), Vol. 1 – as for Elliot and Scott (1659) above

Innes, C, *Origines Parochiales Scotaiae* (T Constable, Edinburgh, 1850)

Manwood, J, (1598), *A Treatise and Discourse on the Laws of the Forest,* 4th edn (London, 1717), in Anderson (1967) as above

Morrison, I A, 'Prehistoric Scotland', *A Historical Geography of Scotland,* eds. Whittington, G W and Whyte, I (Academic Press, London, 1983), pp. 1–24

O'Dell, A C, 'A View of Scotland in the Middle of the 18th Century', *Scottish Geographical Magazine,* 69 (1953), 58–63

Peterken, G F, 'The Status of Native Woods in the Scottish Uplands', *Ecological Change in the Uplands,* eds. Usher, M B A and Thompson, D B A (Blackwell, London, 1985), pp. 14–19

Peterken, G F, *Woodland Conservation and Management,* 2nd edn (Chapman and Hall, London, 1993)

Piggott, S, *Scotland Before History* (Edinburgh University Press, Edinburgh, 1982)

Rackham, O, *The History of the Countryside* (J M Dent, London, 1986)

Rackham, O, *Trees and Woodland in the British Landscape*, 1st revised edn (J M Dent, London, 1993)

Royal Commission on the Ancient and Historical Monuments of Scotland (RCAHMS), Archaeology Aerial Photographs; BOX NT33 SW.SE. (1983)

Skelton, R A, 'The Military Survey of Scotland', *Scottish Geographical Magazine*, 83 (1967), 5–16

Stevenson, J F, 'How ancient is the woodland of Mugdock?', *Scottish Forestry*, 44 (1990), 161–72

Tittensor, R M, 'History of the Loch Lomond Oakwoods', *Scottish Forestry*, 24 (1970), 100–118

Topping, P, 'Early Cultivation in Northumberland and the Borders', *Proceedings of the Society of Antiquaries of Scotland*, 119 (1989), 161–79

Walker, G J and Kirby, K J, 'An Historical Approach to Woodland Conservation in Scotland', *Scottish Forestry*, 41 (1987), 87–97

Walker, G J and Badenoch, C O, *Inventory of Ancient, Long-established and Semi-natural Woodland (Provisional)*, (Nature Conservancy Council, Edinburgh, 1989)

Whyte, I D, *Agriculture and Society in 17th Century Scotland* (John Donald, Edinburgh, 1979)

Whyte, I D, 'Early Modern Scotland: Continuity and Change', *A Historical Geography of Scotland*, eds. Whittington, G W and Whyte, I D, (1983), pp. 119–40

Whyte, I and K, *The Changing Scottish Landscape 1500–1800* (Routledge, London, 1991)

Maps and Estate plans

Ainslie, J, 1773. A Map of Selkirkshire or Ettrick Forest, Sc. 1" = 1 mile, Scottish Records Office (RHP 9446).

Blaeu, J, 1654. *Atlas*, Vol. 6, No. 4, Teviota, Sc. 3.5" = 5 miles, National Library of Scotland.

Crawford 1810. Plans of the Duke of Buccleuch's Estates in North Britain, in the Counties of Edinburgh, Selkirk, Roxburgh, Dumfries and Peebles with the Island of Inchkeith in the County of Fife, Sc. 3" = 1 mile, Manuscript, Bowhill.

Crawford and Brooke *c.* 1830. Map of Counties of Roxburgh, Selkirk, Midlothian and part of Northumberland, surveyed by Order of the Duke of Buccleuch and Queensberry, Forrester, Edinburgh, Register House Plan 46125.

Board of Ordnance 1758. The Military Survey of Scotland, 1" = circa 0.5 miles, National Library of Scotland.

Ladd, E, 1718. Two Volumes of Plans of Dalkeith, Ettrick Forest, Liddesdale...Selkirk Parish, Yarrow Parish, Ettrick Parish and Canonby Parish, SC. 1.25" = circa 2 miles, Manuscript, Scottish Records Office (RHP 9629).

Ordnance Survey 1858. *Sheet XI*, 6" First Edition, Ordnance Survey, Southampton.

Thomson, J, 1824. *Atlas*, Map No. 5, Selkirkshire, Butterworth.

Scottish Record Office: Buccleuch Muniments

SRO: GD 224

83/2: Hints towards a plan for the future management of the woods on the Duke of Buccleuch's Estates.

Report made by Wm. Laing concerning the wood in his charge.

Copy of the Report made by James Thompson and Adam Hogg of the Woods and Planting in the forest under Mr Laing's charge.

85/12: Mr Townshend with Mr Murray of Philliphaugh's proposals for exchanging of Lands and desires it may be carried into execution.

253/1-69: Accounts and Vouchers of Ettrick Forest 1636–1766.

285/13: Accounts of Ettrick Forest 1678–1689.

345: Papers relating to Wm. Kerr, Manager of Accounts and Director of Improvements.

399/4: Accounts and Vouchers of Ettrick Forest 1662.

400/3: Accounts and Vouchers of Ettrick Forest 1665–70.

403/2: Accounts and Vouchers of Ettrick Forest 1686.

459: Memorials, proposals and estimates 1768–1804.

503/7: Report on Estate Management at Bowhill by T Binnie 28/08/1833.

510/9/12: Estate Papers – Bowhill – return of work and wages for four weeks 28/05/ – 23/06/1838.

522/1/5: Estimate of the expense of the plantations proposed to be done this season 1772.

564/15-20: Wood Accounts Ettrick Forest 1798–1807.

590/1: Report by Wm. Kerr to the Duke of Buccleuch of a plan and estimates of the expense of improvements which it seems proper for His Grace's tenants in the County of Selkirk to make upon their respective farms.

590/2: Estimate for sawmill for Bowhill 9/12/1817

618/1-5: Bowhill Accounts Charge and Discharge 1838-8.

619/1-23: Bowhill Accounts 1838/9–1869.

935/4: Sederunt Book of the Buccleuch Commissioners 1710–22, 10/8/1715.

943/1: Accounts of Ettrick Forest 1625-29.

943/2: Accounts of Ettrick Forest 1638-41.

962/5: Miscellaneous Estate Papers including Vouchers for Surveying.

1005/2/6: Townshend Correspondence – State of the Wood of Ettrick Forest – Wm. Laing 16/02/1760.

1105: Bowhill Estate Ledger 1839–42.

1112: Bowhill Cash Book 1864–1889.

1117: Bowhill Estate Ledger 1864–70.

1118: Bowhill Estate Ledger 1880–92.

Acknowledgements

The author wishes to thank His Grace, the Duke of Buccleuch; Chris Badenoch; Graham Booth, and Professor M L Anderson (1895–1961). Parts of this study were initially submitted in partial fulfilment of the requirement for the Degree of B.Sc. in Ecological Science with Honours in Forestry at the Institute of Ecology and Resource Management, University of Edinburgh, May 1994.

13. Coppice Management in Highland Perthshire

Christopher Dingwall

Much has been made of the words written by that old curmudgeon Dr Samuel Johnson following his tour of the Scotland in the autumn of 1773, in which he stated that 'there is no tree for either shelter or timber', that 'the whole country is extended in uniform nakedness', and that 'a tree might be a show in Scotland as a horse in Venice'. Johnson went on to deplore the denudation of the landscape where, he supposed, 'many centuries must have passed without the least thought of future supply' (Johnson 1775). In reading the account of his journey, made in the company of James Boswell, we must allow for a degree of hyperbole, arising from the author's undoubted prejudice against the Scots. We ought also to take account of the fact that his northward journey from Edinburgh took him through Fife to St Andrews, and from there along the east coast via Dundee, Montrose, Aberdeen, Banff, Elgin and Forres to Inverness – a route which, even today, might give one a rather distorted impression of the character of the country as a whole. We cannot be certain what prompted his choice of route – the prospect of a few good dinners and some lively company along the way, perhaps. What is certain, however, is that, had he followed a more direct route to Inverness via Perth, Dunkeld and the military road over the Pass of Drumochter to Speyside, Johnson's impression of the country may well have been very different.

Highland Perthshire, in particular, had long been noted for surviving fragments of the ancient forest cover which it contained. William Camden, writing in the latter part of the sixteenth century, had singled out the district of Atholl, not only for its 'abundance of witches and wicked women', but also for

> That Wood Caledonia, dreadfull to see and for the sundrie turnings and windings in and out therein, for the hideous horrours of dark shades, for the burrowes and dennes of wild bulls with thick manes (Camden 1637).

It is clear even from a cursory glance at General Roy's military survey of about 1750 that substantial fragments of natural or semi-natural woodland survived in Highland Perthshire well into the eighteenth century, even in some of the more densely populated areas.

This chapter focuses on one such locality around Dunkeld at the southern edge of the Highlands, and puts forward evidence to suggest that some of the semi-natural broadleaved woods in the area were managed on a broadly sustainable basis, until at least the middle of the nineteenth century. After this time economic pressures and changing fashion saw many of them evolve into commercial, mostly coniferous, forestry plantations.

With so much attention given to new planting, comparatively little has been written about the management of native woodland by traditional techniques such as coppicing and pollarding. Surviving records do not clearly reveal to what extent such techniques were used in pre-Reformation Scotland to manage the woods belonging, for example, to the numerous religious houses – though woods and forests were evidently seen as a vital part of the overall monastic economy and were generally protected from grazing by hedges or dykes. In one of several cases described by Anderson (1967), the donor of a wood to the Abbey of Coupar Angus in 1292 reserved the right to 'take wands for making ploughs, wagons, harrows and hedges'. Lindsay (1975a) cites what he considers to be good evidence for the coppicing of lowland woods owned by the same abbey around 1550.

There can be no doubt that, like the monks of earlier times, the nobility and other major landed proprietors had a major part to play in determining the character of the land under their control from the late seventeenth century onwards. Some of these men were noted for the 'enlightened' management of their estates and for the energy which they put into the planting of trees from the late seventeenth century onwards. Great impetus was given to improvements in agriculture and forestry with the formation in 1723 of the Honourable Society of Improvers in the Knowledge of Agriculture in Scotland. Among its founder members were a number Perthshire proprietors – the Dukes of Atholl and Perth, and the Earls of Breadalbane, Kinnoull and Strathmore, together with many of the lesser gentry.

In 1813 the Rev. James Robertson reported that there were many landowners in Perthshire who had 'saved what remained of their woods, and made new plantations in places convenient for that purpose'. Comments made by Robertson may help to explain, at least in part, why remnants of the natural oakwoods survived for longer and in greater quantity in this part of Scotland than they did further south. This was that

> Scotch oak has been found in general to be too close in the grain to bend into planks for the sides of ships, and even for the same reason it is found to snap over when used as ribs to a ship; its closeness in the grain is the effect of slower growth, owing to frequent checks by early and late frosts.

Another reason must have been the distance of many of these woods from the potential markets, and the problems of carriage on what was still a very rudimentary road system.

In the early eighteenth century the ownership of the woods in the vicinity of Dunkeld was divided between the Murrays of Atholl and Stewarts of Murthly. Roy's map of about 1750 shows the relict natural woodland to have been concentrated in three main areas – to the east of Dunkeld on Newtyle Hill, to the west of Dunkeld on the eastern and southern slopes of Craigvinean, and on the lower slopes of Birnam Hill to the south of the River Braan. These areas of woodland are also seen on a manuscript map by James Stobie, dating from 1780 (Figure 1). We can get a good impression of the character of this area at the time from an oil painting made in 1765 by Charles Steuart for John Murray, Third Duke of Atholl, in which a large area to the west of Inver and on the south side of the River Braan is seen to be heavily wooded (Figure 2). Thomas Gray, visiting the Highlands later that same year, was struck by the abundance of trees all around Dunkeld, remarking that 'the River Tay… seem'd to issue out of woods thick and tall, that rose on either hand, and were overhung by broken rock crags of vast height' (Beresford, ed. 1925).

That the Murrays of Atholl had long been concerned with the management of the woodland in their ownership is clear from papers dating from as early as 1708, cited by Lindsay (1975b). A slightly later memorandum sent to John, First Duke of Atholl, in 1723 was concerned with damage done to oak coppice in the Wood of Logierait, a few miles to the north of Dunkeld. This arose from an incident in which broom had been 'coutte down from nuirshing the young oak cop; for it is a gratt lose to the wood to coutte dounne the broom'. An inspection was organised to 'look howe the young growth is craped or eatten' (AP: 46(3)222).

Three years later Alexander Murray, factor to James, Second Duke of Atholl, asked Thomas Bissett and Charles Murray of Dunkeld to 'inspect his Grace's woods and report their opinion of them.' Their opinion of the woods was less than favourable:

> The said woods being cutt about 8 or 9 years agoe, there were by farr too many reserves left in them, and tho' the wood would be the better that many of the reserves were cutt, yet for fear of spoiling the under growth 'tis thought not advisable to cut the reserves except in some particular places.

They concluded that the wood which could be cut would 'not amount to any considerable value' (AP: Cartulary, II, 1726–1729).

A series of documents in the Atholl archives relating to the Wood of Inver throws a fascinating light on the way in which the 'sale' of a coppice wood was arranged at the time. The series began on 15 November 1757 with a memorandum which observed that Wood of Inver had last 'begun to be cutt in the year 1735', that cutting had continued for thirteen years, and that its sale at that time had realised the sum of eighteen hundred pounds and twenty guineas. The 'two James Johnstons' from Dunkeld were asked to 'view the wood first good weather, and to give their oppinion how it should be divided… and to take

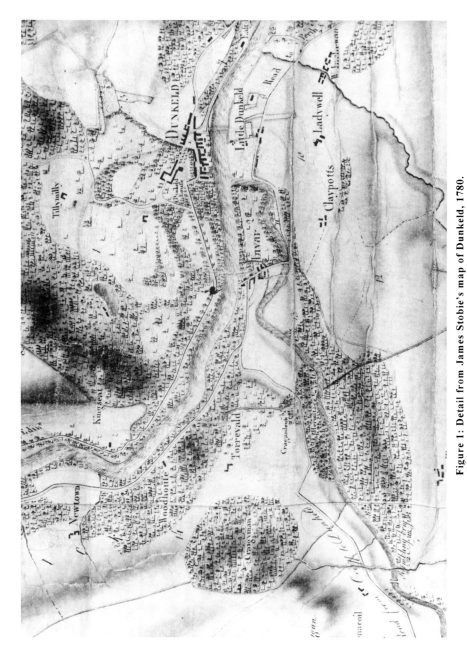

Figure 1: Detail from James Stobie's map of Dunkeld, 1780.

The main areas of oak and birch coppice were to be found to the north of Torrevald and on the south side of the River Braan.

Figure 2: Detail from Charles Steuart's painting of Dunkeld from the east, 1765.
The coppice wood on the south side of the River Braan is seen on the left of the picture. To the right are Creagan Loisgte and Torvald, with Craigvinean beyond.

the number of all the old trees that is to be reserved'. The Johnstons duly delivered their report on 20 November, estimating the value of the wood to be cut at a little over £2555. A public roup was arranged for 6 December 1757, with a reserve price of £1800. Commissary Thomas Bissett was employed 'to write to different people to acquaint them of the above resolution' (AP: 70.II.C.28).

An offer for the wood from 'Loaning and Company' of just over £2222 was recorded on 25 November 1757, but does not appear to have been acted upon. The public roup took place in Dunkeld on 6 December 1757, as planned, with the successive tenders from the four bidders all recorded (AP: 70.II.C.29). A Contract of Sale for the sum of £2375 was subsequently agreed with the successful bidders, Charles Mercer and Alexander Liston, on 26 December 1757 (AP: 70.II.C.30). A description of those trees which were to be excluded from the contract gives one a good impression of the variety of trees making up the wood at that time. These included:

> The old Oak trees which were left as reserves preceeding the beginning of last cutting... the whole Birch trees growing be-east Torryvald both up hill and down from the Water of Tay to the top of the hill... all the Elm trees growing near to the said wood called the Toar, together with the whole Roan trees (and) the whole Firrs and other planted timber growing within the said bounds.

Fifteen years was the time allowed for the cutting of the wood. The main crop was evidently oak in this case, though the purchasers were also granted the right to remove 'ash and other barren timbers'. They were allowed to build 'houses and hutts within the said wood for their convenience' and to 'make pitts for burning of charcoall'. Details were given of the preferred method of cutting, and of the reserves which were to be left. Any wood not carried off by the purchasers within the agreed time period would revert to the Duke.

Though oak was seen as the main crop from woods in the area, there was evidently a good deal of birch to be found in Strathtay alongside the northern approaches to Dunkeld. As evidence for this we have Sir William Burrell's description of this in 1758 as 'the pleasantest ride in this part of Scotland, being chiefly through woods of birch on the side of a mountain' (NLS: MS.2911).

Birch must also have made up a significant part of the woods to the south of the River Braan, close to where John Murray, later the Third Duke of Atholl, had established his Hermitage in 1757. A letter written by one of the Duke's agents from Edinburgh in 1768 refers to negotiations with the neighbouring Murthly Estate for a lease of 'that little piece of birch-wood opposite the Hermitage – fifty-seven years will do for the living, and those unborn may renew the struggle for themselves' (AP: 49.7.60). There can be no doubt that this was the same piece of ground which had prompted an exchange of letters a few years earlier between Sir John Stewart of Murthly and John Murray, after the latter had been obliged to purchase some trees in order to protect the setting of his beloved Hermitage. As well as revealing Stewart's acute embarrassment, the correspondence makes it clear that this wood was then being cropped on a regular basis. Sir John Stewart wrote in July of 1763:

> Sir – I have the honour of yours of the 6th inst. this moment. The contents surprizes me and gives me great concern, finding that you have been obliged to purchase the few trees of the wood of Tarfowack from the people had purchased the wood at last cutting. For I declare upon my honour I gave particular and strict orders... that the trees opposite the Hermitage should be excepted from the sale... I am sorry that by the entail, it is not in my power to give or sell you the property of that tryfling bank which contributes to the beauty of your charming Hermitage. (AP: 49.2.147)

Another small oil painting executed by Charles Steuart in 1765 is almost exactly contemporary with this letter. This shows the view of the Black Lynn Falls on the River Braan, as seen from the Hermitage before the surrounding plantations were established (Figure 3) – a view which includes the 'tryfling bank' which had been the subject of the earlier exchange of letters. There is an interesting comparison to be made between different parts of the woodland seen on the left side of this picture. In the middle-ground is a dense plantation of trees which appears to be of about 20 or 30 years growth, some of them apparently multi-stemmed – presumably the 'few trees' which John Murray had been obliged to purchase. Beyond this is a more open area with a thin scattering of rather skeletal trees arising from ground which is spotted here and there with dense tufts of foliage. This must surely be the coppice-wood cut a few years earlier, with a few standards left to provide seed, and with young growth bursting out from the cut stools.

With the documentary evidence to support it, there can be no doubt that Steuart's painting, perhaps unintentionally, depicts in some detail a mid-eighteenth century coppice-wood under active management. A much larger and slightly modified version of this view was made by Charles Steuart in 1766, as the first in a series of canvases which form part of the grand decorative scheme in the main dining room at Blair Castle.

An interesting detail of the smaller painting is the presence of several goats in the foreground – replaced in the larger and later picture by the figures of a highlander standing and a seated lady spinning. There is good documentary evidence for the goats, too. Dunkeld was well-known as a summer holiday resort, even in the mid-eighteenth century. Many of those who came did so in order to enjoy the combined benefits of fresh air and of goats' whey. These holiday-makers were the cause of some vexation to James Johnston, overseer of John Murray's new garden at the Hermitage. He complained to John Murray in 1862:

> There being such a croud of goat-whey people in Dunkeld, they imagined I had nothing to doe but goe at their desire to show them it. I found there was no keeping their hands off after they once entered. (AP: 49.1.146)

Figure 3: Detail from Charles Steuart's painting of the Black Lynn Falls on the River Braan, 1765.
The land to the left of the falls was the 'try fling bank' which became the subject of correspondence between John Murray and Sir John Stewart of Murthly. Three goats are to be seen in the foreground.

The garden at the Hermitage was securely fenced to prevent the goats adding to this human depredation. A letter from John Murray's brother James describes one occasion in 1863 when the defences failed.

> About two weeks ago a michevious goat broke in a little below the grotto and peeled about a dozen of the Spallie trees, but luckily the animal only did it on the side next the walks, and upon nearer examination found it only to be the outer rind... the place was mended where the goat came in at so hope no more such accidents will happen, but I could wish the walls about it were made securer, especially the thatched house, as it is very accessible to goats to climb over from the outside. (AP: 49.2.20)

Though controlled grazing seems to have been used as a tool in the management of some coppice woods, unrestricted access for livestock, especially for goats, would surely have resulted in damage being done to the young trees.

We are fortunate that the Rev. John Robertson, minister of Little Dunkeld, and contributor to the *Statistical Account* (1792), had an interest in woodland management. He gives us a detailed description of the woodland in his parish, which included both Inver Wood and the piece of ground on the Murthly Estate seen in Steuart's painting.

> The natural woods, which make no trifling part of the wealth of the parish, consist mostly of oak; and grow in smaller and larger clumps along the banks of the Tay, all except one wood in the east end of Strathbraan. The grounds that produce them are, for the most part, of very poor quality, so steep as to be inaccessible to the plough, and incapable of cultivation. These woods are treated in the way of coppice, being commonly sold to woodcutters, and felled when from 20 to 25 years old. Where the oak grows thick and unmixed with other wood, it sells at the rate of from £25 to £40, and has lately sold so high as £54 per acre. Where it grows thin, or interspersed with birch, the acre is not of near so much value. But a crop, 24 years old, of all the oak coppice in the parish would fetch at least £10,000 sterling. It occupies about 800 acres of ground. The proprietors are improving their oak woods by inclosing them with stone walls, and filling up the vacant spaces with planted oak. The extirpation of the birch and other baser woods, would also be a great improvement. The birch woods of which there are near 200 acres, and treated also as coppice, are not worth, at 22 years old, above £2 per acre. (OSA.XII: 402)

The *Statistical Accounts* for other parishes close to the Highland margin help to fill out this picture. In Aberfoyle (1793), for example, the woodland was divided into 24 separate lots, one lot being cut each year on a 24 year cycle. Regulations then in force required the purchasers of the wood to leave 400 trees of 24 years growth, eight trees of 48 years growth and eight trees of 72 years growth. A 24 or 25 year cycle was also practised in Callander (1791), where the value of each cutting was calculated to be about £15,000. In Moulin (1791), not far to the north of Dunkeld, the oak-woods yielded about £4500 at each cutting, the birch only about £500. The sale of oak bark for tanning was said to be second only to linen in its contribution to the local economy. From the neighbouring Dowally (1797), where the Duke of Atholl had imposed a 25 year cycle on the cutting of his woods, and the neighbouring proprietors a twenty year cycle, oak bark was being supplied to the tan-yards of Dunkeld, Perth, Forfar and Dundee. (OSA.XII: 13,163,754,382–3)

There is another detailed account of Clunie (1791), to the east, where twenty or 24 year cycles were the norm. Here the Rev. William MacRitchie described the changes which were occurring in the local economy at the time, with much of the work now being done by 'wood cutting companies who purchase it, with certain reservations, from the proprietors, and send the bark to a great distance, to Dundee, Forfar, Brechin etc.' He goes on to note that:

> The wood-cutters do not draw such profits from this business now, as they did formerly, owing partly to the proprietors of the oak becoming of late more sensible of its value, partly to different companies setting up in opposition to one another, and partly due to some members of the same company not paying due attention to their particular departments.

That coppice management was seen as a long-established practice in the area is implied in a footnote which states that 'This country does not produce one half of the natural wood now that it appears to have produced some hundred years ago'. The same footnote suggests that the extension of arable cultivation, combined with uncontrolled grazing by cattle and a failure to thin the young stocks properly, were all contributing to a gradual fall in the value of the surviving woods in the parish. MacRitchie also makes the interesting observation that coppicing itself exhausts the ground and may ultimately prove unsustainable without a fallow period.

> The ground that produces trees, like the ground that successively produces any other exhaustive crop, must, in a certain number of years, become wasted and fatigued, and consequently must require a certain period of repose. (OSA.XII: 231–2)

A detailed account of the management of coppice woods in Perthshire is to be found in the *General View of the Agriculture in the County of Perth* by the Rev. James Robertson, first published by the Board of Agriculture and Internal Improvement in 1799, and revised in 1813. Robertson's comments reveal that some older practices continued, while others were changing. Where there was no broom to provide shelter for the young oaks, he recommended that larch and birch be used together as a nurse crop, to be cut out as the oaks gained in strength. Thorough weeding was considered essential, to prevent the oak-woods becoming 'infested with hazel, birch and other trumpery'. He opined that 'ornament and utility ought to be the chief objects in planting'.

By this time John Murray, Fourth Duke of Atholl – nick-named 'Planter John' by his friends – was well into his stride. His thoughts are set down in a forestry notebook, compiled in about 1815, entitled 'Woods and Forests as they were, As they are, As in all probability they will be' (AP: 70.vol.14). Inheriting his father's passion for trees, he favoured a more commercial style of planting than the Third Duke. At one point he sought to sum up his planting philosophy with the simple statement that planting should be done 'for beauty, effect and profit' – a view close to that of the Rev. James Robertson.

Despite these changes, and some of the other pressures described by Lindsay (1975b), reference to a plan of the Atholl plantations of Little Dunkeld, Claypotts and Ladywell drawn by T Steuart and dating from 1820 (Figure 4) makes it clear that substantial areas of old oak and birch coppice were still in production at this time (AP: Plans.VII,7). The same was almost certainly true of adjacent woods on the neighbouring Murthly Estate. Of the 800 acres embraced by the 1820 survey of the Atholl woods, 104 acres were listed as being under 'oak' – whether older coppice or new plantation we cannot be sure. This compares with 350 acres under 'mixed' plantation, 25 acres under 'Scotch fir', 21 acres under 'birch', and fifteen acres under 'spruce'. The remaining area was divided between just over 116 acres of 'larch' – the Fourth Duke's private obsession – and about 168 acres of arable and pasture land.

Though none of the oak in these blocks was recorded as being more than 50 years old, the fact that its distribution is virtually the same as that of the woodland seen on Roy's map of about 1750 strongly suggests continuing management of the old coppice wood. The main areas of oak-wood are shown as having been on the east side of Craigvinean (62 acres), on Torryvald to the south-east of Craigvinean (eleven acres), and within the grounds of the Hermitage (three-fifths of an acre). A broad strip of woodland running along the south side of the River Braan was divided between a birch-wood in the name of Dr Niven (just over 21 acres) and an oak-wood listed as belonging to the Inver Inn (some ten acres).

If proof were needed of the continuing viability of these coppice-woods into the middle of the nineteenth century, then this may be found in the *New Statistical Account* for Little Dunkeld. This states that:

> In the districts of Murthly and the Bishoprick [the area to the north of the River Braan] there is a considerable extent of woods. The planted trees are, oak, ash, Scotch fir, larch and plane. The indigenous are birch and hazel. The oak and fir are of most extent, and also the most profitable. The former is divided into coppices, which are successively cut down once in twenty years, and affords a good return for land in other respects of little value. It fetches a good price for the sake of the bark; and, in the summer season, gives employment to a good many people. (NSA: X,1005-6)

Both the First Edition Ordnance Survey of 1863, and the Second Edition Ordnance Survey of 1900 show the Atholl woods south of the River Braan to have been entirely broadleaved, while the Murthly woods are shown as mixed plantation. Hunter (1883), writing between these two dates, talks of 'passing through the Hermitage coppice' during a visit to the Atholl plantations.

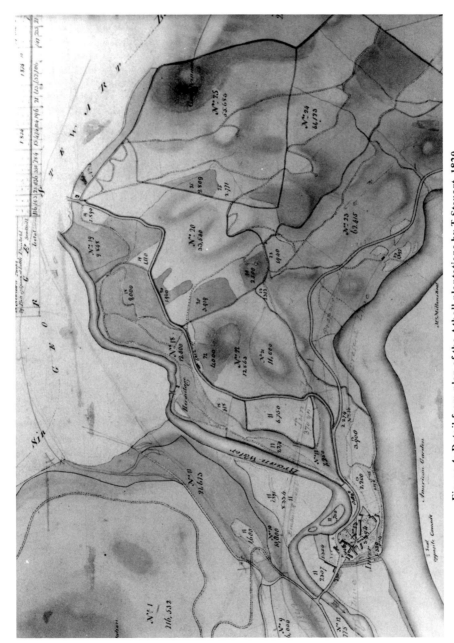

Figure 4: Detail from plan of the Atholl plantations by T Steuart, 1820.

Lots No. 10, 15, 18, 21 and 23 are listed as being of oak, and part of Lot No. 11 as being of birch.

There are occasional mentions of these same oak-woods in the annual 'Atholl Woods – Forestry Reports' which stretch in an unbroken sequence from 1867 to 1923. These include, for example, occasional references to 'pruning and thinning in the oak coppice south side of the Braan' in 1868, to 'thinning oak in the Hermitage coppice south side of the Braan' in 1886 and to 'cutting blown and broken oak in the Hermitage' in 1910 (AP: Bundles 149,167,191). Further and more detailed analysis of the Atholl papers might reveal whether oak was being sold during this period and, if so, whether it yielded a return to the estate. Lindsay (1975a) has cited a number of authors to support his view that the practice of oak coppicing had died out by the end of the nineteenth century as the market for its products declined and management was scaled down. Nothing has so far been found in the Atholl records to challenge this view, though much of the documentary evidence still remains to be explored.

The most recent chapter in the story of the woods in this part of Highland Perthshire begins with the death of John Stewart-Murray, the Seventh Duke of Atholl, in 1917. Crippled by massive death duties, the Atholl Estates were plunged into a financial crisis which was to last for several decades. One consequence of this was the felling of much of the woodland around Dunkeld and the subsequent sale of the land to the Forestry Commission in 1937 (Edlin 1969). Only the core of the Hermitage plantation around the Black Linn Falls was retained by the estate. This was given to the National Trust for Scotland in 1944, following the death John Stewart-Murray, Eighth Duke of Atholl, who had served as the Trust's founding president.

Commercial and other considerations mean that most of the woodland in this area is now coniferous. Even so, a few old oak trees can still be found here and there to bear witness to the several centuries during which the woods thereabouts were managed as oak coppice. There is also some physical evidence that birch was being coppiced on the south side of the River Braan until more recently.

It may never be possible to say whether these woodlands were truly self-sustaining, or whether their continuity was ensured only by interplanting with new stock from time to time. What we can be certain of, thanks to a unique combination of pictorial, documentary and cartographic evidence, is that the native oak and birch woods around Dunkeld, while managed as coppice, can be shown to have persisted on the same site, and to have remained continuously productive for well over two hundred years.

References

AP = Atholl Papers, Blair Castle. Some of these are reproduced in Murray, J, *Chronicles of the Atholl and Tullibardine Families* (Edinburgh, 1908)
Anderson, M L, *A History of Scottish Forestry* (London, 1967)
Beresford, J, *Letters of Thomas Gray* (Oxford, 1925)
Camden, W, *Britannia, or a Chorographical Description of Great Britain and Ireland*, 2nd

edn, trans. Holland, P (London, 1637)

Edlin, H L, *Forests of Central and Southern Scotland*, Forestry Commission Booklet No. 25 (HMSO, Edinburgh, 1969)

Hunter, T, *Woods, Forests and Estates of Perthshire* (Perth, 1883)

Johnson, S, *A Journey to the Western Isles of Scotland* (London, 1775)

Lindsay, J M, 'The History of Oak Coppice in Scotland', *Scottish Forestry*, vol. 29 (1975a), pp. 87–93

Lindsay, J M, 'Some Aspects of the Timber Supply in the Highlands 1700–1850', *Scottish Studies*, vol. 19 (1975b), pp. 39–53

NLS – National Library of Scotland MS

NSA – *New Statistical Account*, Vol. X, *Perth* (Edinburgh, 1845)

OSA – Sinclair, J (ed.), *Statistical Account of Scotland*, Vol. XII, *North and West Perthshire*, gen. eds. Withrington D J and Grant, I R (Wakefield, 1977)

Robertson, J, *General View of the Agriculture in the County of Perth* (Perth, 1813)

Acknowledgements

The illustrations used in this chapter are reproduced by kind permission of the late Duke of Atholl. The author also wishes to thank Jane Anderson, archivist at Blair Castle, for her advice and assistance.

14. The Woods of Strathspey in the Nineteenth and Twentieth Centuries

B M S Dunlop

1800 – Napoleonic Wars

At the turn of the century, the exploitation of the Strathspey forests was at its peak. The international upheaval severely restricted timber imports, and as many of the early plantings had not yet matured, the natural forests had to supply the needs of the nation. At Glenmore, the 1784 contract, considered the first profitable exploitative felling in Strathspey, was completed in 1805. To aid extraction by floating, sluices had been constructed at the mouth of Loch Morlich to provide a sufficient flow of water whenever required for transporting the trees (minimum girth 18 inches) to the sawmills at Inverdruie.

This principle was extended to other parts of the forests by the creation of dams where conditions were suitable. Bulwarks were built across watercourses at the narrowest point between terraces, wooden sluices placed in the bed of the stream, and the land upstream allowed to flood.

The period of this innovation is known from a letter (SRO: Seafield Muniments) dated June 1800 to Sir James Grant of Grant, from his Factor, describing the construction of a bulwark in Abernethy which he was confident would 'raise a flood on the Nethy as occasion requires'. The letter also indicates that dams were being constructed at 'Rothymurchus and Glenmore'. Some nineteenth century maps show the location of dams, of which the remains of many are still visible. Cuts were sometimes dug to transfer water to sections where the terrain was unsuitable for dam construction, or to utilise the same dam for two different watercourses.

When timber – which had been hauled by horses or sometimes cattle to the side of the watercourse below the dam – was ready to be extracted, the sluice was opened to create an artificial spate. The timber was rolled into the water, and floated down to the nearest sawmill for conversion, or to the Spey for binding, with sawn timber, into large rafts destined for the sawmills and shipyards of Garmouth and Kingston.

In her diaries (Strachey (ed.) 1911) Elizabeth Grant of Rothiemurchus gives

176

a detailed account of timber operations between 1797 and 1830. The scale of operations is illustrated by a list of woods (SRO: Seafield Muniments) prepared for a proposed sale by Strathspey Estate in 1805; it was endorsed 'that part of the Natural Fir Woods of Abernethy and Dulnainside... being nearly one third of the former and one half of the latter'. At this time these forests extended to about 13,500 and 6000 acres (5400 and 2400 ha) gross respectively, but there is some doubt as to whether these sales were effected. One of the last of the exploitative sales was at Inshriach and Glenfeshie in 1819, when Sir Aeneas Mackintosh of Mackintosh sold 10,000 trees, which were floated down the Feshie (Skelton 1994).

1843 – Regeneration

Elizabeth Grant recorded widespread regeneration in Glenmore by 1830, and Grigor (1843) observed large numbers of young pine along the edges of the forests. He noted 'seldom can a young plant be seen coming up near the remains of the old trees, but extensive masses of them are rising along the borders of the forests' on *Calluna*. At Glenmore 'in the interior of the forest, a young plant is rarely met with' but 'along the outside of this forest, particularly at the west end, and on the east of Rothiemurchus forest, the young wood, to the extent of several square miles, is fast advancing. The largest of these are about 30 years old'. He also records 'many large and thriving pines' on Craigowrie, between Glenmore and the Spey.

Grigor thus confirms the 'moving forest' principle, and the lack of regeneration within the old stands as at present. He refutes the suggestion that the forests were normally composed of scattered coarse trees, by recording that in Rothiemurchus 'a stranger to these Highland forests cannot but be surprised at the closeness of the trunks to each other' and 'the pines here are not so remarkable for their girth as for their extraordinarily tall and smooth trunks'. These were evidently descriptions of the unexploited stands, much of the natural forest having been devastated, as he himself confirms in his 1868 treatise.

1850 – Changes in Timber Manufacturing

While timber sales continued, there is evidence of the beginning of a decline. In his annual report for 1850 W G Bryson, Factor of Strathspey, stated that generally timber was sold to locals, with 'no enquiries from extensive wood merchants except Mr McKenzie, Elgin'. He records that 'not much has been done in the Natural Forests... the good timber near the dams and floating places having been already cut down, there is not much available timber with easy access.' However he also records 'young plants springing up vigorously in many places throughout the forests', but in need of protection from tenants' sheep and cattle. Bryson mentions that a Mr McIntosh, Wood Merchant, Nairn, has a mobile Steam Saw Mill, which he could bring to Strathspey to manufacture barrel staves etc. from the smaller coarser trees (Strathspey Estate Records).

Previously much timber had been cut, extracted and converted by the Strathspey Estate labour force, and sold as spars and deals. From 1851 almost all the timber was sold standing to merchants, who were then responsible for the harvesting operations, and often they leased Estate sawmills. They also set-up temporary mills in the section of forest being cut, and in 1852 Bryson's annual report stated that at Granish plantation 'Mr Caldwell (of Findhorn) has erected a steam saw-mill which executes the work very rapidly, the trees are principally sawn into small pieces for barrel staves etc.'(Strathspey Estate Records).

At this time there were 15,907 acres (6362 ha) of woodland on the Strathspey Estate, which stretched from Advie to Aviemore. Of this 9850 acres (3940 ha) were natural pinewood, 5087 acres (2034 ha) mainly pine plantation, and 970 acres (388 ha) broadleaved woodland, mainly birch. The early plantations were now beginning to produce significant volumes of timber, reducing the need to seek supplies from the areas of difficult access in the natural forests.

Timber sales continued but in the natural pinewoods the only large trees available were those left uncut at the time of the exploitation fellings. In 1856 in Tulloch 'over-mature thinly scattered' trees were felled, and in the upper Dulnan very old trees. In 1857 in Abernethy the largest trees in the lower forest and 8000 trees in the upper forest were offered for sale, but difficult access reduced the attractiveness of this parcel to merchants. All species were utilised – birch produced wood for barrel staves, turning and carpentry, alder for clogs, and oak for shipbuilding (Strathspey Estate Records).

Pine continued to account for about 90 percent of sales, mainly for construction timber, and a new market developed during the 1850s with the rapid expansion of the railway network. By the early 1860s the railways had arrived in Strathspey, and timber was required for sleepers and buildings. Wooden bridges were constructed over the Spey, for example at Broomhill, so that Abernethy timber could gain access to the new transportation network. A considerable quantity of stone was required for bridges, underpasses and platforms, and much of the bulk material was obtained locally by the removal of surface boulders and rock outcrops in nearby woodland, and rock faces.

In 1863 the Highland Railway was opened, linking Perth and Inverness via Aviemore, Grantown and Forres. Existing roads were improved and new ones constructed, so that timber could be carried overland by road and rail, more reliable but more expensive than floating. The Great North of Scotland Railway from Boat of Garten to Craigellachie was also opened at this time.

1866 – Fall in Timber Values

In 1866 the Government removed the duty on imported timber, and supplies from the Baltic and America recommenced. The results were not immediate, but eventually the price of home-grown timber fell, and the extraction of timber in the less accessible sections of the natural forests became uneconomical.

Grigor (1868) describes Strathspey as having 'magnificent specimens' of Scots pine and 'on the banks of the Spey at Rothiemurchus, Glenmore, Abernethy, and Duthil, and along the northern slopes of the Cairngorm mountains, native Scotch pine timber is produced'. However he states they have 'lately been greatly reduced, owing to the high price of timber, enhanced by the introduction of two railways into the district' and 'a great quantity of fine timber has disappeared'. At Glenmore there were 'still a great many fine trees... They stood at great distances, commonly from 50 to 100 yards apart, and evidently had not been considered of consequence when the intermediate ones had been felled. In other parts they were in patches... on hillsides'. This gives a clear indication that the forest had been felled but trees had been left, almost certainly as seed trees for forest regeneration.

Timber reserves in the once extensive natural forests were becoming depleted, according to the type of tree which was now being marketed. In 1870 a sale was described as 'trees, not large, scattered over a large piece of ground, part of them a good distance from the floating streams' and in upper Abernethy in 1873 'small stunted trees' from 'partly wet ground' were sold mainly because of a good pitwood market (Strathspey Estate Records).

1869 – Creation of Deer Forests

As timber prices fell, sporting values rose, and ever greater numbers of upper and middle class Victorians came north by train to shoot, fish and stalk in the Highlands; the tourist industry developed. Farm tenants and crofters were moved out of forests such as Kinveachy and the upper forest of Abernethy in 1869, the area being then fenced against domestic stock, and designated deer forest. This was not for conservation, to save young trees from browsing, but to reserve the vegetation for deer, which were not excluded by the stock fence. Deer proof fences were generally erected only on the lower margins of the natural forests, to prevent damage to adjacent farm/croft crops, and to reduce deer losses from poaching. In some areas enclosures were built to control farm animals – at Rothiemurchus domestic stock had been removed from regenerating areas by 1848, with a sophisticated system of dykes (Smout 1994).

Some of the felled areas had failed to regenerate, others, and especially the margins, developed dense even-aged pine. Due to ground disturbance, the absence of domestic stock, and low deer numbers initially (a legacy of poaching by the previous occupants) the forests rapidly regenerated on a large scale. Most of the even-aged stands of mature timber of which the forests are now composed date from this time.

Sporting income was now so important to estate owners that new priorities were set, and timber operations were prohibited in the summer in the Abernethy upper forest to avoid conflict with the shooting tenants. However this new type of land use resulted in road improvements. Angling interests downstream complained that floating 'injured' their fishing, despite being given notice of releases one or two days in advance, and floating had for some time been prohibited in the summer from 15 May to 26 August by Act of Parliament. Now Lord Seafield instructed that no dams were to be released on the Nethy while he stayed at Castle Grant, and timber sale agreements contained a clause 'when Lord Seafield or other gentlemen may be fishing the dams are to be run once a week' (Strathspey Estate Records).

By the turn of the century, floating was discontinued. There were some special floats in the Druie in 1903, but the last true Spey float seems to have been a few years earlier. The main reasons for cessation appear to have been the legal actions of angling interests, and the development of better roads and methods of transport, notably traction engines and railways (Dunlop 1994).

1870 – Planting

The second half of the eighteenth century was notable for the amount of planting which was carried out on almost every estate. This was achieved through the restocking of the most accessible felled woods and the establishment of new blocks, mainly with Scots pine. Natural regeneration continued to be encouraged, outwith the deer forests, but where it failed or was incomplete parts of previously natural forest, for example lower Abernethy, were planted or infilled.

While Scots pine plants were raised in the district, from seed gathered locally, some were purchased from other nurseries mainly in the North East. However estates such as Strathspey supplied local provenance seed to such nurseries, or allowed them to collect cones from the natural forests, and often bought seedlings from them to grow on into transplants in estate nurseries. As many as 2,000,000 plants per annum were being despatched to the hill, sufficient for the planting of about 1000 acres (400 ha) depending on spacing. The rate of planting decreased from about 1880, probably due to financial constraints, but on the Strathspey Estate it was recorded in 1878 that 'the ground laid aside for planting in Strathspey is nearly all filled up'.

Francis William, the son of Sir James Grant of Grant who had initiated the first commercial plantings in 1763, became the 6th Earl of Seafield in 1840, on the death of his brother Sir Lewis Alexander, who had inherited the Ogilvie titles and lands at Cullen in 1811 (Fraser 1883). He continued the massive afforestation programme of his father, and was credited with planting over 31,000,000 trees on the Grant/Seafield estates, for which he was awarded the Gold Medal of the Highland and Agricultural Society. On his death in 1853 his son John Charles inherited the estates and titles, and continued the work of his forefathers. By the time he died in 1881 some 30,000 acres (12,000 ha) were reputed to have been planted over the previous 65 years in Strathspey, probably including the Rothes area.

Sir John Ramsden was also a very keen forester, and around 1870 established many woods of North American conifers at Ardverikie, Loch Laggan. He also planted about 1000 acres (400 ha) of Deeside origin Scots pine there and on other local estates which he owned at the time (Dunlop 1994).

1914 – First World War

Between the beginning of the century and the outbreak of war, felling and planting levels were low. The emergency prevented further timber importation and once again British woodlands had to meet the needs of the nation. The result was the large-scale clearance of mature and sometimes immature woods. On the Strathspey estate alone, fellings associated with the war amounted to over 5000 acres (2000 ha), including over 1000 acres (400 ha) accidently burnt. The fellings included parts of the natural pinewoods in Abernethy, Kinveachy, Rothiemurchus and Glenmore, where a tramway was used in the Sluggan Pass (Steven and Carlisle 1959).

Elsewhere narrow gauge railways were constructed by the War Office Directorate of Timber Supply in 1917 and 1918, to carry timber over wet ground to the mainline railways. One ran from Aviemore Station through Rothiemurchus to Glenmore, round the south side of Loch Morlich to the Allt Mor, where men of the Canadian Forestry Service assisted with the timber harvesting operations (Cox and Krupa 1992).

From Duackbridge (by Nethybridge) another light railway was laid into part of the lower forest called Abernethy Central, and John McDonald, who later became Head Forester, recalled that German prisoners-of-war were used to assist in the operations until repatriated, when locals were recruited until the operations ceased in 1921. He revealed that the workforce distrusted the temperamental steam locomotives, and sometimes used horses to haul the bogies (Dunlop 1994). The route of the railway can be seen in some parts, and even the indentations where the sleepers lay.

A third light railway was constructed from Carrbridge across the wet ground at Tordhu, and around the south side of Inverlaidnan hill. The trees there, badly damaged by squirrels, were prematurely felled for pitwood, as were many other plantations. The route of this line was rediscovered after a fire in 1976.

1919 – Forestry Commission

The war highlighted the deficiencies of forestry in Britain regarding the poor quality and low quantity of woodland, and to prevent the same shortages and devastation in the future, a state forestry service was set up. In 1919 the Forestry Commission was formed, with the primary aim of establishing a strategic reserve of timber. The FC purchased Glenmore in 1923, and in 1924 commenced a long programme of planting with a mixture of Scots pine and non-indigenous conifers. They also purchased Inshriach, and carried out a large planting programme until the war.

In the period between the wars there was little activity in the privately owned woods, other than the replanting of felled areas. On the Strathspey estate restocking by natural regeneration was encouraged, but to the regret of Gilbert Brown, the woodland manager, the Directorate of Timber Supply had not left seed trees in many areas. Those which did not self-seed after a few years were planted, and where natural regeneration was incomplete, as in parts of the Abernethy lower forest, the areas were infilled with planted trees (Strathspey Estate Records).

Forest fires were not uncommon, and could cause serious damage. In 1920 an outbreak in the Mineral Well area on the Rothiemurchus plain south of the river Luineag spread up to the Loch an Eilean area. Much of it has now regenerated.

1939 – Second World War

Yet again conflict in Europe disrupted timber imports, and the 90 percent of needs normally supplied from abroad had to be obtained from British woods and forests. This led to even greater devastation than during the First World War to the wooded areas of Strathspey.

As so many men had joined the armed forces, there was a shortage of labour, many women joined the Land Army or the Women's Timber Corps., and volunteers from mainly Commonwealth countries came to Britain to help the war effort. A large contingent of Canadians from Newfoundland were based in Strathspey, and these 'Newfies' built some very good forest roads, many of which are still in use, as part of their timber harvesting operations.

One of the areas felled by them was the large block of pine on the lower part of Kinveachy hill, stretching continuously from Aviemore to Carrbridge. At 2308 acres (923 ha) this was believed to be the largest single felling in the UK. It is reputed that King George VI, on viewing the devastation from a passing train after the war, asked why it had not been replanted. On being informed that there were not enough estate foresters to undertake the work, he instructed that the Forestry Commission provide labour to assist. The replanting was completed by 1967, with the assistance of FC men on contract (Dunlop 1994).

The war associated fellings did not come to an end until 1949. By this time Strathspey's contribution to the war effort, and the high cost to the environment, was apparent. On the Strathspey estate alone 16,131 acres (6450 ha), just over half the then stocked area, had been felled – three times the area felled in the First World War. However some of the natural pinewoods on the lower slopes of Cairngorm, mainly Abernethy and most of Rothiemurchus, escaped almost unscathed, because they were used as training areas for commandos – notably the Norwegian Linge.

Not all of the felling was intentional – once again large areas had been destroyed by fire, and had to be cleared. The worst was in the Dulnan/Kinveachy natural forest where, in 1948, some 3000 acres (1200 ha) of land most of which contained mature trees and young regeneration, were destroyed. The fire appeared to have started in brushwood in a felling area, and burned for six days due to frequent changes in wind direction, spreading into almost every part of the forest. The forest has never recovered – the loss of young saplings and seed trees, plus the browsing of red deer, has prevented regeneration (Dunlop 1994).

Elsewhere the natural forests suffered great losses. Inshriach, Invereshie and Glen Feshie were severely depleted, and the felling margin is still obvious in Invereshie. In Glenmore there was little left to cut, but 80 hectares were felled after the war, and a fire on the south side of Loch Morlich destroyed some of the old forest (Steven and Carlisle 1959).

1954 – Cairngorms NNR

The Nature Conservancy was set up in 1949, and in 1954 declared the Cairngorms National Nature Reserve, which has since expanded. Almost all of the Reserve area is still privately owned, and management is by agreement with the various landowners. The Nature Conservancy later purchased part of the natural pine forest at Invereshie, above Inshriach, and carried out some research there. Conservation of the ecology of the ancient Caledonian pine-birch woodlands is one of the key concerns, but not all of the Cairngorms pinewoods are within the NNR boundary.

In the post war period there was little natural regeneration, probably due to browsing by red deer, but in the Rothiemurchus lower forest large areas restocked naturally. In the same forest in 1959 a disastrous fire started at the side of the Glenmore road, and spread through the mature pine, into the Forestry Commission's plantations at the Sluggan Pass. After a period of 35 years the area near the road is now showing good regeneration.

1950–80 – Planting Expansion

In the 1950s the Forestry Commission's schemes to grant aid private forestry were developed, and in particular the Dedication scheme was welcomed and entered into by many landowners. By signing a legally binding document, owners could dedicate specific areas of land to the growing of trees, managed according to an agreed Plan of Operations, and in return receive grants for planting and management. In addition, areas programmed for felling and thinning in the plan did not require a felling licence.

The scheme took little account of the distinctive nature and requirements of the natural forest, and allowed the felling and replacement of native pine with non-indigenous conifers. On the Seafield Strathspey estate the natural forest in upper Abernethy was included in the Dedication Scheme, as was the mixed natural and planted lower forest, but Kinveachy forest was not. The owner, the Countess of Seafield, and her woodland managers appreciated the value of this rare ecosystem, and the early Plans of Operation stipulated natural regeneration as the method to be used for restocking the Abernethy upper forest.

During the period the restocking of the vast wartime fellings was completed, and new blocks were established. Some of them were on ancient woodland sites, where pine and birch was cleared and in many cases exotic conifers were planted. Wetter sites were ploughed and planted with Sitka spruce and Lodgepole pine, for example in state owned forests at Glenmore, Inshriach and Strathmashie, which was mainly completed in the 1950s and 1960s.

In the private sector, the main driving force behind the steady rise in planting totals was an advantageous tax concession – under Schedule D the costs of establishing and maintaining plantations could be set off against tax due on profits from other business interests. Areas could be planted at virtually no net cost to owners, and concern was expressed at some of the damage being caused to ancient woods and by the planting of sensitive sites. In order to claim the full planting grant, areas of self-seeded local origin pine were infilled by planting, sometimes with pine of foreign or unknown origin, lowering their status and conservation value.

From the end of the 1960s there was a major change in land ownership, due mainly to inflation and death duties. The largest landowner in Strathspey, the Countess of Seafield, died unexpectedly in 1969. The Muckrach area had already been sold in 1968, but now upper Abernethy, and other sections in the early 1970s from Tulchan to Lochindorb and Carrbridge were sold.

Plantations, birchwoods and bare muir throughout Strathspey were purchased by forestry investment companies. Some of the new owners and forestry managers had little knowledge or interest in ecology or forest history, and did not appreciate the rarity and value of the old Caledonian pinewood remnants. They applied normal commercial forestry practices, to the detriment of forests such as upper Abernethy.

Woods grazing agreements, where tenants on adjacent farmland were permitted to graze their stock in commercial plantations and woods on a modest rental, were gradually discontinued. This was mainly due to the rapid rise in fencing costs, and only birchwoods within farm boundaries, generally unfenced, continued to be grazed. This prevented regeneration within or adjacent to the woods, as seedlings were browsed.

In 1976 there was a large fire at Blackmount, north of Carrbridge. A number of outbreaks on the mainline railwayside linked up and swept across the muir to

Tordhu, destroying plantations and some of the last remnants of ancient Caledonian pinewood in this locality.

By the end of the period high inflation resulted in redundancies on even the largest estates, forestry operations were carried out by heavily mechanised non-local contractors instead of local employees, and management was from a distance. The overall effect was a steady reduction in the area of ancient woodland and forest.

1981 – Wildlife and Countryside Act

The decade began with the Wildlife and Countryside Act of 1981 which was eventually to give much greater recognition and protection to the ancient woodlands which had managed to survive. Over the next few years designations such as Site of Special Scientific Interest (SSSI) and National Scenic Area were applied to more and more of the district's assets. However the same year part of the Abernethy lower forest was ploughed for the first time, and planted with lodgepole pine, by a distant management company 'as an investment in a renewable resource'! Nearby a large area of mature pine was clear felled in 1984.

By this time the RSPB had purchased parts of Abernethy forest, and were taking steps to restore the area. In designated areas Nature Conservancy Council grant aid financed the fencing of native woodland, particularly birch, to encourage natural regeneration.

Knowledge of the natural pinewoods was increased by a series of surveys which mapped the stocked ground, classifying and quantifying the area of forest according to age class and stocking density (Dunlop 1985–94).

1987 – Ancient Woodland Inventory

When Strathspey (including Badenoch) was assessed for the national *Inventory of Ancient, Long-established and Semi-Natural Woodland* (NCC 1987), a total of 22,251 hectares of woodland was listed in the various categories. Only 11,362 ha (51 percent) could still be classed as semi-natural. The balance of 49 percent was planted, 9291 ha (41.7 percent) with exotic conifers. Conversion to plantation has caused the greatest loss of natural woodland this century.

The 1988 budget removed the Schedule D tax concession, after an interim period. While this prevented further widespread conversion of ancient and natural woods to plantation, and the planting of valuable wildlife habitat such as the Flow Country, it had a serious retrograde effect on forestry investment, and private sector planting and employment. At a national level, and in the Highlands, annual planting totals dropped dramatically from 1988, but in Strathspey the use of native species and natural regeneration kept annual rates at a more even level.

Changes in forestry grant structures eventually led to the Woodland Grant Scheme (WGS) by the end of the decade. Conservation, landscape and recreation became important elements which had to be incorporated into afforestation schemes in order to receive grants.

1990s – Present Trends and Pressures

The WGS has proved particularly beneficial in the management, restoration and expansion of extant native woodlands, and in increasing the use of native species in new plantations. While large areas of moorland are still being purchased, ploughed and planted mainly with exotic conifers, for example in the Dalwhinnie area, they are required to meet higher design criteria, and to incorporate areas of native species.

In the private sector, schemes – sometimes large – are being implemented to plant native species (many under the confusing title of New Native Pinewoods) and naturally regenerate areas within or adjacent to natural woods. Recent changes in the WGS include the discontinuance of advance grants on natural regeneration – only existing regeneration now qualifies. This may result in a drop in planting/regeneration levels, and could inhibit moves to expand the natural Caledonian pine/birchwoods.

In Glenmore, Forest Enterprise, the state forest wing of the Forestry Commission, has been restoring parts of the old forest. Where old Caledonian pines had been underplanted (or younger regeneration had been infilled) with exotic conifers, the latter have been removed. On the Strathspey Estate, some areas of Lodgepole pine are being prematurely felled in order to achieve regeneration by more natural local origin Scots pine, and planted trees are being removed on RSPB reserves.

The community and recreational use of many woods is being increased. Those adjacent to settlements at Grantown, Dulnain Bridge, Boat of Garten, Carrbridge and Aviemore, and many in between, have been proposed for increased recreational use and as walking routes by Strathspey estate in a Woodland Recreation Initiative, in partnership with other public bodies.

In the pinewoods where culling keeps deer numbers to sustainable levels, such as Abernethy, lower Rothiemurchus and parts of Invereshie, natural regeneration is locally prolific. Pine and birch woodland is spreading onto adjacent land where sheep and deer pressure is low. A recent major survey (Dunlop 1994) has quantified the younger age classes in the natural pinewoods at 38 percent of the land under trees, and in the birchwoods at 30 percent.

Threats to natural woodland survival remain, these being associated with the prevention of regeneration. Existing regeneration, mainly on grouse moors, is destroyed during heather management by muirburn. Trees which survive the flames due to size are felled. In some forests, notably Kinveachy, upper

Rothiemurchus and Glen Feshie, high red deer numbers prevent restocking by browsing seedlings.

Conclusions

Over the last two centuries, some ancient woods have disappeared, and most of the others have been reduced in area. Many natural woods have vanished under a blanket of (often exotic) planted conifers, while others appear to have become extinct. There are many examples of the former, such as the late Coille Chluanaidh birchwood at Cluny, Laggan, which is now a mixed conifer plantation. As to other examples of loss, former woodland between Duthil and Lochindorb is no longer evident, probably lost in the early nineteenth century, and between Loch Ericht and Loch Laggan, and in the Gaick 'Forest', areas which appear to be birchwood on the 1867 OS map are not now evident. The Caledonian pine remnants north of Foregin and Baddengorm, shown on the 1867 OS map, have gone, although there is currently new regeneration springing up in places, mainly from planted pine.

Many of the pinewood areas felled in the last two centuries have been planted, quantified in Badenoch and Strathspey as 49 percent (10,903 ha) of the total area of semi-natural woodland of which 9291 ha involved exotic species. In Inshriach very few areas of ancient woodland remain after felling and planting in the 1930s and after the last war.

Some fellings have not regenerated, giving a reduction in ancient woodland area. Included in this category in upper Abernethy are Revoan and the section south of Loch a' Chnuik where stumps are still visible. There was a massive loss of forest in Kinveachy (1200 ha) as a result of the wartime fellings and associated fire in 1948, as detailed above.

The supply of timber for local use in the past has generally been sustainable, and overall has not caused significant woodland depletion. But exploitation fellings with associated fires, especially in times of national emergency, have caused considerable damage to the pinewood ecosystem. However it would appear that the long-term effect has been less than previously believed. This century the two World Wars were of short duration, and in the context of 7000 years of forest development, the exploitation of less than 100 years centred on the Napoleonic Wars was relatively short.

There certainly was devastation at the time, and large volumes of timber were removed, but it was mainly restricted to one generation of trees. The record shows that areas regenerated and the forest recovered where seed trees were retained, and most of the ancient forests have survived the fellings, albeit down to remnant status in many cases, and with a dearth of over-mature trees.

While timber extraction stimulates regeneration by disturbing ground vegetation and ensuring adequate light, this is only required to regenerate stocked areas. Pinewood dynamics are based on the moving forest principle –

stocked areas seldom regenerate naturally, the regeneration zones are open glades and forest margins, where the ground vegetation has reverted to Calluna heath with full light. For this reason it is essential to maintain wide zones on the forest margins for expansion.

The complete loss of some forests and woodland areas was mainly due to exploitation or abuse where there was no regeneration to replace them. The primary cause of failure was the browsing of seedlings by farm stock or deer, especially in combination with fire. Without recruitment, in the long-term the remaining usually scattered mature trees died from natural causes.

The value of timber ensured that pine trees in plantations were protected from the worst abuses – fire, browsing and theft. In deer forests they were partially protected from fire and felling, but not deer damage. Paradoxically birch, which has had a very low timber value for almost 50 years, has survived and is spreading unaided in many locations, sometimes despite sheep and deer presence, but high value natural oak is practically extinct. This indicates that survival is not totally dependent on timber value.

Fencing and the removal of domestic stock was sufficient to allow forest recovery where deer numbers were low. This is evident from the large areas of now mature Caledonian pinewood which regenerated because they were converted to Deer Forest. It is however clear that such action was not effected to conserve the forest ecosystem in these areas. Elsewhere the protection of susceptible young woodland from fire, animal and human damage was to safeguard trees for their high commodity value. Pine and birch is now spreading wherever seedlings are not over-grazed or burnt.

The main losses, certainly this century, have been from planting, especially after clearance. Current controls will ensure that replacement by exotic conifers is prevented, but naturally regenerated woods could still be planted with native species. This would reduce their status and probably their conservation value, and break their continuity.

With the formation of the Cairngorms Partnership and possible funding from the Millennium Forest for Scotland, the political and financial climates are favourable. If current threats are properly addressed, the turn of the century will present the best ever opportunity to assist nature in restoring ancient woodlands. This could increase their biodiversity and extent, enhancing a superb local asset, to the benefit of wildlife, amenity, recreation and employment.

References

Anderson, M L, *A History of Scottish Forestry* (2 vols., Nelson, London, 1967)

Cox, D and Krupa, C, *The Kerry Tramway and other Timber Light Railways* (Plateway Press, Brighton, 1992)

Dunlop, B M S, *Native Pinewood Surveys & Reports for Nature Conservancy Council* (Aberdeen, 1985–94)

Dunlop, B M S, *The Native Woodlands of Strathspey* (Scottish Natural Heritage Research, Survey and Monitoring Report No 33, 1994)

Fraser, W, *The Chiefs of Grant* (3 vols., Edinburgh, 1883)

Grigor, J, 'Report on the Native Pine Forests of Scotland'. Silver medal essay, *Trans. Highland and Agricultural Society* (1843)

Grigor J, *Arboriculture or A Practical Treatise on Raising and Managing Forest Trees and on the Profitable Extension of the Woods & Forests of Great Britain* (Edmonston & Douglas, Edinburgh, 1868)

NCC 1987, *Inventory of Ancient, Long-established and Semi-Natural Woodland, Badenoch & Strathspey*. Nature Conservancy Council

SRO: Seafield Muniments, Scottish Records Office GD248, Edinburgh.

Skelton, J, *Speybuilt – the story of a forgotten industry* (W Skelton, Garmouth, Moray, 1994)

Smout, T C, 'The History of the Rothiemurchus Woods in the Eighteenth Century', *Northern Scotland*, 15 (1995), 19–31

Steven, H M and Carlisle, A, *The Native Pinewoods of Scotland* (Oliver & Boyd, Edinburgh, 1959)

Stratchey, Lady (ed.), *Memoires of a Highland Lady* (Murray, London, 1911)

Strathspey Estate Records. Estate Office, Grantown-on-Spey

15. Beinn Eighe National Nature Reserve:
Woodland Management Policy and Practice 1944-1994

Tim Clifford and Andrew Forster

Introduction

This chapter briefly discusses changes in woodland management policy at Beinn Eighe National Nature Reserve (NNR) over the 50 years between 1944 and 1994, illustrates how this has influenced management action on the ground and attempts to draw some broad conclusions which may be relevant to the future management of the woodland.

During this time a distinct bipartite approach to the restoration of the Reserve's native woodland has evolved centred on:

1. The conservation and regeneration of the extant ancient semi-natural woodland.
2. The re-construction of 'natural-type' woodland on suitable de-forested ground below the current tree line.

These two elements have long been primary management objectives for the Reserve but ideas on how they might be achieved and the time-scale involved have developed through a number of distinct phases. To understand the gradual development and refinement of thinking it is necessary to outline some of the background to the interest and importance of the Reserve.

The Beinn Eighe massif was established as the first NNR in Britain in 1951 as part of the developing 'Key Site Strategy'. The philosophy behind this, enshrined in the 1949 National Parks and Access to the Countryside Act, was founded on the principle that nature conservation in Britain should be centred on the safeguarding of key areas representing the major examples of natural and semi-natural habitats with their characteristic flora and fauna. NNRs were seen as the cornerstone of this philosophy, designed to ensure that sites were managed specifically for nature conservation through direct ownership, Nature Reserve Agreement or lease.

At the time of acquisition by the then Nature Conservancy, the Reserve, comprising a substantial area of relict Caledonian Scots pine forest and the associated mountain massif of Beinn Eighe extending to 4230 hectares, was purchased for £4000. Today it extends to 4700 hectares, of which approximately 90 percent is owned by Scottish Natural Heritage. The main stand of ancient pinewood covers an area of about 180 hectares with an additional ten hectares in three small, isolated gorges and about 50 hectares of birch-dominated woodland bisecting the main pinewood stand. This pine woodland is one of a group of five relict pinewoods in Wester Ross which may have an endemic origin, are genetically distinct from other native pinewoods in the Highlands and show adaptive genetic differentiation in response to the cool oceanic conditions of north-west Scotland. These woods, of which the Beinn Eighe woodland is the largest and most diverse, are important examples of one of Scotland's most ancient and least disturbed habitats occurring at the extreme western edge of the world distribution of Scots pine. As such they may legitimately be described as 'temperate rain forest' and represent a unique segment of the world variation in Scots pine-dominated woodlands and forest.

On the northern slopes of the Reserve there is a relatively undisturbed altitudinal zonation from woodland through small fragments of sub-alpine type scrub clinging to inaccessible cliffs, to extensive dwarf shrub heaths and ultimately to montane grasslands and heaths on the summits. Conversely the southern and eastern slopes of the Reserve have been de-forested through a combination of climatic change, burning and overgrazing, with small relicts of the original woodland cover only persisting in three relatively steep-sided gorges. This large de-forested area has provided opportunities for the experimental re-creation of native woodland and sub-alpine scrub habitats.

The international importance of the Reserve was first formally recognised in 1976 when it was declared a Biosphere Reserve under UNESCO's 'Man and the Biosphere Programme' and in 1983 with the award of a European Diploma, placing it under the sponsorship of the Council of Europe who make a series of recommendations for its management. Additionally the importance of 'Caledonian Forest', which is a uniquely Scottish habitat, has recently been recognised in European Directive 92/43/EC, the 'Habitats Directive' and the Reserve is included on the list of candidate sites submitted to Brussels for consideration for designation as 'Special Areas of Conservation'. It is against this broad back-ground that the management of the woodland component of the NNR should be assessed.

Woodland management 1944–51: the early debate

The importance of the Scots pine woodland on Beinn Eighe was first recognised in 1939 when the prominent British ecologist Sir Arthur Tansley wrote:

> The best existing natural pinewood left in the north-west Highlands is undoubtedly that on the south-western shore of Loch Maree, some of which is

still regenerating well, and here one can still study the natural behaviour of
native pine.

Ten years later in 1949 the wood was listed as a 'Desired National Park
Reserve' by the Scottish National Parks Committee (Cmnd. 7814, 1949) and it
was proposed that if the National Parks option was not taken up in Scotland,
then the wood should transfer to the list of recommended National Nature
Reserves. At the time it was only the woodland that was considered to be of
national importance. In a letter dated 12 August 1952 from the Earl of Weymss,
a member of the Nature Conservancy Scottish Committee, to Dr John Berry the
then Director for Scotland of the Nature Conservancy, it was stated that the
additional area of the Reserve has been 'only in fact acquired because it was
thrown in cheap'. Nevertheless the value of the additional habitats when
considered in association with the Caledonian pinewood was realised, albeit
primarily in relation to the natural range of red deer and the opportunities
offered for their 'ecological study'. Professor W H Pearsall of the Nature
Conservancy in his 'Draft Recommendations for General Policy of
Management' presented in 1951 concluded that: 'The scientific interest of the
Reserve lies in its possible merit as a deer forest and in the existence of pine and
birch'.

In the same document he went on to describe the value of the woodland itself
as being threefold:

1 'As a surviving relict of the old Caledonian pine forest'.
2. 'As part of the biological unit of the deer forest supplying the necessary
   harbourage for deer'.
3. 'As part of a system including woodland and the transitional moorland types
   which replace it in a wet climate'.

He also recognised the concept of the 'Highland moving forest' and the
importance of the relationship between natural regeneration and deer wintering
pressure and suggested a tripartite management strategy based on the cessation
of burning, the rotational establishment of small deer-proof exclosures
combined with a reduction in the wintering deer population and 'judicious'
planting of native trees within the ancient wood.

As far as practical 'management' of the wood prior to the purchase of the
Reserve by the Nature Conservancy in 1951 is concerned, this amounted to the
wintering of deer, sheep and goats and the felling and extraction of two quite
large areas of Scots pine during the period 1939–1944 by the 'Pioneer Corps' (D
Grieg, pers. comm.). However, although Mrs Grieg, the previous owner of the
area designated an NNR, recalls felled timber lying in the wood when she
purchased it in 1945 there appear to be no surviving estate records recording the
volume of timber extracted and the Forestry Commission Census (1947–49)
records only that the south-east end of the wood was classified as 'devastated'.

Woodland management 1951–58: a policy of minimal intervention

The years 1951–1953 saw the commencement of survey work designed to assess the condition and quality of the woodland as a basis from which to determine management policy. The first survey of the age-structure of the pinewood was completed in 1953 (McVean 1953) and showed quite a varied age distribution with pulses of natural regeneration occurring at about 1888, 1853 and 1763 although these did not occur throughout the wood (Figure 1). Young trees around the outskirts at the western end of the wood were thought to represent a fourth period of regeneration around 1935. However, the wood as a whole did not show the classic 'reverse J' age distribution which indicates a sustained input of young trees into the population.

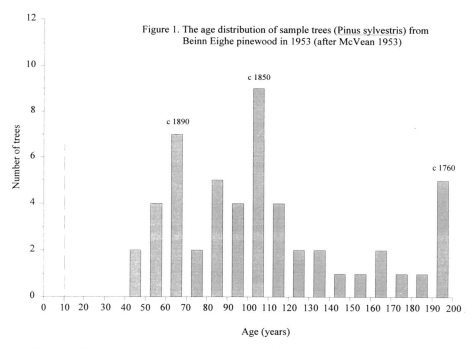

Figure 1. The age distribution of sample trees (Pinus sylvestris) from Beinn Eighe pinewood in 1953 (after McVean 1953)

Figure 1: The age distribution of sample trees *(Pinus sylvestris)* from Beinn Eighe pinewood in 1953 (after McVean 1953).
The number of seedlings under ten years old is unknown.

The two key issues which would underpin all subsequent woodland management on the NNR emerged at the beginning of this period; the ability of the wood to regenerate naturally was the central discussion point with the idea of extending a 'natural type' forest onto formerly wooded parts of the Reserve as a secondary area of concern. The debate between interventionists and non-interventionists became quite heated at times. At a site meeting in July 1952 lead by Professor Pearsall and attended by senior staff of the Nature Conservancy and Scottish Committee members it was agreed after much debate that:

1. The first essential for regeneration of the woodland was a deer and sheep-proof fence ringing the whole wood.
2. 'Artificial' planting would be necessary using locally native species in small groups and patches throughout the wood.
3. The experimental re-creation of woodland in deforested areas on the southern slopes of the Reserve should commence under the guidance of the Forestry Commission (probably using some form of nurse crop which would also act to improve soil conditions).

It was at this point that the Forestry Commission declared their hand when Sir Henry Beresford-Peirse their Director for Scotland, stated:

> I take it that the object of the Nature Conservancy in buying Beinn Eighe was to preserve a good example of a deer forest in a particularly fine part of the Highlands and to secure the regeneration of the natural pine and birch woods there. The Forestry Commission too, have an interest in these woodlands because it is their duty to achieve the maximum productivity of the woodlands of the country of which this forms a part. I see no reason, however, why the interests of the Nature Conservancy and the Forestry Commission need cut across each other... I believe, however, that the method of achieving this might be done rather differently; namely, by handing over the main woodland area of some 300 or 400 acres to the Forestry Commission... The actual regeneration of this area could then be done by the Forestry Commission so that the views and interests of the Nature Conservancy could be taken into full account. The advantages of this suggestion are: First, that what is, in fact, a forestry project would be carried out by the Forestry Commission which is the country's forest authority; Secondly, that the Nature Conservancy would be relieved of a heavy expenditure on work which is really in the sphere of another organisation, while at the same time their own particular interests would be safeguarded. Not only would they save expenditure, but they could also count on a small amount by way of rent feu or capital sum; Thirdly, the Nature Conservancy would not have the difficulty of arranging for management and supervision of the woodlands.

The fledgling Nature Conservancy was perilously close to being swallowed whole by the Forestry Commission and there was some concern amongst Nature Conservancy Scottish Committee members exemplified by Professor Yonge. In a letter to John Berry following the July site meeting he wrote:

> I am by no means certain that what Pearsall suggested and what Sir Henry was prepared to do really amounted to the same thing... There is a gulf between the outlook of the botanical ecologist and that of the forester.

Strong reservations were also expressed by Captain C Diver, Director General of the Nature Conservancy, who in a letter to John Berry dated September 1952 described the report of the July site meeting as 'disingenious'. In a scathing attack on the outcome of the July meeting he wrote:

> The discussion, as reported, appears to have been based on the tacit assumption that the Conservancy's function should be so to modify the pinewood at Coille na Glas Leitire so as to make it, as nearly as possible in the circumstances, by silvicultural standards a good wood. This would connote forest management directed towards the production, in reasonable profusion, of tall straight boled trees that are 'well grown' in terms of the timber they would yield if harvested as a crop. Such a programme would naturally, and very properly, receive support from the Forestry Commission and others concerned about the rehabilitation of British woodlands as a vital asset in the nation's economy. But that this assumption necessarily provides a valid basis for considering the regime of biological management which should be applied to one of the Conservancy's few first class national reserves, I must categorically deny.

Diver urged extreme caution in considering the management of what he termed 'an ecologically first class richly varied conservation unit'. He posed a series of searching questions to the Nature Conservancy Scottish Committee on the value of an artificially created close canopy pinewood habitat and suggested that an active interventionist approach involving ground disturbance, large scale fencing and planting...' would undermine the confidence that is now being placed in them (the Nature Conservancy) by the many who are deeply concerned about safeguarding scientifically valuable places'. He saw the primary value of the woodland as an outdoor laboratory 'presenting first class opportunities' for the study of natural regeneration and the impact of deer browsing on the woodland, and was adamant that any artificial interference should be postponed until 'an adequate ecological and topographical survey has been made' (Nature Conservancy, internal files).

In a letter to Captain Diver dated October 1952 John Berry encapsulated the diversity of opinion on the optimal management strategy for the woodland when he wrote:

> The hopes I had a couple of months ago that I was beginning to learn how ecologists view an area such as the Beinn Eighe pinewood, have been somewhat shaken by discovering how fundamentally opposed eminent ecologists appear to be on the subject.

Nevertheless Captain Diver's intervention heralded a re-think and by early 1953 there was wide recognition that priority should be given to survey and experimental work '...aiming at establishing a long-term programme to restore the woodland' (Nicholson 1953). It also saw the start of the pioneering work of Donald McVean on the ecology of Scots pine and the experimental establishment of native tree species on highly degraded soils, culminating in a range of benchmark scientific papers which still form the basis of the Reserve's woodland management strategy today (Durno & McVean 1959; McVean 1959; McVean, 1961a & b; McVean 1963a & b; McVean 1963; McVean 1966).

McVean believed that large-scale silvicultural operations were not necessary to ensure the continued existence of the wood and that the management strategy for the ancient woodland 'should be broadly one of laissez-faire'. He stressed however the importance of experimental work which should be 'directed towards finding ways in which the ill effects of former mis-management can be mitigated and the full biological potential of the habitat realised'. To support him in his work a small tree nursery was established at the Reserve in 1953 primarily to provide seedling trees for experimental work and in 1954 a 110 acre enclosure was established on the northern edge of the ancient wood to provide a range of soil types on which experimental establishment techniques could be tested free from the effects of grazing animals.

Following a period of intense discussion, debate, and in some cases disagreement, during these early years as to the best strategy for managing what was widely recognised as a priceless resource, by 1954 the policy had finally crystallised out as being one of minimal intervention, observation and small scale experimentation. However, there was still an underlying sense of pessimism regarding the ability of the wood to naturally regenerate and a widely held belief that intervention, including planting was inevitable (Forster 1991).

Woodland management 1958–84: a policy of positive intervention

The investigations and experimental work carried out between 1951 and 1958 suggested that the problem of regeneration of the Caledonian pine woodland was more complex than just the excessive browsing by sheep and deer and that the degradation of soils as a result of man's past mismanagement made seedling and sapling establishment extremely difficult. It was therefore widely accepted that intervention would be necessary to sustain and enhance the woodland. The 1957 Management Plan (McVean, Arbuthnott and Boyd 1957), although recognising the continued importance of scientific study in understanding the dynamics of the woodland, represented the first move towards an actively interventionist policy involving fencing, draining, ploughing and fertiliser application within the main pinewood and elsewhere on de-forested areas of the Reserve. The plan stated:

> The object of management of the Beinn Eighe Reserve is to maintain this area as a field laboratory for the continuous ecological study of the forest, moorland and montane habitats.

This ecological study was to be directed towards:

1. The regeneration of natural climax forest from the existing woodland. (High forest is not the primary, nor necessarily even the ultimate, aim on all low ground; the main object is the production of a scrub or woodland cover of birch, rowan, pine etc., on all sites capable of supporting woody vegetation).
2. The encouragement above the tree line of montane climax communities of the greatest possible variety.
3. The diversification of the Reserve by afforestation.

The 'diversification' of the Reserve was to be achieved through:

> The gradual extension of woodland to cover most of the Reserve below 1000 feet, except where afforestation by the Forestry Commission has been agreed.

'Afforestation by the Forestry Commission' applied to 220 acres of deforested ground on the lower south-eastern slopes of the Reserve leased to the Commission in 1958 for the planting of a commercial conifer crop and the establishment of joint Nature Conservancy–Forestry Commission soil fertilisation experiments. In retrospect this seems to be a sop to the Commission following their unsuccessful attempt to persuade the Nature Conservancy of the merits of Commission management of the Reserve's total woodland resource. However, at the time it was felt that there were tangible benefits to the Reserve in that the established plantation would 'contribute to the diversification of the reserve' (Boyd and Campbell 1964) and would assist in the rehabilitation of degraded soils (Boyd 1961).

At first it was intended that rehabilitation and gradual extension of native woodland would involve 'ecological' planting with minimal ground preparation to produce woodland with a diversity of species, structure and spatial pattern. However, by about 1960 this vision had evolved further to become a policy of intervention to achieve rapid tree cover, which continued into the early 1980s.

Progress with the achievement of the objectives identified in the 1957 plan was reviewed in the 1964 Management Plan revision (Boyd and Campbell 1964) which stated:

> After six years of observation it became apparent that there was no hope of achieving restoration of the Coille na Glas Leitire by natural regeneration alone. Therefore, since 1957, the positive policy has been adopted of fencing, draining, ploughing and planting (with the use of fertilisers where necessary) to achieve rapid tree cover. To achieve the primary object of re-creating a natural-type forest it has been necessary to modify the conventional methods of commercial forestry to meet the special requirements of the Conservancy.

The last sentence regarding the use of conventional methods of commercial forestry is critical and marks a change in philosophy away from 'natural processes' and the selection of tree species to suit particular soils and drainage conditions towards the artificial modification of soils and drainage patterns to allow trees (particularly Scots pine) to grow almost anywhere. Further support for this approach was evident fifteen years later in an internal Nature Conservancy discussion paper (Tilbrook 1979) which stated that the aim should be to cover 75 percent of the ground below 1000 feet with trees, apparently without consideration of the existing soils and drainage. Although not explicitly stated it also appears to mark a move away from the main objective of the 1957 plan which advocated '...the production of a scrub or woodland cover of birch, rowan and pine on all sites capable of supporting woody vegetation', towards some idealised concept of a pine forest at the post-glacial climatic optimum.

The prime reason for the acceleration of the Reserve's afforestation programme from its conservative beginnings appears to have been the success of establishment experiments, particularly three small 'diversification plots' on the south side of the Reserve in Glen Torridon, where commercial forestry techniques had produced good growth and survival of planted native Scots pine on poor degraded soils. At a practical level this change in philosophy gave rise to ploughing and planting within a sixteen hectare deer-proof exclosure within the main native pinewood in 1960 and the establishment of a further nine exclosures totalling 196 hectares on de-forested moorland between 1960 and 1980, within which over 300,000 Scots pine and 100,000 broadleaved trees were planted using largely commercial forestry establishment techniques.

Drainage and ploughing took place on poorly drained ground to help achieve a high percentage tree cover and trees were planted at uniformly high densities as it was felt necessary to suppress ground vegetation. Attempts were made to create a diverse woodland structure, especially in the earlier exclosures. Well drained areas with bracken were often turf-planted with oak and bird cherry, whilst some wet flushes were planted with alder and willows. Additionally birch and rowan were sometimes mixed in with Scots pine and areas were left unplanted to form glades and provide sheltered woodland edge habitat. However, diversity of species and woodland structure was to some extent compromised by the aim of achieving rapid tree cover and the financial implications of maintaining fences in the longer term. Planting was further skewed towards Scots pine as this was easier to grow in the tree nursery than most other native species and difficulties were experienced at times in obtaining sufficient broadleaved planting stock from elsewhere. Another important spin-off from both the change in management philosophy and the difficulties in obtaining broadleaved seedling trees was that the origin of Scots pine planted on the Reserve appeared to become a less important issue and trees of Glen Affric stock and other origins outside Wester Ross were planted in quite large numbers.

Whilst it was acknowledged that red deer were a component of the native woodland ecosystem, the prominence they received in the early debate on woodland management strategy and in the first management plan was not maintained and they were largely considered as a hindrance to woodland regeneration. Nevertheless their potential as a management tool to diversify young plantations in the establishment phase was recognised and two of the exclosures were used to assess the effects of deer browsing by releasing known numbers of red deer into them and measuring their impact on planted native trees of different species. A secondary objective was to determine at what stage the plantations could be opened up to provide wintering for deer. The main conclusions from these studies (Cumming & Miller 1982; Mitchell, MacGowan & Willcox 1982) were that Scots pine suffered limited damage and deer browsing had little impact on survival and a negligible thinning effect, whilst deciduous trees, particularly rowan and willow, sustained significant damage and were unlikely to form more than scrub where browsing was prolonged.

A gradual return to minimal intervention

In 1980 two events halted the Reserve's woodland restoration programme in its tracks and instigated a review of both policy and practice. The first of these was the publication of work on the genotypic variation amongst native Scots pine populations in Scotland (Forrest 1980) which suggested that populations of Scots pines situated quite close geographically could be genetically different and that, as a group, the pinewoods of Wester Ross were significantly different from other native pine populations in Scotland. The second less dramatic event was the closure of the Forestry Commission tree nursery at Blackstand on the Black Isle which had provided seedling trees for the woodland restoration programme since the closure of the Reserve's own nursery in the 1960s.

In 1984 a Nature Conservancy Council internal discussion paper was produced (MacLennan 1984) outlining the importance of the maintenance of local origin Scots pine on the Reserve and suggesting a zonation policy for both seed collection and subsequent planting. This, when combined with the recommendation of the Council of Europe in 1983 that a gene-based seed bank should be established at the Reserve, the re-establishment of a tree nursery at the Reserve in 1985, work on the reproductive potential of Beinn Eighe's small, isolated Scots pine populations (Clifford 1991) and the development of the National Vegetation Classification (Rodwell 1991) as a predictive tool to assist woodland re-creation, gave a new impetus and direction to the Reserve's woodland restoration programme. Minimal intervention and the precautionary principle again became the key management principles giving rise to the following broad woodland management objectives (Clifford 1994):

1. The management of the existing ancient woodland, in the presence of native deer, to maximise natural processes (nutrient cycling, natural regeneration, competition/predation/self thinning).
2. The restoration of a natural altitudinal zonation with woodland grading into sub-alpine type scrub and ultimately to dwarf shrub heath vegetation.
3. The extension of the area of woodland by the re-creation of natural-type pine/birch forest of varied structure and pattern on deforested ground below the climatic tree line (where soils and drainage will allow the eventual re-

establishment of a woodland ecosystem).
4. The maintenance of the genetic integrity of the native Scots pine woodland by the eradication of alien origin Scots pine from within and adjacent to the Reserve.
5. The eradication of exotic conifers and shrubs from the Reserve and the conversion of plantation woods to native-type woodland.
6. The undertaking of monitoring to evaluate the effectiveness of management and to detect natural changes, and the encouragement of research that will provide a better understanding of ecosystem processes.
7. The interpretation of the significance and value of the ancient woodland to the public and the provision of low key recreational opportunities that do not conflict with the conservation objectives.

The key to the current thinking on the management of the Reserve's woodland which is encapsulated in the last two Reserve management plans (Clifford 1990; Forster 1995), is a move away from any attempt to re-create some idealised concept of pine-dominated woodland at the post-glacial climatic optimum, towards the restoration of woodland processes as they would function under the climatic and edaphic regimes prevalent today. This approach now underpins both the management of the existing ancient woodland and the re-creation of natural-type woodland habitats on de-forested ground.

The importance of deer as a positive factor in the regeneration dynamics of these woods is also now widely accepted. The forest floor in most western pinewoods is almost completely covered with a thick carpet of sphagnum moss in damp areas and hypnaceous mosses in drier areas. For seedlings of native trees and shrubs to germinate and establish successfully it is important that there is some disturbance to expose the soil surface. In the absence of fire and windblow, deer play a major role in natural regeneration by creating small 'safe sites' where conditions favour the establishment of seedlings. Complete removal of deer from woodland by fencing in the oceanic north-west will give rise to conditions where only those seedlings already established below the field layer vegetation will recruit to the population. Deer are also important in these woods as they act as an 'ecological sieve', differentially targeting some species such as rowan for browsing and influencing both the structure and spatial pattern of the woodland. Whilst Scottish Natural Heritage recognises the value of small rotational exclosures in 'kick-starting' the process of natural regeneration, it is now felt that the key to the long-term sustainable management of these woods lies in the careful management of deer rather than fencing (SNH 1994), although the deleterious effect of excessive deer numbers are equally clear.

The fencing of 1100 hectares of de-forested ground on the Reserve in 1987, and the consequent loss of deer wintering ground necessitated a marked reduction in the red deer population to prevent displaced animals being concentrated in the unfenced ancient woodland and presented the opportunity to monitor the response of the woodland to a further reduction in deer wintering pressure. From 1988 a heavy annual cull of red deer averaging about 35–40 percent of hinds and 20–25 percent of stags has been implemented and the overall red deer density has been reduced to about two animals per hundred hectares.

Although it is too early to draw firm conclusions about the response of the woodland vegetation to this reduction in red deer density, permanent monitoring plots established within the woodland in 1992 (McLeod *et al.* 1993) have indicated seedling densities of 6000 rowan, 1700 birch and 500 Scots pine per hectare in areas of open canopy, with an overall average stocking of about 8200 stems per hectare. Whilst browsing exceeded 50 percent for each of these three species, overall there was still an average of 3300 undamaged seedling trees per hectare. These seedlings, the majority of which are above the height of the surrounding heather, have been established without the need for planting and provide the 'capital' for a significant pulse of natural regeneration if low deer densities can be maintained. Figure 2 shows the current size structure of the main ancient Scots pine population. As there is a fairly good relationship between age and size for native Scots pine at Beinn Eighe (Clifford 1991) this

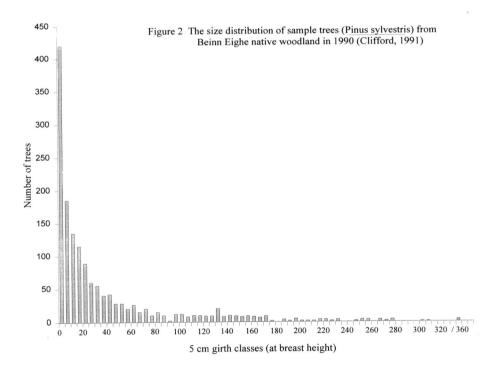

Figure 2 The size distribution of sample trees (Pinus sylvestris) from
Beinn Eighe native woodland in 1990 (Clifford, 1991)

Figure 2: The size distribution of sample trees *(Pinus sylvestris)* from Beinn Eighe native woodland in 1990 (Clifford 1991).

can be interpreted in broad terms as an age structure curve and it shows that there is now a healthy age distribution of pine trees with a sustained input of young trees to the population.

The philosophy of minimal intervention has been applied equally to the re-creation of woodland habitats on de-forested ground below the current climatic treeline. The primary aim in enclosing the 1100 hectares of largely de-forested ground has been to allow natural regeneration of the three small relict gorge pinewoods within the deer-proof fence and to re-create native type woodland by planting on suitable soils in areas distant from existing seed sources.

Before any planting was undertaken a vegetation map was drawn up for the enclosed area using the National Vegetation Classification (NVC) (Pennington 1992), in order to identify important open ground habitats that should not be planted and to identify the range of soils and drainage conditions where it would be possible eventually to re-establish a woodland ecosystem, rather than a generation of planted trees on highly degraded soils. This map indicated that about twenty percent of the total area was suitable for the re-establishment of native woodland and the differing vegetation types and drainage conditions, when combined with existing knowledge of the ecology of native trees and shrubs, gave a good indication as to which species and species mixes should be planted in different areas. This information has been condensed into simple guidelines for the planting teams actually doing the work. For example alder, willow species and a little downy birch have been planted in purple moor grass *(Molinia)* flushes, where there is movement of nutrient-rich drainage water through the soil profile, whilst Scots pine, upright juniper and a little holly have been planted on better drained morainic knolls and hummocks with heather and bell heather. Most planting stock has been grown, from locally collected seed, in SNH's tree nursery at Anancaun adjacent to the Reserve and ground preparation has been limited to light hand screefing, turfing and hand mounding. There has been much debate about the use of ground mineral phosphate fertiliser but, as phosphate deficiency has been identified as a major limiting factor on tree growth and survival at Beinn Eighe (McVean 1963a), it has been considered necessary to provide a small amount to each individual tree at planting, other than where close to wetland and open water habitats.

Planting has mimicked the natural regeneration strategy of each tree species, rather than being guided by some arbitrary pre-determined stocking, so that species that regenerate in dense stands such as alder, willows, birch and Scots pine have been planted at densities of up to 3000 stems per hectare allowing natural thinning to take place. To date about 50,000 locally native trees and shrubs of eleven species have been planted in this way and survival rates have been quite high at about 90 percent for Scots pine and 70 percent for broadleaved species (Webb *et al.* 1995). The aim has not been to create an almost 'instant' woodland of a pre-determined structure and pattern, but to provide a kick-start to the woodland ecosystem by establishing small groups of mixed seed-parent trees which will gradually modify their own environment and provide loci for natural regeneration and expansion. The long term objective today for the de-forested ground on the Reserve is to create a dynamic mosaic of mixed woodland and open peatland habitats, grading into sub-alpine scrub and ultimately to dispense with the fence and allow deer back into the woodland.

Discussion and Conclusions

From the acquisition of the Reserve in 1951 to the present day the dual objectives for the management of native woodland have remained constant. However, the means by which these objectives have been achieved and the time-scales associated with management prescriptions have been the subject of prolonged and often heated debate.

The great mass of documentation spanning forty five years indicates that the development of woodland management policy and related practice has evolved through three distinct phases. During the first seven years of the history of the National Nature Reserve those Nature Conservancy officers and Scottish Committee members favouring a policy of minimal intervention held sway. Despite strong reservations about this approach and a desire amongst some Committee members to re-create Caledonian forest as rapidly as possible, this period was characterised by careful observation and small scale experimentation in an attempt to understand the processes of degradation prior to any firm decision about the level of management intervention required.

This epitomises the 'precautionary principle' and, in retrospect, certainly seems a sensible and logical approach. What is perhaps slightly surprising in relation to the relatively long ecological time scales over which woodland processes operate, is that this period was so short.

However, at the end of the period there was still very real concern about the possible loss of elements of the 'old pine forest' ground flora and an underlying pessimism about the ability of the wood to regenerate naturally even if deer and sheep were excluded. This time also marks the commencement of a period of rapid change in commercial forestry practices away from the selection of timber trees to suit specific soils and drainage conditions towards the wholesale modification by intensive ground disturbance so that a limited range of exotic conifers could be grown quickly almost anywhere. These new techniques, when combined with the application of fertiliser, offered the promise of the establishment of native trees quickly and effectively almost regardless of the level of soil degradation. Under these circumstances it is hardly surprising that a policy of positive intervention to achieve rapid tree cover ensued.

The gradual return to a policy of minimal intervention was precipitated in 1980 by a simple and ostensibly unremarkable event, the closure of the Forestry Commission tree nursery on the Black Isle which had been producing all the trees for the Beinn Eighe woodland restoration programme since the closure of the Reserve's own nursery in the early 1960s. This gave a breathing space to review progress and plan for the future. It also coincided with the gradual emergence of new scientific information shedding further light on the ecology and dynamics of native pinewoods and the evolution of ideas on sustainability and biodiversity, culminating at the international level with the United Nations Conference on Environment and Development in Rio in 1992 and at the domestic level with the establishment of Scottish Natural Heritage in the same year. The wheel had turned almost full circle and the 'precautionary principle', 'ecological time-scales' and 'natural processes' again became the cornerstones of woodland management policy.

At this point in a review of past management it would be fair to ask what the cumulative effect of these changes in policy and practice has been on the ancient wood itself. Even with the benefit of hindsight it is not possible to say that one approach would have worked better than any other at the particular time. Both policy makers and managers worked with the best information available at the time and common sense and pragmatism would dictate that management policy would be bound to change as new information became available. The management plans for the Reserve have always been viewed as highly dynamic documents designed to provide a 'feedback loop' whereby new knowledge gained from research, survey and monitoring could flow into management decision making.

The question is perhaps best answered by a comparison of the general shapes of the curves shown in Figures 1 and 2. The earlier bell-shaped age distribution shown in Figure 1 which shows a complete absence of pine trees between ten and 40 years of age has been replaced by the classic 'reverse J' age distribution shown in Figure 2 with large numbers of pine trees in all the younger age classes. This change in the age structure of the pine population has taken place over a period of just under 40 years and is the result of all previous management action, which in this area of the Reserve has focused primarily on natural regeneration. Although it says nothing directly about changes in biodiversity it does indicate that the potential for the ancient woodland to sustain itself over the longer term is now assured.

Having undertaken this review and one of us having been involved as Reserve Manager at Beinn Eighe NNR for a period of almost twelve years, the authors tentatively suggest that the following broad conclusions applicable to future woodland management may be drawn from the 'Beinn Eighe experience':

1. Science does not always give absolute answers on which policy can be based.
2. However, policy should be informed by the best scientific evidence available at the time, tempered with pragmatism.
3. Where the resource is particularly valuable the precautionary principle should be adopted when absolute answers are not available.
4. Management planning is by its very nature a dynamic process. The proper monitoring of the effects of management action is essential to provide a 'feedback loop' and allow the development of best practice.
5. It is essential that managers record and date all management action and that

these records survive long periods of time.

References

Boyd, J M, *Conserving Nature* (Scottish Field, 1961)

Boyd, J M and Campbell, R N, 'Beinn Eighe National Nature Reserve; Management Plan, First Revision, 1965–69' (unpublished manuscript, Nature Conservancy, 1964)

Cmd. 7814, *Final Report of the Scottish Wild Life Conservation Committee* (HMSO, 1949)

Clifford, T, 'North-West Scotland Region. Beinn Eighe National Nature Reserve. Management Plan for 5 year period 1990–94' (unpublished manuscript, Nature Conservancy Council, Inverness, 1990)

Clifford, T, 'The history of Scots pine (*Pinus sylvestris* L. var. Scotica.) on the Beinn Eighe National Nature Reserve, and aspects of the demography of two isolated gorge pinewoods' (masters dissertation, University of London, 1991)

Clifford, T, *Beinn Eighe – 43 years a Pinewood Laboratory*. Poster title. In: Our Pinewood Heritage. Conference Proceedings, 1994, ed. Aldous, J R, pp. 257–58. Forestry Commission.

Cumming, R P and Miller, G R, 'Damage by Red Deer (*Cervus elaphus*) enclosed in a planted woodland', *Scottish Forestry*, 36 (1982), No. 1

Durno, S E, and McVean, D N, 'Forest History of the Beinn Eighe Nature Reserve' *New Phytologist*, 58 (1959), 228–36

Forrest, G I, 'Genotypic variation among native Scots pine populations in Scotland based on Monoterpene Analysis', *Forestry*, 53, No. 2 (1980) 101–28

Forster, A N, 'A report on the woodland management policy at Beinn Eighe National Nature Reserve 1951–1970' (unpublished report, NCCS, Inverness, 1991)

Forster, A N (ed. Clifford), 'Beinn Eighe National Nature Reserve. Ten Year management Plan, 1995–2005' (unpublished manuscript, SNH, Inverness, 1995)

MacLennan, A S, 'Pine Provenance in Wester Ross – a Discussion Paper' (unpublished report, NCC, Inverness, 1981)

McLeod, D, Routavitz, E, Murray, J, Ramsey, S, Christie, H, McWhinnie, J and Clifford, T, 'Beinn Eighe NNR, Coille na Glas-Leitire Woodland. A survey of seedling and sapling populations within an area proposed for management under a Woodland Grant Scheme' (unpublished report, SNH, Inverness, 1993)

McVean, D N, 'Coille na Glas-Leitire, 1953 Investigations', Reserve Record, 21 (Nature Conservancy, 1953)

McVean, D N, 'Ecology of *Alnus glutinosa* L VII. Establishment of alder by direct seeding of shallow blanket bog', *Journal of Ecology*, 47 (1959), 615–18

McVean, D N, 'Experiments on the direct sowing of Scots pine', *Empire Forestry Review*, 40 (1961a), 217–27

McVean, D N, 'Experiments on the ecology of Scots pine seedlings', *Empire Forestry Review*, 40 (1961b), 291–300

McVean, D N, 'Growth and mineral nutrition of Scots pine seedlings on some common peat types', *Journal of Ecology*, 51 (1963a), 657–69

McVean, D N, 'Direct sowing of Scots pine on ploughed land in Wester Ross', *Scottish Forestry*, 17 (1963b), 24–25

McVean, D N, 'Establishment of native trees and shrubs on Scottish nature reserves by direct seed sowing', *Scottish Forestry*, 20, No. 1 (1966), 26–36

McVean, D N, Arbuthnott, J C and Morton-Boyd, J, 'Management Plan. Beinn Eighe Nature Reserve, Wester Ross' (unpublished manuscript, Nature Conservancy, Edinburgh, 1957)

Mitchell, B, McGowan, D and Willcox, N A, 'Effects of Deer in a Woodland Restoration Enclosure', *Scottish Forestry*, 36, No. 2 (1982)

Nature Conservancy. 1951–1962. Internal files. Beinn Eighe NNR archive. Anancaun Field Station, Kinlochewe.

Nicholson, E M, 'Scientific Management of the Conservancy's Woodlands (SP/M/53/3), Annex IV', (unpublished manuscript, Nature Conservancy, Edinburgh, 1953)

Pearsall, W H, 'Kinlochewe Nature Reserve: draft recommendations for general policy of management. Reserve Record 1' (unpublished manuscript, Nature Conservancy, Edinburgh, 1951)

Pennington, R A, 'Vegetation survey of the Beinn Eighe ring-fenced area' (unpublished report, NCCS, Inverness, 1992)

Rodwell, J S (ed.), *British Plant Communities, Volume 1 Woodlands and Scrub* (Cambridge University Press, Cambridge, 1991)

SNH, *Red deer and the natural heritage* (SNH Policy Paper, SNH, Edinburgh, 1994)

Tansley, A G, *British Islands and their Vegetation* (Cambridge University Press, Cambridge, 1939)

Tilbrook, P J, 'The Beinn Eighe Re-afforestation Programme' (unpublished discussion paper, NCC, Inverness, 1979)

Webb, J, Milnes, K and Pierce, L, 'Beinn Eighe NNR: A survey of the success of tree planting carried out between 1989 and 1994 within the ring-fenced area' (unpublished report, SNH, Inverness, 1995)

Acknowledgements

We thank Professor T C Smout for inviting us to contribute this paper to the conference report. TC is also indebted to AF for the original idea to carry out the review and for the long hours he spent searching through old files and manuscripts. Any opinions expressed in this paper do not necessarily reflect SNH policy and are those of the authors alone.

Index

Aberdeen, 119, 136, 162; Bishops of, 136, 139
Aberdeenshire, 18, 136
Aberfeldy, 102
Aberfoyle, 170
Abernethy, 12, 17, 92, 98, 115, 117–19, 176–87
Aboyne, Earl of, 139
Achmelvich, 127, 132
Achnacarry, 119
Achnatra Wood, 27
Advie, 178
Agricola, Julius, 47, 49; campaigns of, 48
alder, 18, 26, 66, 69, 76, 88, 90, 103, 109, 116, 148, 154, 155, 178, 198, 202
Aldwark, 152
Allander Water, 76
Allt Mor, 181
Allt na h'Airbe, 132
Amat, 117
America, 179
An Abha, 127
An Coimhleum, 131
ancient forest, 162; reduction of, 185
ancient pinewood, 191
Ancient Tree Forum (formerly Veteran Tree Group), 26
ancient tree stem forms, 27–32; maiden, 27–8; coppice, 28–9; pollard, 30–2
ancient trees, 24–39; ageing of, 32; species, 26–7
ancient woods/woodland, 1, 2, 24–39, 41, 44, 45, 76–85, 147, 184, 185, 187, 188, 192, 196, 199, 200, 204
angling, 180
animals, 2, 6, 16–19, 67, 90–92, 94, 95, 97, 103, 104, 110, 111, 149, 179; domestic stock, 87, 90, 95, 143, 150, 179, 188; livestock, 113, 170, 184, 188; pressure of increasing numbers, 19
Antonine Wall, 50
Appin of Dull, 102, 103, 105, 106, 110
apple tree, 69
archaeologist, 1
archaeology, 1, 2, 6, 7
Ardtallaig estate, 108
Ardgour, 93
Ardradnaig estate, 108
Ardvar, 129
Ardverikie, 181
Argyle, Earl of, 115
Argyll, 90, 91, 93, 94, 95; Dukes of, 12
Arinacrinachd, 132
Arrochar, 112

ash, 18, 24, 25, 26, 28, 30, 31, 69, 88, 90, 103, 110, 119, 133, 147, 150, 151, 153, 154, 155, 156, 157, 167
aspen, 11, 16, 26, 90, 129
Association of Certified Field Archaeologists, 82
Assynt, 2, 16, 21, 98, 126–34
Atholl, 162
    archives, 164
    castle, 168
    Dukes of, 12, 163
        First Duke of, John, 164
        Second Duke of, James, 164
    estate, 2, 12, 174
    papers, 174
    plantations, 172
        Claypotts, 172
        Ladywell, 172
        Little Dunkeld, 172
    woods, 172
Auld Wark, 149
auroch, 20
Avenel, Robert, 70
Aviemore, 178, 181, 182, 186
Ayrshire, 7

Badachro, 132
Baddengorm, 187
Badenoch, 185, 187; Wolf of, 6
Badluarach, 132
Bailefuil Wood, 28
Balliknock, 119
Baltic, 179
Banchory, 41, 42
Banff, 118, 119, 162
bark, 103, 109, 112, 158
baron courts, 19, 101–14, 124; records, 2, 93, 95
Battleby, 1, 3
bear, 20, 50
Bearsden, 81
Beauly, 90, 91, 93, 120; ~ Firth, 48
beaver, 20
beech, 26, 27, 30, 157
Beinn Eighe, 2, 132; ~ National Nature Reserve, 190–206
Beinn Gharbh, 131
Beinn Shieldaig, 132
Benderloch, 102, 108, 110, 113
Berry, Dr John, 192, 194, 195
Berwick, 71
Bialowieza National Park, 25, 26
biodiversity, 25, 86, 87, 94, 97, 188, 204

Biosphere Reserve, 191
biotic history, 40
birch, 2, 6, 7, 11, 16, 18, 19, 24, 26, 27, 29, 41,
    66, 69, 76, 88, 90, 92, 94, 95, 96, 98, 103,
    109, 116, 119, 127, 129, 130, 132, 135–46,
    148, 150, 153, 154, 155, 158, 165, 167, 170,
    171, 172, 173, 174, 178, 183, 184, 185, 186,
    187, 188, 191, 192, 194, 197, 198, 199, 201,
    202
Birnam Hill, 164
Birse, 136, 139, 140; Forest of ~, 136, 139
Bissett, Thomas, 164, 167
Black Andrew, 147, 151–8
Black Isle, 199, 203
Black Lynn Falls, 168, 169, 174
Black Wood of Rannoch, 17, 18, 93
Blackmount, 184
Blackstand, 199
Blaeu, John, 10, 11, 12; Blaeu's map, 77, 139
Blair Atholl (see Atholl)
Boat of Garten, 178, 186
bog, 6
Boonies, 54, 65
Borders, 2, 76, 88, 147–61
Boswell, James, 162
Bowhill, 157
bracken, 24, 198
Branxholm Wood, 89
Breadalbane, 2, 16; Earls of, 163; estate, 107,
    110, 113; John, Second Earl of, 108, 111,
    112
Britain, 6, 40, 47, 49, 53, 66, 181, 182, 190
broadleaved trees/woodland, 40, 42, 44, 45,
    157, 163, 178, 198
broadleaves, 2, 17, 18, 24, 26, 147, 151, 156,
    158
Bronze Age, 6
Broomhill, 178
Brown, Gilbert, 182
Bruce, Robert the, 34
Brundtland Report, 86
Brussels, 191
bryophyte, 25
Buccleuch estate, 2, 89; lands, 151
Buccleuch, Francis, Second Duke of, 155
Buccleuch, Scotts of, 149, 150
bundle planting, 30, 33
Butter, Henry, 124

Cadzow, 2, 27, 33, 34; ~ Oaks, 34, 77–81
Caesar, Julius, 81
Cairngorm, 18, 183
Cairngorms:
    forests, 144; mountains, 179; National
    Nature Reserve, 183; ~ Partnership, 188
Caithness, 7, 11
Caledon, 1, 5, 47–51
Caledonia, 47, 48, 49
Caledonian:

~ forest, 16, 47–50, 111, 191, 203; ~ pine, 3,
    91, 115–18, 123, 124, 187, 190; ~
    pinewoods, 2, 3, 16, 17, 184, 185, 186, 188,
    192, 196
Caledonii, 47, 48
Callander, 170
Callart, 93, 120
Cameron, Alexander, 124
Cameron, Donald, 119
Cameron, Dugald, 124
Cameron, Ewen, of Glenevis, 121
Cameron, John, of Fassifern, 122
Cameron, John, of Lochiel, 119
Cameron, Sir Ewen, 119
Campbell, Colin, of Glenlyon, 110
Campbell lairds of Glenorchy, 106, 109–11
Campbell of Barcaldine, 102
Campbell of Glenfalloch, 102, 112
Campbell of Monzie, 102
Campbell, Patrick, 122
Campbell, Robert, 108
Campbells of Argyll, 102
Campbeltown, 121
Canadian Forestry Service, 181
Canadians, 182
Capella, Martianus, 48
capercaillie, 18, 97, 118
Carnachy, 10
Carrbridge, 181, 182, 184, 186
Carstramon Wood, 30
Castle Grant, 180
Castle O'er, 65
cattle, 5, 7, 12, 16, 18, 19, 20, 21, 49, 66, 70,
    78, 81, 88, 89, 93, 94, 96, 97, 110, 111, 124,
    156, 176, 178; Highland black, 18
Celidon Wood, 49
cereals, 65
charcoal, 25, 94, 95, 120, 167; reserves, 16
Chatelherault Country Park, 78
cherry, 18, 69; bird ~, 66, 198; dwarf ~, 67;
    wild ~, 66
Chisholm, Roderick, 120, 121
Chisholm woods, 120
Churchill, General, 124
Claggan estate, 108
Clashnessie Bay, 127
Claudian invasion, 49
Clunie, 171
Cluny, 187
Clyde, 121, 123
Coigach, 93, 131, 132
Coille Chluanaidh, 187
Coille ne Glas Leitire, 132
Coille Phuisteachain, 122
Commissioners of Annexed Estates, 17, 115,
    121, 122, 123, 124
Commonwealth countries, 182
Comrie Golf Course, 32
conifer, 2, 12, 42, 44, 45, 147, 158, 163, 174,

181, 182, 184, 185, 186, 187, 188, 197, 200, 203; non-indigenous, 182, 184; North American, 181; plantation, 147, 187
conservationist, 1, 21, 25, 26, 116
coppice, 1, 2, 16, 17, 21, 24–9, 32, 35, 66, 88, 92, 94, 103, 162–75; fused ~, 29; natural ~, 29; singled ~, 28–9; bundle planting, 30; management, 162–75; stool, 28, 29, 32, 76, 81, 94; ~ wood, 168, 170, 171, 172; sale of, 164
coppicing, 28, 65, 69, 77, 82, 88–91, 111, 163, 171; ~ with standards, 28, 33
corn, 148
Coronelli's map, 111
Coryloid pollen, 64, 66, 67, 68
Council of Europe, 191, 199
County Antrim, 119
County Down, 119
County Meath, 119
Coupar Angus, Abbey of, 163
Craigellachie, 178
Craigowrie, 177
Craigvinean, 164, 166, 172
Crathes, 42
crofters, 179
Cromarty, 119
crops, 65, 67, 70, 167, 171, 179
Cul Mor, 131
Culdares estate, 110
Culloden, 115, 120
Cumbria, 53
Currently Unwooded Roy's Sites (CURS), 24

Dalkeith Park, 35, 36
Dalmore Woods, 117
Dalwhinnie, 186
dams, 176, 177, 180; creation of, 176
Darling, Frank Fraser, 5, 7, 16, 20
David I, 34, 70, 78, 149
Davidson, John, 119
deadwood, 25, 26, 27; benefits of, 25–6
Deans Cleugh, 151, 156, 157, 158
Dedication scheme, 183, 184
Dee, 136
deer, 2, 5, 7, 12, 18, 20, 25, 30, 31, 33, 81, 91, 93, 95, 96, 98, 110, 116, 133, 148, 150, 179, 180, 186, 188, 192, 195, 199, 200, 203
browsing, 198, 200; impact of browsing, 195–6, 199
culling, 186, 200, 201
~ proof exclosures, 192, 198
~ proof fence, 194, 202
forest, 179, 180, 188, 192; creation of, 179–80
medieval deerparks, 31
red ~, 20, 130, 132, 183, 187, 192, 198, 199, 200, 201; browsing, 183; hindrance to woodland regeneration, 198
roe ~, 19, 129, 130, 132

role in natural regeneration, 200
stalking, 179
wintering, 199; wintering pressure, 192, 200
Deeside, 2, 17, 18, 98, 117, 135–46, 181
deforestation, 88–97, 148; causes of, 92
dendrochronological, 31, 78, 80
disafforestation, causes of, 6
distal volcanic deposits (tephras), 53
ditches, 82; drainage, 82
Diver, Captain C, 195
domestic stock (see animals)
Doune, 119
Dowally, 171
Drogheda, 119
Druim na Doire Duibhe, 131
Drumchapel, 2, 81, 82, 84
Duackbridge, 181
Duchess Anna, 152
Duecaledonius Ocean, 48
Dulnain Bridge, 186
Dulnainside, 177
Dulnan, 178; forest, 183
Dumfries, 49, 88
Dunbar, 32
Dundee, 162, 171
Dunkeld, 2, 48, 162, 163, 164, 167, 168, 170, 171, 174; summer holiday resort, 168
Dunvegan, 12
Duthil, 179, 187
dykes, 18, 156, 163, 179; boundary, 32; faill (turf), 155; stone, 153, 157

East Anglia, 71
Easter Ross, 91
ecologist, 1, 16, 21, 40
Economic and Social Research Council, 2
Eddrachillis Bay, 127
Edinburgh, 122, 126, 162, 167
eels, 12
Effgill, 68
Eilean a' Ghamhna, 130
Eilean na Gartaig, 130
Elgin, 162
elm, 26, 28, 29, 30, 31, 88, 147, 150, 154, 156, 157
Elphin, 126, 127, 130, 131
Emperor Constantius Chlorus, 49
Emperor Septimius Severus, 49
Emperor Vespasian, 49
enclosure (see also dykes, fencing), 53, 67, 89, 90, 92, 95, 98, 103, 110–12, 152, 153, 155, 159, 179; neglect of in the Highlands, 92; to protect plantations, 141
England, 6, 18, 30, 31, 41, 53, 67, 71, 84, 86, 87, 88, 92, 97
Enniskillen, 119
epiphytes, 25, 42
Eskdale, 53, 65, 66, 69, 70, 71
Ettrick, 150, 153; forest, 89, 149, 150, 155;

valley, 148; woods, 90
Europe, 25, 31, 32, 40, 66, 86, 87, 88, 182

farmer, 6, 19, 30, 31, 106, 107, 113, 114, 148, 155
farming, 6, 20, 65, 70, 71, 88, 95, 97, 104, 136, 150; medieval, 2
farmland, 184
farmsteads, 150
Farquharsons, 140
Farrar River, 48
Fastheugh, 149, 151, 152, 153, 156, 158; woods, 153
fauna, 50, 190
Fellend, 66
fences, 69, 95, 198; deer proof, 179, 194; sheep proof, 194
fencing, 17, 19, 20, 21, 25, 91, 92, 94, 104, 140, 195, 196, 200; of native woodland, 185; costs, 184
ferns, 25, 32, 42
Feshie, 177
Feugh valley, 139
Fife, 6, 76, 88, 162
Finzean, 135, 136, 140, 143–5; estate, 136, 139–41, 143
fir (see also pine and Scots pine), 119, 120, 124, 154, 156, 177; silver ~, 26
Firbush Point, 18
fire, 6, 7, 17, 29, 82, 90, 93, 94, 112, 116, 139, 181, 183, 184, 187, 188, 200; forest ~s, 182
Firth of Forth, 47
fish, fisheries, 86; fish farm, 129
fishing, 179, 180
Flanders, 88
flora, 1, 7, 20, 21, 24, 25, 41, 50, 190, 203
flowering plants, 42
foggage, tolls of, 149
Foregin, 187
Forest Habitat Network, 135, 144
Forest of Bowland, 53
Forest of Selkirk, 149
Forest of Traquair, 149
forester, 1, 17, 26, 28, 29, 104, 106–11, 124, 150, 152, 153
forestry, 2, 3, 6, 7, 16, 18, 19, 47, 86, 94, 116, 143, 145, 155, 163, 185, 198; commercial, 203; private, 183
Forestry Commission, 3, 174, 181, 182, 183, 186, 194, 197; ~ Census, 192; Forest Enterprise, 186; plantations, 183; tree nursery, 199, 203
Forfar, 171
Forres, 119, 162, 178
Fort William, 115, 120, 123
Fortingall Yew, 32
Foulshiels, 154
France, 33, 87, 88
Fullartoun, Henry, 119

fungi, 25, 27; bracket ~, 27

Gairloch, 132
Galloway, 88
Galloway, R Angus, 3
game, 18, 21
Garbh Doire, 131
Garmouth, 118, 119, 176
Garscadden, 2; wood, 76, 81–4
Gatehouse of Fleet, 30
gean, 26, 29, 90
geomorphological factors, 133
George VI, 182
glaciation, 40, 52
glaciolacustrine terrace, 53
Glasgow, 2, 76–85, 121; University of, 82
Glen:
    Affric, 18, 116, 198; Ardvar, 130; Derry, 91; Ferrick 139, 143; Feshie, 177, 183, 187; Garry, 116; Kinglass, 93; Kishorn, 133; Leraig, 127, 129, 130, 131, 132; Loy, 3, 115, 117, 122; Lui, 91; Moriston, 116; Orchy, 90, 93, 95; Tanar, 135, 139, 141; Torridon, 198
Glencalvie, 118
Glenceitlein, 109
Glencoe, 12, 91, 93
Glenetive, 109
Glenevis, 123
Glenkinglass forest, 111
Glenmallie, 115
Glenmore, 93, 176, 177, 181, 182, 183, 184, 186; forest, 117, 184
Glenorchy, 109–14; estate, 104, 107, 113; ~ wood, 110
Glentanar forest, 93
Global Environmental Change Initiative, 2
goats, 7, 18, 20, 93, 95, 96, 109, 168, 169, 170, 192
Godwin, Sir Harry, 52
Gordon, Robert, of Straloch, 11, 91, 139
Gordon, Duke of, 117
Grampian, 48
Granish plantation, 178
Grant, Dr William, 117
Grant, Elizabeth, of Rothiemurchus, 176, 177
grants, forestry, 185; Woodland Grant Scheme, 185
Grant, James, 116, 119
Grant, Sir Archibald, of Monymusk, 124
Grant, Sir James, of Grant, 176, 180
Grantown, 178
Grants of Rothiemurchus, 115, 121
grass, 20, 67, 69, 70, 71, 96, 97, 130, 155, 156; purple moor ~, 202
grassland, 50, 67, 69, 191
grazing, 24, 28, 29, 30, 32, 40, 66, 67, 69, 70, 77, 78, 89, 90, 94–7, 110, 148, 153, 163, 170; by cattle, 171; controlled, 171; over~, 191; permits, 149; pressure, 18, 20, 129,

150; summer ~, 130; wood ~ agreements, 184
grazing animals, 16, 18, 67, 129, 130, 133; damage of, 6; effects of, 196
Great Glen, 48, 91, 123
Green Party, 5
grouse moors, 186
Guisach wood, 124

Hadrian's Wall, 66
Hamilton, 77
Hamilton, Dukes of, 81
hawthorn, 69, 148
Hay, Sir George, 94
hazel, 6, 24, 28, 29, 65, 66, 67, 69, 88, 90, 92, 94, 103, 110, 116, 136, 148, 150, 171
heather, 20, 91, 93, 97, 124, 201, 202; management, 186; moorland, 136
heathland, 20
hedged enclosures, 67, 70
hedgerow, 24, 26, 29, 30, 69
hedges, 30, 67, 163
herbage, 20
herbs, 66
Highland clearances, 19
Highland Planning Department, 7
Highlanders, 2
Highlands, 5–23, 25, 47, 48, 87, 90, 91, 92, 94, 95, 96, 97, 98, 101, 102, 112, 133, 135, 140, 143, 179, 185, 191; ecological history of, 5, 7
holly, 11, 12, 16, 69, 90, 92, 94, 148, 202
Home, John, 126, 127, 129, 130, 131
Honourable Society of Improvers in the Knowledge of Agriculture in Scotland, 163
horse, 11, 18, 19, 21, 87, 89, 93, 96, 122, 123, 176, 181
Hull, 118, 119, 120
hunting, 18, 70, 81, 88, 118, 149; reserves, 149; rights, 150

Ice-Age, 5, 6
Iceland, 53; volcanic eruptions in, 133
Inchcailloch, 28
Innerkip, 89
Innerleithen, 29
Innerpeffery, 92
Innis Chonain, 112
insects, 25; saproxylic, 25, 27
Inshriach, 177, 182; ~ forest, 183, 184, 187
Institute for Environmental History, 1
interglacial, 52
Inver, 164; Wood of, 164, 170
Inver Inn, 172
Inverarary, 12, 27; castle, 123
Invercauld, 98, 117, 118
Inverdruie, 176
Invereshie forest, 183, 186
Invergarry, 94

Inverlaidnan hill, 181
Inverlochy, 122
Invermaille, 124
Inverness, 119, 123, 162, 178
Ireland, 16, 120, 121
Iron Age, 48, 53, 55, 63, 65, 68, 148
iron: furnace, 17, 93; masters, 16, 17, 94; mill, 119; podzols, 42; smelting, 7, 11, 16, 19; works, 6, 119
ivy, 69

Jacobite rising, 120; failure of, 20
Jacobite Robertsons of Struan, 17
James I, 150
Johnson, Dr Samuel, 162
Johnston, James, 168
juniper, 11, 148, 202

Kenmore, 132
Kincardine, 118; Wood of ~, 89
Kingston, 176
Kinlochleven, 12
Kinnoull, Earls of, 163
Kinveachy, 181, 182; forest, 179, 183, 184, 186, 187
Kippen, 89
Kirkaig River, 127, 132
Kirkpatrick Fleming, 66

Lady Park Wood, 26
Laggan, 187
Lake District, 30, 31
lake sediments, 52
laminated silts, 55, 61
Lancashire, 53
Land Army, 182
Langholm, 89
larch, 26, 27, 44, 45, 140, 157, 158, 171, 172
Lauderdale, Earl of, 86
Ledmore Oakwood, 29
Lemannonius gulf, 48
Letterbeg, 10, 19
Lewenshope Rig, 148, 149
Lewis, 6
Lewisian Gneiss, 126
lichens, 25, 27, 32
Liddesdale, 153
lime, 25, 28, 29, 33; common ~, 26, 27
Lincolnshire, 40, 44
Little Dunkeld, 170, 172
Liverpool, 120
liverworts, 32
Loch: a' Chairn Bhain, 127, 130, 131; a' Chnuik, 187; an Doire Duibh, 132; an Draing, 132; an Eilean, 115, 116, 118, 182; Ardvar, 129, 130; Arkaig, 115–25; Assynt, 127, 131; Awe, 102, 109, 112, 130; Bada na-h-

Achlaise, 132; Borralan, 130; Broom, 132;
Cam, 127, 130; Carron, 12, 13; Coulside, 8;
Doire na h'Airbhe, 132; Drumbeg, 127; Eil,
12; Ericht, 187; Etive, 21, 94; Ewe, 16;
Fyne, 21, 48, 94, 123; Garten, 6; Glencoul,
127, 131; Glendhu, 131; Inver, 127; Laggan,
181, 187; Leven, 12, 17, 93, 120; Linnhe,
48, 93; Lochy, 119; Lomondside, 12, 16, 28;
Long, 48; Loyal, 8, 9, 10, 11, 19; Lurgainn,
132; Maree, 12, 16, 132; Morlich, 176, 181,
183; Nedd, 127, 129; Osgaig, 132;
Pityoulish, 6; Rannoch, 102; Roe, 127, 132;
Sealge, 11; Stack, 11; Tay, 12, 15, 18, 110;
Tayside, 30, 38, 39, 92; Torridon, 132;
Toscaig, 133; Urigill, 127, 130, 131;
Veyatie, 130, 131
Lochan na Dubh Leitir, 130
Lochaweside wood, 111
Lochiel, 121, 124; ~ woods, 119
Lochindorb, 184, 187
Lochlomondside, 112
Lochniver, 126
Lochwood, Beattock, 31
Lodgepole pine, 184, 185, 186
London, 18, 117, 118, 119
Long Knowe, 65
Lothian, 148
Lovat, Lord, 121
Lower Diabaig, 132
Lowlands, 6, 87, 88, 89, 90, 91, 92, 97, 148
lucerne, 67, 70, 71
Luineag river, 182
Lummis, John, 120, 121
Lyneholm, 68

McDonald, John, 181
McInnes, John, 104, 106
McInskellich, Ewen, 104
Mackenzie of Seaforth Estate, 97
Mackintosh, Sir Aeneas of Mackintosh, 177
Macleod of Macleod, 12
McPhee, John, 122
McVean, Donald, 195, 196
Mamlorne, 110
Mamore, 91
Mar Lodge Estate, 91
marshland, 49
Mason, Captain John, 92
meadow, 66, 70
Meallard, 130
medieval, 52–75, 77, 101; baron courts, 101; ~
earthworks, 82
Melrose Abbey, 149
Menzies, estate of, 2, 104, 106, 108, 109, 112,
113
Menzies lairds of Weem & Rannoch, 102, 103,
106, 109
Merlin, 49
Mesolithic, 6, 7, 21; ~ occupation, 148

Methven Wood, 28
microliths, 148
Middle Ages, 6, 7, 71, 88, 91
Millennium Forest, 3, 188
Milngavie, 76
Moffat, George, 154
Monadhliath, 48
monastic economy, 163
monks, 70, 149, 163; Cistercian, 68, 70
Mons Graupius, battle of, 50
Monteath, 91
Montrose, 12, 16, 162; estate, 89
moorland, 42, 44, 186; deforested, 198
Moray, 48
Moray plain, 119
Mortoun Wood, 89
mosses, 32, 42, 126; sphagnum, 200;
hypnaceous, 200
Moulin, 170
Mugdock Castle, 76
Mugdock wood, 76, 77
muir, 184
muirburn, 186
multi-stemmed, 168
Munro, William, 119
Murphy, Roger, 119
Murray, Charles, 164
Murray, John, Fourth Duke of Atholl, 171
Murray, John, of Broughton, 121
Murray, John, Third Duke of Atholl, 164, 167
Murrays of Atholl, 164
Murthly estates, 167, 170, 172
Murthly woods, 172

Nairn, 119
Napoleonic Wars, 176–77, 187
National Forestry Policy, 135
National Nature Reserve, 192, 193, 203; Beinn
Eighe, 190–206; Cairngorms, 183
National Parks and Access to the Countryside
Act, 190
National Register of Archives, 12
National Scenic Area, 185
National Trust for Scotland, 3, 174
National Vegetation Classification, 199, 202
native woodland, changes in, 126–34
Native Woodland Discussion Group, 33
natural regeneration, 86, 192–3, 195, 200, 201–
2, 204; prevented, 18
Nature Conservancy, 2, 183, 190, 192, 194,
195, 197, 199, 203; Council, 47, 185
Nebraska, 40
Nedd, 130
Neolithic, 6, 87
Newark, 149, 150, 152, 153, 154, 155, 158
Newfoundland, 182
Newtyle Hill, 164
Norfolk, 70
Normandy, 29

Norway, 95, 123

oak, 2, 5, 16, 17, 21, 24, 25, 26, 27, 28, 29, 33, 35, 36, 37, 39, 76–85, 88, 89, 90, 91, 92, 94, 96, 98, 103, 109, 110, 111, 112, 113, 115, 116, 119, 124, 129, 136, 147, 150, 153, 155, 156, 157, 163, 167, 170, 171, 172, 174, 178, 188, 198; ~ bark, 17, 109, 119, 171; coppice, 164; coppicing, 174
oats, 19; growing of, 19
old growth, benefits of, 25–6
Oldany Island, 127, 132
Ordnance Survey maps, 41, 103, 126, 152, 172
Orkney, 48
Over Rig, 52–75
Oxford, 68, 71

palaeoecological reconstructions, 69
palaeoecological record (at Over Rig), 65–7; Romano-British period, 65–6; Dark Age, 66; Anglo-Norman Economic Recrudescence, 66–7
palaeoenvironmental analyses, 53
palynological changes, 63, 65; ~ indicators, 65, 67, 68
palynologist, 1
palynology, 63–5
pannage, 88; rights of, 149
parkland, 24
parks, 26, 27, 30, 31
Parsons, Benjamin, 115, 118
Pass of Drumochter, 162
pastoralism, 65
pasture, 7, 24, 42, 44, 49, 65, 70, 78, 88, 91, 92, 95, 97, 110, 111, 124, 126, 149, 172
pasture flora, 20
peat, 6, 17, 52, 53, 55, 61, 63, 65, 66, 67, 76, 87, 115; formation of, 6
Peebles, 49
Pennant, Thomas, 117
Perrott and Field, 118, 119, 120
Perth, 28, 162, 171, 178; Dukes of, 163
Perthshire, 1, 12, 30, 32, 48, 90, 92, 106, 162–75
phytosociology, 40
Picts, 49
pigs, 88
Pinchot, Gifford, 86
pine, 2, 3, 5, 6, 16, 17, 24, 25, 41, 92, 93, 98, 103, 109, 110, 111, 113, 115–25, 127, 130, 136, 139, 140, 141, 143, 144, 177, 178, 179, 180, 182, 183, 184, 185, 186, 187, 188, 191–204; plantation, 178, 188
plant indicators, 40–6
plantation forestry, 135, 140
plantations, 26, 41, 136, 140, 141, 157, 158, 168, 172, 178, 181, 183–5, 186, 187, 197, 199, 201
Pliny, 47

Plora Wood, 29
poaching, 179
Poland, 25, 26
pollard, 26, 27, 30–1, 80; restoration, 31–2
pollarding, 27, 30, 31, 32, 79, 80, 88, 163
pollen, 7, 52–75
Pont, Timothy, 1, 10–21, 91, 93, 115
poplar, 69, 115
potato, 20
pre-Reformation Scotland, 163
Preston, 120
Preston Company, 120
primaeval woods, 40
Ptolemy, 47, 48

Quinag, 131

railways, 178, 179, 180, 181; Great North of Scotland Railway, 178
Ramsden, Sir John, 181
Rannoch, 17, 18, 102, 103, 106, 114; Black Wood of, 17, 18, 93
raptor, slaughter of, 21
Rassell, 18
recreation, 186, 188
Reforesting Scotland, 3
regeneration, forest, 24, 177, 179, 183, 184, 186, 187–8, 190, 194, 196, 197, 198, 200; natural ~, 180, 182, 183, 184, 185, 186, 192, 193, 195, 202, 204
Revoan, 187
Riccaby, Mathew, 119
Richaby, Thomas, 119
Riddel, James, of Ardnamurchan, 107
River Braan, 164, 167, 168, 172, 174
River Feugh, 136
River Tay, 164
River White Esk, 53
roads, 164, 178, 182; improvement of, 180
Robertson, James, 116, 117
Rohallion, 48
Romans, 47, 48, 49, 50, 53, 66; arrival in Scotland, 6; invasion, 148; writers, 48, 49
Romano-British period, 65–6, 148
Rome, 50
Roosevelt, Theodore, 86
Ross Wood, 28
Rothiemurchus, 93, 98, 115–25, 176, 179, 181, 182, 183, 186; forest, 177, 183
roup, public, 167
rowan, 26, 27, 69, 90, 116, 129, 148, 197, 198, 199, 200, 201
Royal Hunting Reserve, 136
Royal Scottish Forestry Society, 3
Roy's map, 24, 76, 77, 81, 103, 139, 164, 172
Roy's military survey (see Roy's map), 10, 11, 87, 91, 151, 155, 162
RSPB, 185; ~ Reserves, 186
Rubha Reidh, 132

runrig, 82

sainfoin, 67, 69, 70, 71
salmon, 12
sawmills, 176, 178
Scandinavia, 30, 121, 123
Schiehallion, 48
Scoraig peninsula, 132
Scotch fir, 172
Scots pine, 17, 18, 44, 45, 90, 136, 140, 141,
    156, 179–82, 186, 191, 192, 195, 197, 198,
    199, 200, 201, 202; genetic differences, 199
Scottish Department for Agriculture, 7
Scottish History Society, 16, 126
Scottish National Nature Reserve, 2, 3
Scottish National Parks Committee, 192
Scottish Natural Heritage, 135, 144, 191, 200,
    204; Countryside Centre, 1; tree nursery,
    202
Scottish Record Office, 12
Scottish Wildlife Trust, 7
Scottish Woodland History Discussion Group,
    3
Scott, William, 153
Seafield Strathspey Estate, 184
Seafield, Countess of, 184
Seafield, Lord, 180
Selkirkshire, 148
Sellar, Patrick, 18
settlement, 148
sheep, 2, 5, 7, 11, 16, 17, 18, 19, 20, 21, 31, 49,
    70, 71, 78, 88, 89, 93, 94, 95, 96, 97, 98,
    103, 129, 130, 131, 132, 133, 150, 178, 186,
    188, 192, 196, 203
    Blackface, 18, 96
    Cheviot, 18, 96
    farming, 7, 149, 150; deleterious effect of,
    20
    grazing, 7; effect of, 20
    ~ proof fence, 194
shielings, 91, 92, 136, 150
shooting, 179, 180
shredding, 88
sickle medick, 67
silurian mudstone, 55
silver firs, 157
silvicultural, 24, 153, 159, 196
singled coppice, 28–9
Site of Special Scientific Interest, 77, 185;
    Mugdock Wood, 77
sitka spruce, 7, 44, 45, 184
Skye, 98
Sleat, 98
sloe, 66
Sluggan Pass, 181, 183
soils, 25, 28, 29, 32, 90, 91, 198, 202; black,
    129, 130; degeneration, 7; degradation, 7,
    196, 197, 198, 202, 203; disturbance, 43;
    fertilisation, 197; glacial, 115; heavy, 156

Solway Firth, 66
Southern Uplands, 52–75, 88
Southampton, 68
Speed, John, 115, 121
Spey, 90, 92, 93, 176–80
Speyside, 2, 6, 12, 17, 18, 91, 93, 162
Spinningdale, 29
sportsmen, 20
spruce, 17, 172; ~ firs, 157
squirrels, 181
St Andrews, 162; University of, 1
stagheadedness, 78
stalking, 179
Stammie, James, 119
stedes, 150
stems, 24, 25, 26, 27–32
Steng Mosses, 66
Stewart-Murray, John, Eighth Duke of Atholl,
    174
Stewart-Murray, John, Seventh Duke of Atholl,
    174
Stewarts of Murthly, 164
Stewart, Sir John of Murthly, 167
Stoer Point, 127, 132
Stornoway, 123
Strathcarron, 12, 13
Strathclyde, 76
Strathglass, 120
Strathmashie forest, 183
Strathmore, Earl of, 162
Strathnavar, 8, 9, 10, 11, 19
Strathspey, 14, 115, 119, 123, 135, 144, 145,
    176–89; estate, 177, 178, 179, 180, 181,
    182, 186
Strathtay, 167
Strathyre, 28
stub trees, 32
Sussex, 53
sustainability, 103, 204
Sutherland, 7, 10, 11, 19, 90, 96, 97, 98, 117,
    126–34
sweet chestnut, 26
sycamore, 26, 27, 29, 31, 32, 38, 88, 151, 154
Syre, 10

Tacitus, 47, 48, 49, 50
tanbark, 25, 94, 95, 120
tenanted farms, 68, 155
tenants, 2, 68, 90, 92, 95, 96, 97, 101–14, 122,
    124, 136, 140, 150, 154, 177, 179, 180, 184;
    evictions of, 17
Tenby, 71
Thorton, Colonel, 21
Thule, 48, 49
timber, 2, 7, 16, 17, 18, 19, 25, 29, 31, 77, 87,
    88, 89, 92, 93, 95, 103, 104, 107, 108, 110,
    111, 112, 114, 117, 119–23, 139, 140, 150,
    151, 152, 153, 154, 155
    for building, 148